D0843166

HX
288
.Y6
1975

LARRY A. JACKSON LIBRARY
Lander College
Greenwood, S. C. 29646

THE ITALIAN LEFT

THE ITALIAN LEFT

A Short History of Political Socialism in Italy

by

W. HILTON-YOUNG

342361

GREENWOOD PRESS, PUBLISHERS
WESTPORT, CONNECTICUT

LARRY A. JACKSON LIBRARY
Lander College
Greenwood, S. C. 29646

Library of Congress Cataloging in Publication Data

Young, Wayland Hilton, Baron Kennet, 1923-
The Italian left.

Reprint of the 1949 ed. published by Longmans, Green, London, New York.
Includes index.
1. Socialism in Italy. 2. Italy—Politics and government—1870- 3. Partito socialiste italiano.
I. Title.
HX288.Y6 1975 329.9'45 74-33893
ISBN 0-8371-7998-X

The passage from Oggi, domani e mai *by Riccardo Bacchelli is included by kind permission of Aldo Garzanti Editore, Milan.*

Originally published in 1949 by Longmans, Green and Co., London, New York

Reprinted with the permission of Longman Group Limited

Reprinted in 1975 by Greenwood Press, a division of Williamhouse-Regency Inc.

Library of Congress Catalog Card Number 74-33893

ISBN 0-8371-7998-X

Printed in the United States of America

CONTENTS

ILLUSTRATIONS

INTRODUCTION

THE English traveller, used to the narrow and orderly streets of London, will be astonished when he goes to Rome at the behaviour of the traffic there. The streets are very wide, and cars, buses, lorries, carts, carriages, handbarrows, and bicycles may be going in any direction and at any speed. Besides going in the usual direction, that is forwards and on the right-hand side, they may go across, backwards, on either side, and even round in circles. Let us take this conspicuous difference between Italy and England as an allegory of the difference between English and Italian politics. In Piccadilly, there is a general agreement about which way to go; the same narrowness of the street, which makes progress slow, makes it orderly. But in, say, the Via dell' Impero at Rome, the great width of the street invites speed and allows any sort of course. Equally, English politicians are agreed in favour of free debate, of parliamentary action, and whenever possible of traditional procedure. Not so Italian politicians. With such an expanse of tarmac open to the traffic it is not worth while to observe any particular rule of the road; any direction, any speed, any change of either is tolerated. There is no political matter on which all Italians are agreed.

Three types of vehicle which are common in Rome and not in London happen to fit in with this allegory. There is a kind of bus that trails a second bus behind it; these trailers are often dropped off by the roadside and left there or manhandled by a team of pushers until other buses come to pick them up. So Italian political parties will continually split up and the dissident section will join up with some other section or party. Then occasionally one may see a loaded railway truck rumbling along on a sort of framework built to carry it by road; movements and programmes which are not political at all masquerade as politics. Lastly, and too obvious to need any explanation, there are the processions of four boys on tricycles bearing four advertisement placards, for a film perhaps, or a patent medicine. These boys pedal very slowly to the general confusion and wear a trivial uniform and a fixed smile.

With such a wide road and such diversity of purpose, are there not then many accidents? Not very many, for Italian drivers are sure of eye and swift in their reactions and they do not like getting hurt. But there was one accident, so big that Mussolini was able to profit by the concern and alarm of the public to close the road to traffic for twenty years.

It was brought about by the erratic behaviour of one of these big multiple buses, a red bus, the Italian Socialist Party. It was continually dropping trailers all over the road, picking them up again, and zigzagging to and fro in a perilous and annoying manner. Each component part had its destination written on the front, but the labels were continually changing. Sometimes it would just say "Elysium"; sometimes it would describe its route as "Elysium via Revolution" or "Elysium via Constitutional Debate" or "Elysium via Moscow"; sometimes it would say, "You can ask the driver, but he's deaf." The confusion caused by this multiple red bus was such that Mussolini and his fascists blocked the whole road.

Now that war and civil strife have opened the road again, the multiple red bus is back and is again dropping its trailers with their doubtful labels. This book is the history of the red socialist bus in the traffic of Italian politics.

CHAPTER I

PRECURSORS

Until the foundation of the Italian Socialist Party in 1892

IN the middle of the nineteenth century, when England was taking stock of the fact that she had become an industrial country and that her welfare depended on the welfare of the men who worked her iron and coal deposits, Italy was in the throes of the movement for national unification which had come about in England fully three centuries before. The great Italians of that time, Cavour, Mazzini, Garibaldi, were engaged on a work of political and military change; they were throwing out foreign dynasties and making a democratic nation out of a collection of the outlying provinces of old absolutist empires. Not only was there no political working-class movement, there were no national politics; not only were there no trade organizations, there was no industry. The Austrians and the Spaniards were expelled, the Pope was shorn of his temporal power, and in 1870 Rome became the capital of united, democratic, lay Italy. But the Italian working class, which was almost entirely agricultural, remained unrepresented, without the right or indeed the wish to organize itself for collective action, and for the most part untouched by the changes that had taken place. Instead of a remote Austrian or Spanish monarch there was now a remote Piedmontese monarch, but the landlord was still there.

This political apathy was natural enough. Proletarian politics are an industrial phenomenon and develop in the compact masses of a great city. Even now, fifty-six years after the foundation of the Socialist Party, the Italian peasant is in much the same condition as he was in 1870. The long distances between one farm and the next, the long hours which the peasant works, the sluggishness born of monotonous exertion in the open air, all these tend to stop new ideas reaching the peasant at all or to distort them if they do reach him. The Sicilian uprisings of 1893 and 1894[1] are an excellent example of this distortion. Italy was an agricultural country whose foreign rulers had to be driven out before any unified industrial progress could be made. Not only was there no socialism, but there was also no ground suitable for it to grow in.

But during the Risorgimento there was an isolated forerunner, a patriotic leader with something of the socialist in him; this was the Neapolitan nobleman Carlo Pisacane. Already in the seventeenth century Naples was known as a black spot for poverty and undernourishment and even to-day, after nearly a century of modern government both totalitarian and democratic, an English Minister of Health after seeing the *Bassifondi* of Naples would return to clearing up the East End and the Gorbals as to a parlour game. In the middle of the nineteenth century Naples, under a backward dynasty, held the largest and poorest urban proletariat in Italy. The excellent climate was perhaps the only thing that enabled these people to survive unemployment, overcrowding, near-starvation, and their consequences of dirt, cholera, diphtheria, and typhus. This misery, although it did not lead to the wide diffusion of revolutionary ideas among those who suffered it, did lead to an intransigent and bloodthirsty philanthropy among some of the better-off Neapolitans who beheld it. There was too in Naples an old tradition of free and excellent philosophy—it is enough to remember Vico—and of the international exchange of ideas.

Philanthropy and philosophy combined in Pisacane. He was the first of the high-minded heroes of noble family who are scattered through the early history of Italian revolutionary socialism. He abandoned a military career and went with somebody else's young wife to London, where he became acquainted with the

[1] See pages 35–7.

works of Fourier and Proudhon and published polemics against the liberal ideas of his fellow-exile Mazzini. He passed a long exile, sometimes serving with the French Foreign Legion and always attended by the spies of the Bourbon police, more because of his elopement than because of his seditious ideas, and returned temporarily to Italy to take part in the great uprising of 1848 in Milan. He was killed in the abortive Neapolitan uprising of 1857, when the shipload of conspirators which he brought down from Genoa in the steamship *Cagliari* found the Bourbon police waiting for them instead of the barricades they had expected.

In a series of essays written over some years he had set out his ideas on national regeneration through social revolution. He believed that the real unification of Italy could be brought about neither by the international politics of Cavour, nor by the sentimental religious nationalism of Mazzini, nor yet by the heroic feats-at-arms of Garibaldi, but only by a concerted uprising of the peasants. In his letters he poured scorn on the idea of a "national uprising for national honour." He believed that Italy's labouring millions were the only force powerful enough to rid her of her foreign overlords. He knew well enough that the labouring millions could not see as far as an independent united Italy; what they did see was the landlord. Once get the peasants to overthrow the landlords and the dynasties would topple over with them. The peasants would free Italy by freeing themselves; their self-interest was to be the instrument of the patriot's ideal.

To this extent Pisacane was a patriot. He preached proletarian revolution as the best means to the common end of all the leaders of the Risorgimento. But there are indications in his views on revolution and on the nature of the liberation which was to be desired for Italy that he was as much a socialist as a patriot. He taught that the condition of the working masses depends not on political institutions but on the economic system, and that a revolution can only have its origin in earlier happenings and not in an idea translated into abrupt action by strong men. The idea of a revolution is only fertile and can only proceed to the act when the idea itself is implicit in earlier acts. In his

Political Testament,[1] dictated the night before he sailed to his death in the *Cagliari*, he said that if the House of Savoy, under whose aegis the unification of Italy was taking place, had not been a liberal dynasty, the true proletarian revolution might already have come about. These three points, the insistence on the importance of economic conditions, the theorizing over the historical mechanism of revolution, and the impatience of liberalism in high places, are strikingly like Marx, whose writing he knew at most in part.

It has been much discussed whether Pisacane was primarily a socialist or a patriot; it matters very little. He was a man with a socialistic cast of mind and emotions whose ideals overlapped those of the patriots of his day and who lived at a time when all revolutionary effort was harnessed to a patriotic end. His aim was indeed a free and united Italy, but under the direct control of the agricultural proletariat. He died at the height of the movement which established a free and united Italy, but thirty-five years passed before the foundation of a party which preached direct control by the proletariat. In his life he was important only as a minor patriotic leader; after his death his influence was greater. He had urged forcefully the cause of the proletarian revolution and had died gallantly fighting as much for that as for the cause in which so many others died, the cause of national liberation. He was the first and for many years the only socialist martyr; he was by no means the first patriot martyr. Besides this, he set people thinking about class revolution in general, whether it was to be desired, and how it could be brought about.

But, as he realized, class consciousness must precede class revolution, and in his time there was no such thing among the peasants and little enough of it among the few industrial workers. Industrialization, however, railways, and free trade were following Cavour and his successors wherever they ruled. The cotton and silk industries of Austrian Lombardy, already flourishing in the eighteen-forties, were expanded and improved by the Piedmontese innovations of gas-lighting, railways, and steam-power.

[1] Carlo Pisacane, *Testamento politico*; Ancona, 1880.

Foreign coal began to pour in through Genoa. Free-trade treaties, particularly with England and Belgium, promoted vigorous industrial growth all over the north of Italy, and in the 'seventies and 'eighties there were enough urban concentrations for the beginnings of socialism to appear.

The prehistory of the Italian labour movement is little different from that of labour movements in other countries. The medieval Guilds and Arts held on as atrophied, formal bodies until the eighteenth century, when the Pious Unions, *Pie Unioni*, began to appear. The typesetters and the hatters of Turin had theirs already in the seventeen-twenties. These were local trade-assistance societies, centred on a bank with more or less clerical backing. In the eighteen-twenties the Austrians in Lombardy instituted savings banks, *Casse di Risparmio* or more particularly *Monti di Pietà*, and in Piedmont between 1848 and 1860 appeared the Mutual Aid Societies, *Società di Mutuo Soccorso*, which by 1870 had spread all over Italy together with Piedmontese rule and institutions. A characteristic of all these three forms of organization was that they would give assistance in kind, in furniture or clothing, as well as in money. None of them was political, and all were local rather than confined to particular trades. It was only as the new coal-based industries superseded the old quasi-domestic ones that workers' organizations began to concern themselves with terms and conditions of work and later with politics. In the eighteen-seventies and 'eighties the habit of local association was being carried over from insurance and assistance to the first, as yet unrecognized, attempts at collective bargaining. Various types of organization appeared, but that which assimilated the others and has lasted until to-day was the Chamber of Labour, *Camera del Lavoro*, a grouping of all the workers of one town or district irrespective of their trade.[1] On to this movement political socialism grafted

[1] The English equivalent is the Trades Council, but, since the influence wielded in Italy by a great *Camera del Lavoro* can only be compared to that wielded in England by a great Trade Union, I shall use the translation throughout and avoid the equivalent. See pages 47–8.

itself, the latter being more the product of intellectual currents than, as in England, a spontaneous working-class growth.

In 1870, after two decades of colourful and heroic adventure, the Italians found themselves face to face with a liberal and constitutional monarch, a frock-coated parliament, a prosaic civil service, and peace. The Piedmontese constitution, itself an uninspiring combination of English parliamentarianism and French centralized bureaucracy, had been extended to cover all Italy. The organization of new taxes and administrative reforms meant drudgery for the politicians. The unification had cost money, and there was an unhealthy deficit to be made good. In his speech from the throne at the opening of the Italian Parliament in 1870, King Victor Emmanuel II said: "Now the prose must follow the poetry."

The Italians were bored. Cavour was dead, and the other two giants of the Risorgimento, Garibaldi and Mazzini, were thoroughly disgruntled. They never tired of proclaiming that although union had been achieved it was the wrong sort of union. Mazzini would have had it a republic based on a reformed and liberal Church and informed with a fervid poetic belief in the civilizing mission of the Italian people. Garibaldi would have had it far more radical and democratic than it was. Of those who had worked and fought for the union, many more had done so under the influence of Mazzini's and Garibaldi's ideas than under the influence of Cavour's, but it was Cavour's ideas that underlay the new state. Pope Pius IX lived on till 1878 growling out hostility to the Italian government in Rome, and his strict followers were another discontented group.

The hope which united all parties was that once the bickering reactionary dynasties were gone, the natural wealth of Italy would be scientifically exploited and would bring a new prosperity, especially to the south. But a commission of inquiry[1] reported in 1881 that scientific exploitation could do little with a soil as infertile and parched as that of southern Italy. It was well known that deposits of coal and iron were quite inadequate

[1] Under the chairmanship of Count Stefano Jacini.

to support any large-scale industry, so that when this Report exploded the myth of Italy as a natural garden the mood of bored depression became deeper.

The great preoccupation of the eighteen-seventies and 'eighties was the "Social Question." Many suggestions were put forward for improving the lot of the peasant and the industrial worker, and five currents of opinion in particular contributed to the formation of a socialist party; that is to say, most of the early adherents of socialism came to it through these currents. Let us now consider the five leaders of thought identified with those currents: Giuseppe Mazzini, Mikhail Bakunin, Giuseppe Garibaldi, Benoît Malon, and Karl Marx, who all influenced Italian socialism directly or indirectly.

Under Mazzini's influence had grown up in the 'fifties and 'sixties the Artisan Brotherhoods, *Fratellanze Artigiane*, which at the time when no one knew what form the union would take attempted to interest the working classes in achieving national unity in a Mazzinian republic. They had some following among the working men who had leisure and education enough to be interested in politics at all; but the working classes were not going to exert themselves much for Mazzini's reformed christianity, nor for the idea of a national mission, and these organizations were mainly held together by the great warm-hearted effusions, circulated in thousands of copies, with which Mazzini punctuated each new stage of the movement for national unification. In 1871 he forfeited the support of his proletarian following by condemning the Paris Commune, and by then, too, it had become clear that the ideas of Cavour had finally triumphed. The Artisan Brotherhoods, having nothing left of policy or ideals to attach them to the working classes, lost their following, and in 1879 the Mazzinian paper *Il Dovere* (*Duty*) left off publication for want of readers. There had been nothing socialist about Mazzini's teaching, rather the reverse; but he had done a good deal to awaken the working class to politics in general. It was easier to pass to socialism from Mazzinian republicanism than from apathy.

The leader of the first specifically proletarian revolutionary movement to have any following was the Russian anarchist exile Mikhail Bakunin. The movement attracted a great deal of attention and showed at least one way not to approach the "Social Question"; its failure cleared the ground. For this reason Bakunin deserves a rather fuller account than the other four.

He lived in Naples from 1865 to 1868 and was again in Italy, mostly at Florence, from 1872 until his death in 1876. His political character is best summarized by the aphorism of the French revolutionary Caussidière, who was with him in Paris in 1848: "He is a godsend on the first day of a revolution and a menace on the second." He arrived in Naples, large, vehement, with a great beard, surrounded by the glamour of past revolutionary exploits in all the corners of the world and of his escape from Siberia to London via Vladivostok and New York. In Naples he found that combination of cheerful squalor and intransigent philanthropy in which Pisacane had grown up. The Bourbons had gone and Naples by then enjoyed the liberal Piedmontese constitution which was extended to each new part of Italy as it came under the rule of the House of Savoy. Bakunin found his kind of agitation easier than it would have been under the personal police-rule of a few years before. His teaching of a revolution carried to the last extreme, of a holocaust, of Armageddon, found a ready hearing among some of the philanthropic intellectuals of the university city. He set up a section of the First International in Naples and over much of southern Italy his views were diffused through a more or less secret organization known generally as the Alliance, which was one of the Social Democratic Alliances or Bakuninist organizations which existed in several countries. Naturally it had nothing to do with what we should now call social democracy.

Above all Bakunin was an internationalist, and his organizations were mainly active as constituent sections of the Working Men's International Association. During these years the history of this Association, the First International, was that of the struggle between Marx, its authoritarian founder, and the anarchist Bakunin, a struggle which ended with the break-up of the International in 1873, when Marx withdrew his faction to New York. This struggle was not mirrored in Italy; while the International remained intact, the Italian section at Naples—which was incidentally for many years the only one to pay regular subscriptions—was solidly behind Bakunin. The day of Marxism in Italy came later.

Bakunin's agitation was revolutionary and secret, although the existence of the section of the International at Naples was officially permitted. He had a wide knowledge of Italy, but his tactics in each particular country were not adapted to its characteristics. He wanted revolution. When? Some time; it had to come. How? By fire and the sword. With what end? It did not matter; once destroy the state, capitalism, all and every sort of organization, and mankind would be free and happy. Anarchism in Bakunin's day was not the carefully worked out doctrine it became later with Kropotkin, but it derived from his own character a strain of whole-heartedness that made it appeal to that type of Italian intellectual who believes that it matters not so much what views you hold as that you should hold them in their extremest form. Bakunin had very little proletarian following in Italy; his adherents came from the poor students, the intellectual *petit bourgeois*, the literate discontented of all classes. This imitation proletariat drew the fire of Marx, who described them as "*Deklassierte*"—the unclassed. An eminent student of Italian socialism, Robert Michels, has defended them as "*Sichselbstdeklassierende*"—those who unclassed themselves. Marx denounced the Italian section of the International as composed of "lawyers without clients, doctors without knowledge or patients, billiard-playing students, commercial travellers, and various more or less unsavoury journalists of the gutter press."[1] Leonida Bissolati, the moderate socialist leader of later years,

[1] Karl Marx, *L'Alliance de la Democratie Socialiste et l'Association Internationale des Travailleurs*; p. 60; quoted in Robert Michels, *Sozialismus und Fascismus als politische Strömungen in Italien*; 2 vols., Munich, 1925; i, 48.

said it was a matter of "poets and cranks." Behind these polemics was the common knowledge that a workers' revolutionary movement cannot be run without any workers in it.

The most remarkable leader of the Italian Bakuninist movement was another *narodnik* nobleman, Carlo Cafiero. He was of an old Apulian family and was training for a diplomatic career when he was fired by anarchist teaching. Later, as head of his family, he made over to the movement his whole fortune of 700,000 lire, in those days a very large sum; indeed it could have financed the movement for years. Once he had been converted to the cause, Cafiero led a life of the greatest austerity and virtue, getting up very early, eating very little, and preaching violence and bloodshed without respite. His inspiring personal demeanour brought many adherents to his political views. He led the Benevento Affair, to be described later, published later in life a condensed translation of *Capital*, and died in a madhouse in 1892.

A more serious and effective leader was Andrea Costa, a Romagnole who was introduced to politics by the poet Carducci, under whom he studied philology at the University of Bologna. Carducci was a great enemy of all that was Piedmontese and dull, and Costa entered parliament first as a neo-Mazzinian republican. He too was soon converted to anarchism, but, as we shall see, he grew out of it later.

In 1867 during a stay in Florence, then the capital of Italy, Bakunin actually converted two Deputies to his views. In Sicily, which one of them represented, in Florence itself, and at the Congress of the International at Berne in 1868, they cast a certain aura of respectability round the movement which ill befitted the large explosiveness of its tenets.

A revolutionary movement with such a motley, top-heavy following could not accomplish much. The fundamental cause of its decline was simple. The Bakuninists, a body of people held together by political ideas, were urging the working masses, an economic class, to rise in revolution. As is generally the case when a group A tells an unrelated group B how to behave, nothing happened. The immediate causes of the decline of the movement were two. First there was the weakening of its international backing. When in 1873 the First International split into two rival bodies, the Communist International and the Anarchist International, the Italian section, meeting at Rimini under the chairmanship of Andrea Costa, affirmed its continued adherence to anarchism. But the prestige of belonging to the only international workers' organization had gone. When Bakunin died in 1876 the leadership of the Anarchist International passed to Kropotkin, who had not Bakunin's special interest in Italy. The second reason was a series of attempts to begin the revolution which were more picturesque than effective.

Bakunin himself left the Italian scene disguised as a priest after the failure of a rising which he organized with Cafiero and Costa at Bologna in 1874.[1] The Benevento Affair is characteristic of the bomb-and-false-beard atmosphere against which the more disciplined socialists later tried to prevail and it is therefore worth describing in more detail. In 1877, the year after Bakunin's death, a band of internationalists including the austere Carlo Cafiero decided to begin the revolution. An advance guard of two men and a girl took a villa near Benevento, a sizeable agricultural town behind Naples, from which they were to direct operations in the neighbouring countryside. Within twenty-four hours the behaviour of this pretended holiday party had attracted the attention of the police, and as they returned on their second afternoon from a preparatory expedition they came upon a policeman watching their house from behind a hedge. A direct encounter—danger! All was at stake. The hottest spirit among the internationalists fired; the police, reinforced from behind other hedges, returned the fire. A battle developed and the police finally withdrew, bearing their wounded. Clearly there was no time to be lost; once the first revolutionary act had been committed there must be no hesitation. As many of the band as possible were gathered at once and twenty-three of them under the command of Cafiero himself marched on a little

[1] This rising is the subject of Riccardo Bacchelli's historical novel, *Il diavolo al Ponte Lungo.*

neighbouring town. They invaded the town hall, where the town council happened to be in session, and in the name of the Revolution demanded arms. The mayor was alarmed by the pistols, the fierce beards, the flowing cravats. He would like to oblige, but it was clearly most irregular. Perhaps a receipt . . . ? A document was drawn up . . . "under duress . . . accept no responsibility . . ." The mayor's signature was taken to the police station; ". . . if the mayor says so . . ."; a few rifles were distributed to the puzzled peasants. Next must come the total demolition of the capitalist state. The revolutionaries collected all the archives of the town and started a bonfire in the *piazza*. But the common ideals of all humanity must be respected: the archives of the religious congregations were salved from the flames. Since this was the end of an era of oppression, fifty lire was taken from the tax-collector's drawer and scattered among the crowd. At this point the parish priest appeared. But he was no calculating cardinal; within a few minutes he was proclaiming that the twenty-three were the messengers of true religion, divine emissaries come to inaugurate the age of freedom and love. Then the internationalists attacked the next town, this time with the help of the parish priest from the outset, for they had met him on the way there and he returned with them to assure his flock of their good intentions. But by now the Benevento police were closing in and the internationalists had to take to the hills and woods. After a few hours they were all captured sheltering from a rainstorm in a barn. They and the two priests were clapped into prison in Naples and, while awaiting trial, founded a new section of the International among the prisoners. Most of them were released under the amnesty for political offences that followed the accession of Umberto I in 1878, and not long afterwards a jury found the rest not guilty on criminal charges.

In the middle 'seventies there were many such affairs, generally on an even smaller scale, but that which virtually ended the internationalist movement in Italy was the bomb episode at Florence in 1878. This was a complex story of plots and counterplots, demonstrations and counter-demonstrations, with plenty of bombs and shooting. An ugly clash between two hostile processions converging in the same street gave rise to a long series of trials of revolutionaries and near-revolutionaries. These trials were in a sense the end of Bakuninist anarchism and the beginning of modern socialism, for at them the authorities, the public, and what was more important the agitators themselves, began to see the distinctions between nihilism, anarchism, and socialism, words which had hitherto been used indiscriminately for an indiscriminate response of "down with it" to any stimulus.

At those trials a young Russian girl of striking appearance and manner made her first appearance. She was Anna Kulishov,[1] the mistress of Costa and the mother of his child. She lived on until after the war of 1915–18 and was the friend and guide of three generations of Italian socialists. She differed from most of the Russian exiles who at this time devoted themselves to proletarian agitation in western Europe in that she had a clear head as well as a warm heart. During her defence, which she conducted herself, she put her finger on the weakness of Bakuninist anarchism as a revolutionary movement: "Socialism," she said, "does not create armed bands, but it is ready to direct those that are thrown up naturally by social conditions."

When the trials at Florence came to an end in 1880 the supporters of the revolutionary anarchist movement were reduced to a few scattered eccentrics who had, however, a surprising endurance. At the movement's apogee, in 1871, its leaders had claimed for it ten thousand adherents; but whatever their number they were not drawn from the class to whose interests the movement was directed. It had been a kind of fanatical altruism and in action had shown that it did not have the support of the working masses. In the few years of its existence it had demonstrated in practice what could have been perceived in a few seconds of clear thought, that the material interests of the working class are not furthered by the *deraciné* intellectual who places a bomb under a police station. But in sincerity, courage, and

[1] The Italian spelling is Kuliscioff; we shall use the English one.

lofty idealism, the Bakuninists have remained unsurpassed in the history of Italian proletarian agitation.

The historical importance of the Italian Bakuninist movement lies not so much in its own theories or achievements as in that it awoke the Italians to the possibility of proletarian movements in general. It left behind it a belief not in anarchism in particular, but in the possibility of devoting oneself entirely and implacably to the interests of the working class. It may be that the accident of Bakunin's presence in Italy set back for some years the growth of a viable proletarian movement, since very many people came to the real thing by the false start, most notably Andrea Costa.[1]

Garibaldi fostered no organizations, but he had countless followers in the sense that countless Italians watched and listened for his opinions and were influenced by them. Garibaldi, the hero of all free and unfree peoples, before whose redshirts and rifles thrones and empires had crumbled in two continents, was living in these days in retirement on an island and searching his conscience about receiving a pension from King Victor Emmanuel. His work as a patriot completed, he had become a socialist. In 1871 he was made in his absence commander of the National Guard of the Paris Commune, and he was glad of it. During the eighteen-seventies he wrote several letters of support to the first freakish near-socialist candidates to the Italian Parliament. He described socialism as the "sun of the future," and some of the first groups in which socialism was discussed were called "Garibaldi Circles." Although he was sceptical of Bakunin's methods, he successfully founded sections of the International even in black, catholic Rome. He appeared at one meeting of the International when its unity was gravely threatened by the Marx-Bakunin split and his impressive presence, for he made but a short speech, united the delegates of both factions in enthusiasm. Garibaldi was a socialist by instinct, not by reasoning;

[1] This account of the Bakuninist movement in Italy is mainly taken from two sources: Robert Michels, *Sozialismus und Fascismus als politische Strömungen in Italien*; 2 vols., Munich, 1925; and Alfredo Angiolini, *Cinquant' anni di socialismo in Italia*; Florence, 1900.

one might almost say that he was so by force of habit, the habit of always being on the extreme left. But that Garibaldi should have given socialism his blessing was a good enough reason for many Italians to become socialists. The Red Shirt led them to the Red Flag.

A serious socialist programme was formulated for the first time in Italy by Benoît Malon, a Frenchman. He had been one of the communist mayors in Paris in 1871. When the Commune was extinguished he took refuge in northern Italy and there abandoned revolutionary extremism and turned to the idea of a workers' movement devoted to social and industrial reform by democratic methods—adult suffrage, elections, and debates, as opposed to bombs and revolutions. Living in Milan he conducted an energetic press and pamphlet campaign as best he could, being a foreigner and therefore without standing in the labour movement. His was an approach to socialism which was not familiar in Italy, but which was quickly diffused and appreciated. He was the first "reformist" in the Italian proletarian movement as Bakunin was the first "revolutionary." The battle between *riformisti* and *rivoluzionari* did not cease thereafter until the dissensions between them allowed Mussolini to suppress them both. Malon offered a programme of practical reforms for the consideration of those working men and their sympathizers who were for convenience called socialists. Against Armageddon and the holocaust he set up the ideas of the more developed sections of the French and German socialist movements, the right to combine, the right to strike, legislation on hours and conditions of work, legal recognition for the agencies of sickness- and unemployment-insurance and for co-operatives. Many of less fiery temper found Malon's ideas acceptable and it was under their influence that the Italian Workers' Party was founded in 1882.[1] A significant and important convert to Malon's reformism was Andrea Costa, the Bakuninist leader. He was imprisoned in Paris in 1879 for his activities in the French branch of the anarchist movement, for the early agitators cared little in which

[1] See pages 18–20.

country they worked. It was the year of the trials at Florence, and Costa thought much in prison about the propriety of Bakuninist methods. He rejected them in a letter to his Italian colleagues which became famous as a symbol of the transferred allegiance of many people from anarchism to reformism. In it he recognized that the old movement had been a false start, that it had been too much up in the air, founded on emotion not reasoning; "We must come to grips with reality." In 1881, shortly after his return to Italy, he founded the newspaper *Avanti!*, called after the organ of the German Socialist Party, *Vorwärts!* When the Italian Socialist Party was founded in 1892 *Avanti!* became its official organ and after many vicissitudes it is still so to-day.

The Mazzinians and Bakuninists were fast falling off, but the intellectuals among them turned to Marx rather than to Malon. It is impossible to say when Marx first became known in Italy. Students and intellectuals had of course known the *Communist Manifesto* since 1848, and the unscholarly popularizations of a certain Loria were known in the 'seventies. Perhaps more important was the fact that the Italian delegates to the International, though taken there by Bakunin, had heard Marx and brushed up against his ideas. Pisacane and Bakunin had familiarized Italians with a point of Marxism which they both held independently, the doctrine of the increasing misery of the proletariat and the increasing prosperity of the capitalists. By 1880 groups of Marxist publicists—lawyers, journalists, and university teachers—were beginning to appear, but it was not until the eighteen-nineties that Marxism was exhaustively studied.

During these years, the political phenomenon *trasformismo*, transformism, had grown up, a natural concomitant of the current gloom about the industrial and agricultural future of Italy and of the dullness of political life. Until 1876 ministries were taken from the successors of Cavour, the Action Party and its allies; they were upright, hardworking, regarded as being a little right of centre, and above all boring. In 1876 Agostino Depretis became Prime Minister and, as he was supposed to be a man of the left, hopes were high; perhaps at last the new grey age would take fire a little. But not at all; it became clear that there had been no change. And between 1876 and 1887, when Depretis finally left office, there grew up this system of *trasformismo*. The original meaning of the word referred to the transformation of Deputies elected to pursue some clear line into recruits to the amorphous following of Depretis. No matter what the platform on which a Deputy was elected, he supported Depretis. The phenomenon was to survive for long. It was perfected by Giolitti in the first decade of the twentieth century and lasted right up until Mussolini abolished parliamentary rule. The classical exposition of it was given in one sentence by a Deputy of the old right in 1891: "How can we form a serious opposition to a ministry which follows our own road in just the same way as we should, if not better?"[1]

The basis of *trasformismo* was a network of bargains controlled from the Ministry of the Interior: "You vote for this measure of mine and I'll see that you get that new bridge in your constituency." This mild form of corruption was brought to marvellous efficiency by Giolitti, but it was Depretis who invented it. The effect was a lack of definition in parliamentary groups, and the impossibility of discerning whether any particular ministry was fish, flesh, or fowl. Gradually the word *trasformismo* came to mean the inevitable transformation of everything and everybody in politics into something else. Democratic parliamentary rule was vitiated from the start and the country was denied the only healthy relief from the boredoms of democracy which might have been achieved, that of sharply defined and vigorous party debate.

The poverty of the soil made impossible a wealthy agriculture; the lack of coal or iron deposits made impossible a healthy industry; and *trasformismo* had fundamentally enfeebled parliamentary democracy. These were the three main characteristics of the age in which Italian socialism grew up.

[1] Bonghi; quoted in Croce, *Storia dell' Italia, 1871–1915*; Laterza, Bari; p. 20.

In 1882 a small widening of the still very restricted franchise by Depretis gave the signal for the appearance of the first proletarian political party in Italy. It appeared in Milan, already the biggest industrial city and the city where the workers were most prosperous and educated. A group of workers from the old light industries, led by the glovemaker Giuseppe Croce,[1] issued an appeal for local sections to be founded of a *Partito Operaio Italiano*, Italian Workers' Party.[2]

The new party gathered round the remnants of an earlier organization, the *Figli del Lavoro*. The Sons of Labour had had no programme and little organization; they carried on a sporadic and violent political and syndical activity. Cafiero was associated with it for a time, but those who passed to the Workers' Party were of milder temper, for the new party's programme was far from inflammatory; it included the non-intervention of the government in negotiations between labour and management on wages and hours of work, universal suffrage, the right of combination, legal recognition of the Mutual Aid Societies, a single progressive tax, the abolition of the bureaucracy and of the National Lottery, and a foreign policy of universal brotherhood and the freedom of all peoples.[3] Appended was an appeal to all workers, agricultural as well as industrial, for solidarity in the struggle against capitalism. This is by no means a Marxist programme, although some of its phrases indicate that Marxism was already in the air. It is a mixture rather of Malon and idealism.

The history of the Italian Workers' Party can be briefly told. It put up candidates in Milan and a few other towns at the general elections[4] of 1882, though few of its members had a vote themselves. Its failure to get any seats caused it to languish, but it

[1] Not to be confused with the philosopher Benedetto Croce.

[2] The word *operaio* has industrial overtones which it is difficult to render into one English word. The general term "worker" corresponds rather to the Italian word *lavoratore*. An *operaio* is an artisan, mechanic, factory-hand, miner, etc.; not an agricultural worker.

[3] Rinaldo Rigola, *Storia del Movimento Operaio Italiano*; Milan, 1947; p. 76.

[4] Constituency majority voting, not proportional representation as now.

emerged again before the general elections of 1886, strong enough, small provincial group though it was, to draw some words of sympathy from Depretis, who hoped thereby to win for himself some votes from those Milanese electors who were not far enough to the left to vote for the Workers' Party, but would be impressed by a government which tolerated it. Contrary to Depretis' expectations, the Workers' Party was then furiously attacked by the Republicans and the Radicals, hitherto the parties of the extreme left, who accused it of having been bought by Depretis. The newspaper of the Workers' Party concluded from this incident that "democracy is vile," and finally the quarrel had to be submitted to a "jury of honour," a kind of independent arbitration, which decided in favour of the Workers' Party. The Party again failed to get any seats in 1886 and the next year Depretis reversed his attitude, suppressed the Party, and imprisoned its leaders on charges of inciting to strike and disorder which he could have preferred against them at any time he liked since its foundation. But the sympathy enjoyed in Italy by any body subjected to political suppression enabled it to hold on more or less under cover and with its headquarters transferred to Alessandria in Piedmont until 1890, when the polemics began which led two years later to the formation of the Socialist Party.

This was the first attempt by the Italian working class to bring itself to grips with practical politics. It was a purely proletarian attempt, that is to say the leaders of the Party and the editors of its papers were themselves all workers, and that was why it came to nothing. Giuseppe Croce and his colleagues were thoughtful men but they had neither funds nor political nor oratorical skill. They were passionately, but in the long run vainly, opposed to accepting any help or guidance from the bourgeois intellectuals who were only too willing to throw their means and their vigorous and noisy ideas into the scales on the side of the Workers' Party. At that time, when it was a very new conception that a working man should be active in national politics at all, there was no hope that he could make his way in them alone; so this grave and responsible little group of workmen became merged in the growing current of violent and over-intellectual Marxism. In the light of later events the Workers' Party is interesting because it was the first and only political movement confined to the Italian workers themselves, without any bourgeois leadership, and because it was not revolutionary. It was democratic, parliamentary, and reformist; its inspiration came from Malon. If at this time the group of educated men with political vigour who occupied themselves with the well-being of the working class had been attached to Malon's ideas rather than to those of Marx, the whole history of Italian socialism would have been different. Whether it would have been better depends on an opinion of the events to which Italian socialism gave rise; and chief among these was, as we shall see, the twenty years' rule of fascism.

By the late 'eighties Marx was becoming known more widely and in greater detail. *Capital* was available in translation in a series called the "Economists' Library," together with the writings of Robert Owen and others of very different views from Marx. The philosophical and intellectual climate of Italy after the Union was predominantly "positivist." In Italian usage this word has not the same meaning as it has in French or English, for Comte was regarded as an eccentric minor star in comparison with the great stars, Darwin and Herbert Spencer. Italian positivism was what we might call "evolutionary materialism". It conditioned some powerful thinkers, notably the criminologist Cesare Lombroso. Applying the principles of Spencer and Darwin to his own field he played down the moral responsibility of the criminal and played up the effect on him of his environment in youth and society's duty to reform him rather than to protect itself against him. The two most conspicuous diffusers of Marxism, Antonio Labriola and Filippo Turati, grew up in admiration of Lombroso. Into this rationalist and anti-clerical atmosphere, partly perhaps the philosophic expression of the intense political dislike felt by all liberals for the reactionary part played by the papacy from 1850 until the death of Pius IX in

1878, Marxism swept like a religious revival. Proud, self-sufficient knees were bent once more, and the ideal of the open mind gave way, not to the will of God, but to the will of History. After two decades of conscientiously deciding for themselves the intellectuals arrived with relief at the conclusion that, whatever they might do or think, the proletarian revolution was bound to come. In the words of Benedetto Croce: "The will never feels itself so free as when it knows it is in accordance with the will of God or the necessity of things."[1]

In 1889 Antonio Labriola,[2] Professor of Philosophy in the University of Rome, delivered a series of lectures in which he propounded to his students an enthusiastic and rigidly orthodox Marxism. He had previously been a "positivist" who believed that the most fruitful approach to human problems was through philology and ethnology—a not uncommon view in Italy at the time—and his sudden conversion aroused much attention; he was nearly dismissed for his lectures. He corresponded with Engels and induced him to insert in his preface to the third volume of Marx's *Capital*, then in preparation, a sharp condemnation of the adulterated Marxism that had been diffused in Italy by Loria. A series of books and pamphlets written by Labriola over some years fascinated Italian intellectuals with the idea of total adherence to Marxism. Some of his essays were read in prison by the young Trotsky in 1898 and were later praised by him in his autobiography.[3] Labriola was not an original thinker, but his writings have those qualities of enthusiasm, liveliness, and fidelity to the source which are best adapted to introduce into a new country the ideas of a very original thinker indeed.

Labriola's former pupil Benedetto Croce, then comparatively unknown, was fired with enthusiasm for the new gospel and in 1895 he and Labriola were invited by Georges Sorel (not yet a syndicalist) to contribute articles to the Parisian Marxist paper

[1] Croce, *Storia dell' Italia, 1871–1915*; p. 161. q.v., *passim*, for "positivism" and Marxism in Italy in the 1880's and 1890's.

[2] Not to be confused with the politician Arturo Labriola.

[3] Trotsky, *Ma vie*; Paris, 1930; i, 189. Quoted in Croce, *Materialismo storico ed economia marxistica*; Bari, 1946; p. 282 *n.*

Devenir Social.[1] Signor Croce then devoted himself to a detailed study of the doctrine that had so attracted him at first sight. His powerful analytic mind enabled him to see the extraneous elements—economic, moral, and above all prophetic—in the philosophy of Marx, and his great learning enabled him to see the limited application of historical conclusions drawn from a knowledge which went little beyond the period of the Industrial Revolution in England and France. A series of lectures by Signor Croce, becoming more and more heterodox, strained and finally broke his partnership with Labriola, who remained strictly orthodox. It took Signor Croce five years to burn through Marxism; his final conclusions were collected in 1899 under the title of *Historical Materialism and Marxist Economics.*[2] He went straight to the root of the matter at the base of Marx's economics, the Labour Theory of Value, which he said worked very nicely in theory but not in practice. He called it a "hypothesis thought up and assumed as a universal fact."[3] As to the integral interpretation of history in terms of the class struggle, he pointed out that the Marxist view was only tenable for those periods when (*a*) there were classes, (*b*) they had antagonistic interests, and (*c*) they were conscious of this antagonism; and that this was by no means always.[4] Signor Croce's criticisms of

[1] Croce has given an account of these activities in an essay called *Come nacque e come morì il marxismo teorico in Italia: 1895–1900*, which he published first in his monthly *Critica* and later as an appendix both to his own *Materialismo storico ed economia marxistica*; Bari, 1946; and to his edition of Labriola's *La concezione materialistica della storia*; Bari, 1938.

[2] *Materialismo storico ed economia marxistica*; reprinted Bari, 1946.

[3] A translation, necessarily inadequate, of the highly condensed Crocean phrase: "*Un fatto pensato e assunto come tipo.*"

[4] The reaction of a professional socialist historian to these criticisms is interesting. Giacomo Perticone, in his *Storia del socialismo*; Rome, 1945, after condensing Croce's propositions, says they were "simply to put a formal point of view or a canon of interpretation . . . in the place of an evaluative view of life; a logical concept in the place of a myth. Once take away the myth and political reality can only become empty of significance and content, the political struggle can only be degraded into a conflict between individuals and an antagonism of particular and provisional interests and programmes."

Marx were of great significance for the whole European socialist movement. He was one of the first thinkers to react analytically to the communist dogmas; he neither accepted them with reverent and unquestioning devotion nor rejected them with an instinctive shudder. His impartial examination and irrefutable logic was one of the first stimuli of that philosophical movement which Marxists and students of Marxism call "revisionist," i.e. the revision of Marxian doctrine. Bernstein himself, who headed the movement in Germany where the philosophy of Marx was taken even more seriously than in Italy, was influenced by Signor Croce's criticism, and the collaboration between Signor Croce and Sorel and their long correspondence[1] contributed to the latter's abandonment of strict Marxism and to his formulation of syndicalism. The conscientious tackling of Marxism at a high logical level by some Italian professors at this time was important in the light of later events, for it put "philosophical" Marxism once and for all out of the running as a creed for clear-thinking Italians. In 1939 Signor Croce himself made this claim for their work in the eighteen-nineties: "This ninety-year-old historical materialism, returned from Russia, seems a new and important thing to some English professors. . . . The reason for this is perhaps that English political and economic theorists have never thought Marxism worthy of the serious attention which we Italians gave it, and which vaccinated us against the recurrence of the disease."[2] It is true at any rate that Marxism as a philosophic and historical doctrine effectively vanished from Italy about 1900; what remained was political Marxism, that is, a refusal to co-operate with the capitalist state pending the inevitable revolution and the dictatorship of the proletariat.

We have been led rather far ahead in considering the impact of Marxism on the philosophers and we must return to the political Marxists who were gaining influence while the philosophers were worrying their dialectical bone. Most notable of these

[1] Croce published Sorel's letters to him in his monthly *Critica*, Naples, between 1928 and 1931.

[2] *Materialismo storico ed economia marxistica*; Bari, 1946; p. 316 *n.*

was Filippo Turati. Turati was a young Milanese barrister who was brought to a practical sympathy with socialism through his defence of some of the leaders of the Workers' Party when they were prosecuted in 1887. He was the friend and political collaborator of Anna Kulishov, and, when she left Costa, lived with her until her death. Turati's first work in connection with Marxism was the natural result of the incidents of his profession and of his early adherence to Lombroso. He wrote a series of essays on penology in which, on to the Lombrosian idea of the effect of the criminal's environment in general, he grafted the Marxian idea of his economic environment in particular. In these early days he was not afraid of saying that crime was a function of capitalist society and would vanish with it.

During 1890 and 1891 there grew up, partly through the efforts of Turati, the *Lega Socialista Milanese,* the Milanese Socialist League. In composition it was the antithesis of the Workers' Party, for it was made up exclusively of bourgeois intellectuals. Its programme was imposing and grandiloquent. In contrast with the modest list of the Workers' Party, it set out its aims and ideas in six chapters headed Economics, Politics, Family, Education, Religion and Morals, and Method.[1] The programme is full of the fine hopes and uncompromising idealism of a group that has never been tested in practical politics, but there is one interesting point in it. Under the heading "Method" appears the following passage: "Socialism considers as idle, and leaves open, the question whether the unfolding of the great ends of economic and political evolution will make necessary, as has happened so far in the course of history, a violent and bloody clash between opposing interests and between the classes which represent them. For scientific socialism the social revolution does not come about at any particular moment of time; it fills a whole period and draws into itself all the activities of evolution, reflecting itself in events and in thought and making use of even the most hostile forces to help it, each in its turn." Here is already visible a compromise between the views of reformists

[1] Rigola, op. cit., p. 107.

and revolutionaries, the two parties whose dissensions in the succeeding thirty years paralysed the socialist movement and made it fall apart in the hour of trial.

Now a socialist party can logically work for a proletarian revolution, and it can logically work for proletarian reforms, but it cannot logically fail to decide which, or "leave the question open." If it wants a revolution it must reasonably want a successful revolution, a revolution, that is, which embraces as many of the population as possible and is determined and if necessary bloody in action. Reforms therefore will not help, since they make the working masses more contented and act against the widespread spirit of ferocity and determination which a revolutionary must arouse. That is the position of Marx and Lenin. But if a socialist party wants reforms, it must reasonably do all in its power to carry out the reforms by means of whatever machinery there may be available, even if the reforms include a change in the machinery. To preach revolution does not help, because in a parliamentary democracy the achievements of a party depend on the confidence which it is able to inspire in its contemporaries, both as electors and as members of other parties. If it is continually threatening them with liquidation, they will not trust it. This is the position of the British Labour Party, for example. The issue is in no way affected by the quibble on the word "revolution" to which Turati, so nearly a real statesman, was addicted; either revolution means the violent overthrow of one form of society and the violent installation of another, as in the "French Revolution" or the "Russian Revolution," or else it means a fundamental change in the form of society brought about by peaceful reforms or adjustments, as in the "Industrial Revolution" or the "Managerial Revolution." No amount of formulae invented to save unity could succeed in concealing this fundamental duality of purpose.

In 1891 those Italians who held these two opposed views came together in a common admiration of Marx; the fact that the first were Marxists and that the second were not did not prevent it, for there is enough Marxist doctrine to allow one to feel like a

Marxist while rejecting the crux of the whole thing, the revolution. Those thrown together by Marx in 1891 remained together for thirty years out of respect for proletarian unity. The oil-and-water composition of the Italian Socialist Party is already discernible in the Milanese Socialist League.

Also in 1891, Turati and Anna Kulishov founded the *Critica Sociale*, a Milan fortnightly review. It lasted until Mussolini's special laws of 1925 and became the dominating organ of that section of the press and of opinion which accepted socialism but rejected the bloody revolution.

In 1890, on the initiative of a gathering of socialists at Bordeaux, May 1st was for the first time observed as an international labour day, and in the same year the Italian Government sent representatives to an international governmental congress called by the Emperor William II at Berlin to study social legislation "with warm hearts and cool heads." It was this atmosphere of international as well as national interest in socialism that led to the formation of the Italian Socialist Party.

In the late 'eighties the remains of the Workers' Party in Lombardy and Piedmont were debating whether to amalgamate with the intellectuals. This was not so much a question of alliance as of leadership, for to join with the intellectuals would inevitably mean to accept their views and their orders. At first the purists prevailed; there were to be no bourgeois in the Workers' Party. At a Party congress in 1887 a motion to throw open the Party to anyone who accepted its programme was defeated. The Party continued to refuse admittance not only to intellectuals, but even to "those who direct the work of others." But this firm stand did not last; a gradual recession from it ended in a common meeting with the Milan Socialist League in 1891 to choose two men to represent Italy at the international socialist conference at Brussels later in the year. The choice fell on Giuseppe Croce and Filippo Turati; and it was symbolic of the final fusion between working-class and bourgeois socialism.

At Brussels, Turati and Croce found that the live issue was not that of wage-earner versus intellectual, but that of Marxist versus anarchist. The conference resolved the issue by voting down the anarchists, and the two Italians returned well content with an outcome which had not strained their unity. The story repeated itself in Italy the next year, and the Italian Socialist Party found its own unity in opposition to anarchism.

To Genoa in August 1892 came a great concourse of those of all shades of opinion who were concerned to further the interests of the wage-earner. Giuseppe Croce presided provisionally over four hundred delegates from Chambers of Labour and local political groups of various colours, fire-eating anarchists from the Romagna and a few dark men from the unknown south, as well as delegates from the Workers' Party and the Milanese Socialist League. It became evident at once that there was no possibility of co-operation between those who accepted, however provisionally, parliamentary elections as a means to their ends, among them most of the "Marxists," and those, the anarchists, who did not. Things were brought to breaking-point by a legalitarian speaker who addressed the anarchists in these words: "You are as honest as us, but there is no doubt that there is a quarrel between us and that it goes on every day and every hour, because we are different, because we are following a directly opposed course. There is nothing in common between us, so leave us in peace."[1] The meeting dissolved in an uproar, and the next morning the "legalitarians" met in one hall and the "anarchists" in another.

The situation was now thoroughly confused, for the stormy meeting of the day before had omitted to define the differences between the two groups. The experienced and respected Andrea Costa would not go to either hall and a certain number followed his example. Both meetings proceeded to pass resolutions in the name of the *Partito dei Lavoratori Italiani*.[2] It was found that those who had met separately supposing themselves to be anarchists were not as anarchical as they had thought, for they passed a resolution saying that "while they expected nothing

[1] Camillo Prampolini; quoted in Rinaldo Rigola, op. cit., p. 120.
[2] Italian Workers' Party; but see note, page 18.

from legal means, from Parliament, or from the State, they left single sections to conduct themselves as they thought best in the vicissitudes of public life."[1] Single sections of what, is not specified. Nothing came of this meeting; those of true anarchist temper returned to their obscure lives of bomb-throwing and those who were really socialists were slowly absorbed into the new Party.

It was in the other hall that the Italian Socialist Party was formed.[2] Here the Milanese Socialist League was well in control of the situation and the meeting constituted itself into a political party and voted its programme. As this programme remained the official programme of the Socialist Party until 1919, it is worth quoting in full:

Programme

1. WHEREAS under the present dispositions of human society men are constrained to live in two classes, on the one hand that of the exploited workers, and on the other that of the capitalists who hold the wealth of society exclusively to themselves;
2. and by reason of their economic dependence the wage-earners of both sexes and of every age and condition form the Proletariat, which is constrained to a life of poverty, inferiority, and oppression;
3. and all men, provided they contribute according to their abilities to the creation and maintenance of the benefits of society, have an equal right to enjoy those benefits, principally that of an individual existence guaranteed by society;
4. AND RECOGNIZING THAT the present economic and social institutions supported by the political system represent the dominion over the working class of those who monopolize the wealth of society and nature;

[1] Rinaldo Rigola, op. cit., p. 121.

[2] The name *Partito Socialista Italiano* was adopted only in 1895. The party was first called *Partito dei Lavoratori Italiani* and then *Partito Socialista dei Lavoratori Italiani*, but, since its adoption of the present name was accompanied by no change of programme or composition, it will be simpler to call the party the Italian Socialist Party from now on.

5. and that the workers can only effect their emancipation by the socialization of the means of work (land, mines, factories, transport, etc.) and by means of collective control of production;

AND HOLDING THAT these ends can only be achieved by the action of all the proletariat organized in a "class party" independent of all other parties and having a double aspect: (1) of the "professional struggle" for the immediate improvement of the conditions of work (hours, wages, factory regulations, etc.) the carrying on of which would be delegated to the Chambers of Labour and other trade organizations; and (2) of the wider struggle for the conquest of political power (in the state, in the communes, in the civil service, etc.) in order to transform these organs from the instruments of oppression and exploitation which they now are into the instruments of the economic and political expropriation of the ruling class;

the Italian workers, intending to effect their own emancipation,

DETERMINE

to organize themselves into a Party based on the above principles.[1]

A central committee of seven was elected; there were six wage-earners, including Giuseppe Croce and one woman, and a parliamentary Deputy, Antonio Maffi, who had been elected as the candidate of a local Milanese radical group.

It strikes the eye at once that this was not in fact a programme at all, but a statement of the reasons for the formation of the Socialist Party. There is no concrete aim stated, unless it be the socialization of the means of work, and these six words in themselves call up no very clear idea. The "programme" was, of course, the highest common factor of the views of those present at Genoa, who were united in accepting Marx's analysis of the ills of capitalist society but not in accepting his remedy, revolution. Indeed if the "programme" leans either way it leans slightly to the non-Marxist school of reformism. The phrase

[1] Rinaldo Rigola, op. cit., p. 121.

"the conquest of political power," followed by a list of the organs of power to be conquered, suggests elections rather than the absolute and destructive intransigence of Marx. But on the other hand the word "election" is nowhere mentioned, and those who pleased were free to interpret the phrase as conquest by threat and force. In fact the new Party plunged at once into the electoral struggle with success. The programme was a safe, wide resolution voted with full knowledge of the discrepancies of outlook in the nascent Party and designed to hold the Party together for as long as might be, a design which it fulfilled, to the detriment of Italy, until it was superseded in 1919.

CHAPTER II

NATIONAL POLITICS

From the foundation of the Socialist Party in 1892 *until the outbreak of war in* 1914

1. *The governments of Crispi,* 1887–96, *of Rudinì,* 1896–8, *and of Pelloux,* 1898–1900

ON the death of Depretis in 1887, the Sicilian Francesco Crispi had taken office as Prime Minister. At last Italy was assured that the boredom and gloom of political life would be dispersed, for Crispi was the most controversial figure in the country. He had been Garibaldi's lieutenant on his famous Sicilian expedition and had been left in Sicily more or less as a dictator when Garibaldi and the Thousand continued their triumphant march to Naples. Crispi was a man of violent utterance and great instability, characteristics which kept him out of power as long as the influence of Cavour lasted. But his clamorous conversion from Mazzinian republicanism to support of the Savoy Monarchy made him acceptable later as a political leader. He was under continuous fire for supposed bigamy and financial fraud, and his entry into power at once upset the gloomy restraints of the preceding regime. He galvanized parliamentary debates into hectic violence, and for the ten years of his rule lurid accusations and counter-accusations were shot back and forth in the Chamber where Depretis' dignified and equable suppleness had formerly stifled every disagreement before it appeared. In foreign policy Crispi was dominated by an eccentric hatred and suspicion of France. To him France was all Masons and anticlericals, divorce and trade unions; and so he began a tariff war which hurt France very little and Italy very much. The labour troubles which arose partly because of the tariff war were to Crispi more evidence of French wickedness. He was convinced that they were fomented by agitators in French pay. As a complement to his anti-French policy, Crispi joined Germany and Austria in the Triple Alliance which remained the main plank of Italian foreign policy and one of the stable elements in the European situation until 1914.

But for all his turbulence and energy Crispi did not break the tradition of *trasformismo*. Indeed by these very qualities he confirmed it. Whereas it had been impossible to say whether Depretis was right, left, or centre, because his adaptability confused every issue and the price he offered for collaboration emasculated his opponents, it was impossible to say whether Crispi was right, left, or centre, because his violent and illogical reactions created issues where there were none and his sudden changes of position made it impossible for anybody to know whether he was his opponent or not. His most flamboyant *volte-face* and that which created most excitement at the time, although it does not bear directly on the story of socialism, was in his attitude to the Church. He started in office with the intention of reconciling the Italian state with the papacy, but, when he found that the prelate[1] with whom he was negotiating was not the agent of the Vatican at all, he suddenly reversed his policy and was violently anti-clerical for the rest of his time in power. In 1889 he had a statue of Giordano Bruno erected in the very square where that philosopher had been burnt by the Church in the seventeenth century.

Crispi finally came to grief over an imperial adventure. The hated French had taken Tunisia, which he regarded as marked for Italian rule, and so he must compensate Italy by following up a very modest settlement sponsored by Depretis on the Red Sea, and becoming the protector of Abyssinia. But financial timidity and political interference with the military command on the spot

[1] Tosti, Abbot of Monte Cassino.

led to the total defeat of the Italian forces by those of the Abyssinian Emperor Menelik at Adua in 1896. Crispi fell.

The first two years of the Socialist Party were on the whole uneventful. It was busy organizing itself and learning the best way to keep alive in spite of Crispi's tempestuous dislike, to whom all socialists were "atheist anarchists." The second National Congress of the Party, meeting at Reggio Emilia in 1893, was devoted to redefining its position *vis-à-vis* the anarchists and to regulating various affairs which it found necessary now it was a nation-wide party. The latent discrepancy between the revolutionaries and the reformists was not much in evidence and Turati was able to raise a cheer by identifying legalitarian methods with political maturity. He described anarchism as the "teething of the workers' movement," and counterbalanced this with a slap at the right wing: "Socialism has not everywhere broken the umbilical cord which bound it to popular liberalism." In both ways its consciousness was "full of atavisms."[1] In those early years the opposition of the socialists to the anarchists made the former lean towards legal and moderate ideas; compared with an anarchist, an orthodox Marxist was a peaceable fellow. A common hostility to anarchism obscured the conflict between the revolutionaries and the reformists in the Socialist Party.

The main work of the Congress was to regulate the relations of the Party with the handful of parliamentary Deputies who had adhered to it. It voted a resolution which showed all the trepidation and mistrust with which the socialists entered parliamentary politics. It ruled that (1) the socialist Deputies must form a disciplined group in Parliament; (2) they must expound the general views of the Party; (3) they must keep in touch with the Party through its Secretariat and must accept the Party's ruling on particular issues; (4) they must take every opportunity of proclaiming in the Chamber that the Party had no faith in

[1] See the collection of Turati's speeches and articles published at Bologna in 1921 under the title of *Vie maestri del socialismo.*

"adulterated reforms" proposed by the bourgeois to save their own necks; (5) Regional and National Congresses were to be the judges of Deputies' behaviour; (6) the Deputies' conduct was always to be inspired by the Party Line, which was revolutionary; (7) in strikes and disturbances the Deputies were to go to the place and use all their energies and all their privileges to further them; (8) they were under no circumstances ever to vote confidence in any government.[1]

Here again was a compromise. The revolutionaries wanted to have nothing to do with parliament; the reformists wanted to go there and do useful and constructive work. So they agreed that there were to be socialist Deputies, but that in effect they were to do nothing at all, since the eighth article allowed them no power to support any government which they might find less obnoxious than any other.

In 1892 and 1893 the socialists were also beginning to discover the difficulties of keeping going under a hostile government. In Costa's opinion the old Cavourian Right (1870–6) had tolerated Bakunin and his sections of the International as a bogy[2] with which to frighten the centre and to discredit the moderate left. The old Workers' Party had been deceived by Depretis' initial blandishments and had failed to keep its end up under his later persecutions. But the big new party was determined not to go down before Crispi's intermittent attentions. It was not until the Sicilian rising of 1894 that Crispi took determined action against it, but from its foundation it had experienced his milder methods of repression. He had a pinprick technique of indirect action; he would instruct a prefect to requisition a hall for other purposes when the socialists wanted to meet there, or he would try to break their nerve by submitting them to continuous espionage. With characteristic good humour, Turati said in an article early in 1894: "It will be a red-letter day for us if by the special complaisance of our superiors we are allowed to meet at Imola, privately, on tiptoe."[3] As we shall see, they were not.

[1] Giacomo Perticone, *Storia del socialismo*; Rome, 1945.

[2] *Spauracchio* was Costa's word.

[3] Turati, op. cit.

It was in that year that the first trial of strength came, and Crispi played into their hands. Since 1860 there had been in Sicily organizations of the peasants, and to a lesser extent of the sulphur-miners, called the Workers' Groups, *Fasci dei Lavoratori*.[1] They were originally Mazzinian but outlasted Mazzinianism. The Sicilian peasant with his strong strain of Arab blood was probably the poorest and most primitive in Italy, and the *Fasci* survived as an inchoate expression of his solidarity against the landowner, the mayor, the prefect, the policeman, and sometimes against the brigand in the hills. They had been little affected by Bakuninism in the 'seventies and were in 1893 neither trade unions nor mutual assistance societies. They had between two and three hundred thousand members.

The Sicilian system of land-tenure was disgracefully antiquated. The land was for the most part divided into big estates, the *latifondi*, each owned by a nobleman who lived in Rome or in a comfortable villa well away from danger. Between him and the peasant were two and sometimes three layers of lessees and sub-lessees, all of whom had to make a living out of the land. Besides his rent the landlord could exact certain feudal taxes and in practice he paid very little to the state. In 1893 a fall in the price of wine, due at least in part to the withdrawal of French buyers from the market as a result of Crispi's tariff war, combined with the old abuses of the land-tenure to provoke a revolt. The peasants of the whole island rose immediately in sympathy with those of Marsala and other wine-growing districts, and the sulphur-miners quickly joined them. As was natural, they acted through the *Fasci* and it was to these that the socialist agitators addressed themselves. The new organized socialism had not made much headway in the backward, agricultural island, but when the disturbances started socialist demagogues were prompt to organize the peasantry and to try to give a socialist turn of class-consciousness to purely local and spontaneous grievances.

[1] The word *fascio* means nothing but "group" and *fascista* nothing but "grouper." Both words are now of course discredited in Italy and are never likely to be used in their old sense again.

In this they were not wholly successful, for two local landlords, a prince and a duke, whose sympathies lay with their peasants and not with their absentee brothers, led bands in the fighting; and the rioters themselves, far from unanimously accepting socialism as their guide, carried in procession images not only of Marx, but also of Mazzini, Garibaldi, the King, the Queen, and Jesus Christ.[1] It is difficult to guess which of these eminent persons would have been most offended by the proximity of the others. All over Sicily columns of peasants marched on the police-stations, the prefectures and the houses of the landlords. There were a number of deaths in clashes with the police. But for all the attempts of the socialists the movement remained undisciplined and sporadic. The bigger and better organized *Fasci* of the cities, Palermo, Messina, Catania, remained calm, although there were minor disturbances, reflecting those in Sicily, in the marble and silk-producing areas of the north, which had also been hit by Crispi's anti-French trade policy.

In 1892 Crispi had been temporarily thrown out of office because he had provoked the extreme left and Old Right to sink their differences in a common exasperation, and his place had been taken by Giovanni Giolitti, then comparatively young and unknown. Giolitti was inexperienced and a liberal, and all that he did about the Sicilian troubles was to send down a senator to investigate and report. But a growing body of opinion called for more decisive action and in December 1893 Giolitti fell and Crispi returned. The Reggio Emilia motion had ordered the socialist Deputies never to vote confidence in any government. It is interesting to note that the first time they were called upon to obey this order they should by doing so have contributed to the return of their greatest enemy.

Crispi knew exactly what was the matter in Sicily; it was a Franco-Russian plot. The agitators, socialist and others, were in French pay and their aim was to detach Sicily from Italy and set it up as an independent Republic under French and Russian tutelage. The Church, of course, favoured the project as a step

[1] Panfilo Gentile, *50 anni di socialismo in Italia*; Milan, 1948; p. 58.

towards the disintegration of the lay Italian State. Crispi expounded this view in the Chamber and supported it with documents which he believed to be conclusive. The majority naturally did not share his view, but, since it would lead him to the action which they desired, they gave him the powers for which he asked. Instead of a senator, he sent a general to Sicily, and declared a state of siege there and in the disaffected areas of the north. There followed arrests, the suppression of local papers, trials by special tribunal, sentences of imprisonment for major agitators, and house-arrest for minor ones. Finally Crispi suppressed the Socialist Party and at the end of the session, when they no longer enjoyed a constitutional immunity, he arrested the socialist Deputies. When he was an old man in retirement, he claimed that more credit was due to him as the saviour of Italian unity at this time than as Garibaldi's right-hand man.

There followed the general elections of 1895, and several of the imprisoned socialists were elected. Their election was annulled and they were re-elected. A very natural thing had happened; the same moderate opinion which had been shocked and alarmed at the excesses in Sicily had been even more shocked and alarmed at Crispi's unselective repressions. The great body of liberal and peaceful sentiment which had been at first on Crispi's side swung round into sympathy with the persecuted socialists. Crispi had in fact overreached himself and made the socialists the heroes and martyrs of all liberals, a bizarre situation which lasted until 1900 and enabled the socialists to survive the savage persecutions of those years.

The continuation of special tribunals and house-arrest was forgotten in 1896 because of the news from Abyssinia. The socialists now had their first opportunity of trying out the effects of Marxist propaganda in war-time. They proclaimed, as best they could in their harassed situation, that not only was the war against Menelik a manifestation of capitalist imperialism, but also that Crispi had resorted to it to distract attention from his repressive policy at home. They were not, however, able to sow much dissension or alarm, partly because they were a small party and partly because it was a small war; the Italian troops engaged numbered about 15,000 only, so that the campaign was not on a scale to provoke any strong feeling of national unity. They were frankly delighted at the news of the defeat at Adua and their agitators cried: "*Viva Menelik!*"

At the final fall of Crispi, the position of the socialists had changed somewhat since his return to power in 1893, three years before. Between then and their arrest in 1895 the socialist Deputies had found that they were not alone in their rigid abstinence from any glimmer of co-operation with the government; the two parties who sat beside them on the benches of the extreme left were almost equally intransigent. These were the republicans and the radicals.[1] The Republican Party had grown round a nucleus of diehard Mazzinians by the accretion of men who were opposed to the monarchy for various reasons other than the poetic discontent of Mazzini himself. The Party was particularly strong in the Romagna, that territory to the north-east of the Apennine chain, by Forlì and Imola, which had been the most remote and recalcitrant of the Papal States. The rule of papal governors, carried out between 1815 and 1859 through an Austrian garrison, had engendered in the province an automatic aversion from whatever government there might be, an aversion which was transferred from the distant Pope and the distant Emperor to the distant King. It was this tradition of turbulence and disaffection which gave most of its leaders to the Republican Party, fiery, austere, high-minded men, many of whom were called Giuseppe after Mazzini and Garibaldi.

The Radical Party had appeared in 1878 with the first aim of resisting Depretis' *trasformismo*. At all costs it would not allow itself to be disnatured by the wiles of that too reasonable grey-beard. Their two main planks were universal suffrage and the "armed nation", or as we should say a democratic army based on temporary territorial service. They accepted the monarchy, since they thought that they would be able to be more effective by doing so. Except for their attitude to the monarchy the two

[1] Same words in Italian, *Repubblicani* and *Radicali.*

parties were much alike. Neither Party accepted Marx's teaching.

The Republican, Radical, and Socialist Parties were so much alike in their parliamentary action or rather lack of action that they came to be known collectively as the "Extreme Left," *estrema sinistra*, or simply *l'estrema* for short. Their alliance was strengthened by Crispi's suppression of the socialists, which naturally incensed and alarmed the other two Parties.

The acceptance *de facto* by the socialist Deputies of a parliamentary alliance caused mixed feelings in the central organs of the Socialist Party. Turati approved. In an article in 1895 he said that the bourgeois parties, among which socialist doctrine included the republicans and radicals, were their economic but not their political enemies. Political tactics, he said, were the same in principle as personal morals, and for a party to have no allies would be the same thing as for a man to have no friends.[1] But the prevailing opinion was the opposite one, that to smile at a republican was just as much a betrayal of the interests of the working class as to smile at a great industrial monopolist. The issue was largely forgotten under the stress of Crispi's persecution, and the general elections of 1897 came without any decision having been taken.

At the elections the socialists enjoyed the benefits of the liberal reaction in their favour, and they got twenty seats out of some five hundred. Together the three parties of the *estrema* had sixty-seven. Thus the socialists had survived their first encounter with the real political life of the nation, but it must be admitted that Crispi did not make it very difficult for them. The part they played in the disorders of 1893–4 would not have led a wise minister to such extreme measures of repression. The majority of Italians saw this clearly, and, as soon as Crispi had been discredited by the Abyssinian defeat and had fallen, an amnesty was passed and the socialists came out of prison to take part in the elections. The new Prime Minister was Antonio di Rudinì, a Sicilian Marquis who was chosen by reaction from Crispi for his sober caution and

[1] Turati, *Vie maestri del socialismo*; Bologna, 1921; article entitled *La tattica elettorale.*

his unblemished personal character. For a year everything went smoothly. Rudinì embarked on the retrenchment natural after the collapse of Crispi's imperial adventure and sent a commissioner to Sicily to wind up the state of siege. The commissioner eased out the tension by a sensible moderation; on the one hand he forbade strikes and refused to allow the formation of either socialist or catholic organizations among the workers, and on the other he encouraged the formation of a non-political trade union for the sulphur-miners.[1] The socialist Deputies took their seats beside the republicans and radicals, and it seemed that all would go quietly and prosperously for a while.

But violence and civil strife had not burnt themselves out. In 1898 a series of labour disturbances all over Italy culminated in the "four days of Milan," an outburst which put the Sicilian troubles in the shade. The immediate cause of the outbreak was a rise in the price of bread following a bad harvest and the interruption of grain imports consequent on the Spanish-American War, which also disorganized the Italian cotton industry by interrupting the import of cotton. The fighting was much more violent and more organized on both sides than anything that had yet been experienced. Minor stone-throwing incidents turned into full-scale massacres when the police panicked, fired on the crowds, and charged. Thousands of idle onlookers were involved and their presence made it impossible to isolate the trouble. Tramcars were upset to form barricades and there was some arson. At one stage the police and troops thought that they had discovered the "anarchist headquarters" in the convent of Monforte. They stormed it and tried to pull the beards off the Capuchins, whom they supposed to be the disguised leaders of the revolt. The beards were not false, nor were the Capuchins. When it was far too late, the government made a gesture of appeasement by taking all tax off grain for two months.

At the end of four days, it was found that the casualties were two policemen killed, and among the populace 80 killed and 450

[1] The *latifondi* still exist to-day, although they have lost some of their more objectionable aspects since 1897.

wounded.[1] These are the official figures, and it is not likely that the police would have exaggerated their own butchery. A riot in Milan with such a shocking death roll was a very different matter from anything that might happen in rural Sicily. Milan was the biggest city in the land and the centre of its industry, and it was also the headquarters of the Socialist Party. There was no doubt at all that the more extreme socialist leaders had been fostering the disorders, if not by example, at least by continuous and vehement precept. The workers of Milan were to a large extent what the socialists had made them; the riots were the first fruit of socialist propaganda. Earlier in the year, during the increasing labour troubles, Rudinì had said in a speech: "Thus far and no further"; and Leonida Bissolati in his first leading article as editor of *Avanti!* replied: "Thus far and yet further."[2] Yet Bissolati was well known as a leader of the more moderate faction in the Party. Altogether the socialists had been openly asking for trouble. But once again the government had played into their hands. Rudinì's answer to the riots was the same as Crispi's four years before; a state of siege, military tribunals, house-arrest, the suppression of over a hundred left-wing newspapers, and the imprisonment of the socialist leaders who had been in Milan at the time, including Turati, Anna Kulishov, and Bissolati. The King wrote an open letter of congratulation to the general who had suppressed the riot and awarded him a high decoration. But this was all a familiar routine. The issues, which had been obscured after the Sicilian disorders by the Abyssinian War and the dispersed nature of the disorders themselves, were clearer this time, because the disorders of Milan had flared up and been brutally suppressed in only four days, and because Milan was the industrial, financial, and commercial capital of Italy.[3] So the natural liberal reaction came quicker. As soon as the dust had settled Rudinì was succeeded by Luigi Pelloux, a

[1] Elizabeth Wiskemann, *Italy*; O.U.P., 1947; p. 43.

[2] "*Di qui non si passa*" and "*Eppure si passa.*"

[3] It was often called also the "moral capital of Italy." Mussolini forbade this description during his campaign for the glorification of Rome and the Roman Empire.

liberal general who had achieved wide popularity by refusing to proclaim a state of siege in the area under his command when it was ordered by Rudinì. Pelloux started his term of office with a wide amnesty for the socialist agitators and the withdrawal of the press ban. But he too succumbed to the spirit of *trasformismo*. It was his opinion that the Milan disorders called for some legal provision against a recurrence of the violence that had burst out twice in five years.

It was in the first place a mistake to think that either the real grievances of the working class or the demagogy of their socialist leaders could be dealt with by precautionary legislation, but a far graver mistake was the method which he used to get the legislation through. His bills were not in themselves excessively severe. They provided for the prior authorization of open-air meetings by the police, the prohibition of strikes by state and local government employees, the empowering of the courts to dissolve organizations directed to the overthrow of the constitution or to the disintegration of the Italian state, and the liability of a newspaper to suspension for three months if the editor were convicted of seditious falsehood or incitement to violence, and to the surveillance of each issue by the police after a third conviction.[1] The bills passed first and second reading by a large majority. Then the *estrema* opened its attack. Socialist, republican, and radical Deputies began to speak, and it soon appeared that they would never stop. They were, in fact, obstructing. This was the first appearance of parliamentary obstruction in Italy and the Government remembered Gladstone's answer to the Irish members; it proposed to introduce the guillotine and the closure. The *estrema* however continued to filibuster in the debate on the guillotine with as much gusto as they had in the debate on the bills. Pelloux adjourned the sitting in exasperation. He took his bills to the King and they were promulgated as Royal Decrees. By the constitution a Royal Decree could only come into force if approved by parliament within a month, and at the reopening of the session the moderate left, incensed at legislation being

[1] Gentile, op. cit., p. 80.

passed by decree when parliament was in session, joined force with the *estrema.* For some days the debate on the bills proceeded in an uproar. When the stamina of the opposition allowed no more obstruction and the vote was no longer avoidable, they broke the ballot-boxes.[1] The session was again adjourned. During the recess the status of Pelloux's provisions was in doubt until the first case came up for trial under them, that of an anarchist agitator. The Court of Cassation, the supreme organ of the Italian judiciary, declared the decrees illegal, as indeed it could hardly fail to do. After a few months of hang-fire Pelloux returned to the charge in the Chamber of Deputies. The bills were presented again, and the *estrema* obstructed; the guillotine and closure were proposed again, and the *estrema* still obstructed. Finally Pelloux decided he would put the question of the guillotine to the vote, whether or not there were opposition members who still wished to speak. The whole opposition, both moderate and extreme left, walked out of the Chamber. The guillotine and closure were passed, but the opposition had the last word, for they did not come back. Pelloux recognized the impropriety of governing with a rump parliament, dissolved, and went to the country. The whole episode lasted for a year, from the first presentation of the bills in June 1899 to the general elections in June 1900.

The opinion of the country about Pelloux and the obstructors was made clear at the elections. The parties of the *estrema,* in alliance at the polls, increased their seats from 67 to 95, and the socialists in particular from 20 to 32. After a short false start power was assumed by Giuseppe Zanardelli, the libertarian leader of the moderate left, with Giolitti as his Minister of the Interior. The socialists knew therefore that a breathing space had come.

This was the end of the "heroic age" of Italian socialism, an age which is usually presented as all enlightenment and a true passion for liberty on one side and all bayonets and bigotry on

[1] In both houses of the Italian Parliament members still vote by secret ballot, first having their names ticked off on a list.

the other. There is some truth in this presentation; the three ministries which had to deal with the first socialist agitations all made the same mistake of alienating moderate opinion by the severity of their measures. Crispi suppressed the Socialist Party after disorders which, far from being attributable to it, were more attributable to his own fiscal policy, and thereby made socialism the more popular. Rudinì, arriving in power on the wave of liberal feeling provoked by Crispi, mishandled the situation in Milan to the extent shown by the casualty list, and by his repressions made socialism more popular still. Pelloux, arriving in power on the wave of liberal feeling provoked by Rudinì, resorted to unconstitutional methods in an attempt to stop the pendulum, and made the socialists who resisted them so popular that it was once and for all recognized that no government could live that did not expressly tolerate them. On the other hand it is arguable that the socialist Deputies behaved improperly in obstructing debate in the Chamber and in finally breaking the ballot-boxes. But there is this to be said for them, that the suffrage at this time was by no means universal. It would be indefensible for a minority to hold up the proceedings of a parliament which represented the entire population, but when representation is only partial, and on a property qualification, the rights and wrongs are not so clear. If the socialist members had been agitating for universal suffrage, as the old Workers' Party had, or indeed if universal suffrage had been a conspicuous plank in their programme, they would surely have been justified in using violent means to stop the passing in a quasi-oligarchic chamber of measures which they believed not to have the support of the majority of the population. But to agitate for universal suffrage would have been an avowal of the merits of the parliamentary system, and that the majority of the socialists could not stomach. They resorted to violence, therefore, without advancing the only possible justification for it. Their conduct however brought them increased support, which they cared about more than the propriety of their methods. The larger question of the propriety of socialist agitation in the country in Sicily and at Milan is not indeed peculiar to the place and time. It is the question which dominated Europe from 1789 until the terms in which it was posed were turned upside down by the development of Soviet Russia in the nineteen-twenties, and it cannot be answered except in consideration of a wider scene and of more general principles.

The practical effect of the six-years' battle and particularly of the violent parliamentary campaign of 1899–1900, which was contemporary with the Dreyfus Affair in France, was the installation of a liberal government. Repressive policies had been given a full trial and found not to be practicable. The military tribunal and the suspension of newspapers were not seen again in Italy until the time of fascism. This outcome was directly due to the spirited if incorrect behaviour of the *estrema,* of which the socialists were the backbone and the claws. For the socialists of course this was an unforeseen turn. If there is anything a newly founded Marxist Party does not expect or want to do, it is to secure the triumph of liberalism by parliamentary action. But we have seen how the Party was not composed entirely of orthodox Marxists, and although they kept quiet about it, it is likely that the democratic element headed by Bissolati and Turati gladly accepted the buffeting of these years for the sake of the turn of the tide which they rightly guessed would follow. It was a period in which the new Party was forced to answer attacks, made upon it with the weapons of parliamentary democracy, by itself entering the lists in parliament.

But alone they could not have hoped to put up the resistance they did, and from the point of view of their own principles the most important outcome of the whole period was the electoral alliance of 1900. This was the logical conclusion of the increasing co-operation of the three parties of the *estrema* in parliament, and when by their combined boycott of the Chamber they provoked the elections it was hardly to be avoided that they should take the obvious course of thus ensuring that their common effort be put to the best advantage in the next parliament. In those days the Italian electoral system was much like the English; it was based on majorities in single-member geographical constituencies. The alliance therefore took the form of the alliances we know in the English electoral system; the three parties agreed not to run against each other. In this way they were able to turn to the best advantage the republican predominance in the Romagna and the socialist predominance in Milan and in the other industrial cities of Lombardy. But even so limited a compromise with the bourgeois state caused some heart-searching among the purists. That the alliance should have been accepted is a measure of the success of those who were trying to steer the Party into the ways of constitutional democracy.

If we consider the formidable impact of socialism on Italian politics, it is remarkable how small the Socialist Party was, and to what a small extent, even then, it was run by the workers themselves. In 1904 the proportion of the whole population of certain provinces which was inscribed in the Socialist Party was as follows: for every 10,000 inhabitants, Emilia-Romagna, 201; Tuscany, 67; Piedmont, 53; Lombardy, 44; Lazio, 28; Calabria, 7; Sardinia, 5. Perhaps the most interesting thing about these figures is the fact that Lombardy comes fourth. Since Milan was its happy hunting ground, it reflects the failure of the Party to reach the peasants of the middle Po Valley. In 1903 a questionnaire to Party members on their own estimate of their class status gave this result: rural and urban workers, 72·18 per cent; *petit bourgeois*, 14·29 per cent; "educated persons," 3·8 per cent. In the same year, of the 33 parliamentary Deputies 28 were university graduates, 3 were *petit bourgeois*, and only 2 were wage-earners.[1] Of the leaders of the Party who made a name for themselves at this time, only one was a wage-earner, Costantino Lazzari, who was of the revolutionary wing; and he was an accounting clerk. He had been a colleague of Giuseppe Croce in the foundation of the Workers' Party in 1882. All the rest were lawyers, university teachers, journalists, and those like Antonio Maffi who had been Deputies before the foundation of the Party. The issue of wage-earner versus intellectual had been

[1] All these figures come from William Salomone, *Italian Democracy in the Making*; Philadelphia, 1945; p. 54.

settled under the stress of common danger, and much to the advantage of the intellectual.

The headquarters of the Party was still at Milan, and was always to remain there. It was naturally to the great industrial city that the leaders directed their attention, and from it that their solid and useful support came. But socialism, if no stronger, was much more noisy and active among the turbulent folk of the Romagna, at Imola and at Forlì, in the old republican strongholds. These cities under the Apennine mountains were the home of the fiery, the intransigent, the ferocious, the demagogues. The central cities and above all Florence were also beginning to develop their own type of socialism, less noisy than that of the Romagna, less respectable than that of Milan, and notable for a kind of cold savagery. There is some foundation for the view that both socialism and fascism have drawn their orators and agitators from the Romagna, their funds and their wisdom from Milan, and their murderers and blackmailers from Tuscany. Venetia and the south of Italy were not so interested in socialism, although the backward Sicilian peasants were, as we have seen, not deaf to its agitators.

The old local trade assistance societies had taught the habit of local association, and the habit was carried over from matters of insurance to matters of collective bargaining. At the turn of the century the Chambers of Labour were becoming stronger and more numerous.

The *Camere del Lavoro,* local organizations, have always been more important in Italy than the *sindacati,* trade unions. The cause of this is probably to be sought in the general causes of *campanilismo* ("our town hall has a higher tower than yours"). Italy is a mountainous country and communications are still bad. There is also the matter of tradition; every Italian worker knows about the *condottiere* who led out his ancestors in the sixteenth century to fight the ancestors of the worker in the next town. The strength of local organizations as opposed to trade organizations later made difficult the work of strike strategists; for one can paralyse a whole country with a stoppage in a single industry, but one cannot do so with a stoppage in a single city. When Italy was within a hairsbreadth of a socialist revolution in 1920 there was, as we shall see,[1] a trade union in charge of the agitation, not a Chamber of Labour.

There was at this time no body corresponding to the Trades Union Congress in England.

The structure of the Party was democratic. At the bottom came the Local Associations, more or less closely linked with the Chambers of Labour. These Associations sent delegates, each representing a certain number of votes, to Regional Congresses and to an Annual National Congress which elected a Chairman, Secretary, and Direction, or Executive Committee, for the year. The Direction would in turn appoint a permanent secretariat. In close co-operation with the Direction was the staff of the Party's newspaper *Avanti!* Funds came from compulsory subscriptions from members of the Party. There has never been a "political levy" in the Italian labour movement, and so no question of "contracting in" or "contracting out." The Party was always very poor in comparison with the French and German Socialist Parties, and this was a common justification for its representation in parliament by professional men and not by wage-earners. Deputies were not paid until 1912.

The propaganda of the Party was carried out first and foremost by the press. Around the daily *Avanti!* was grouped an exuberance of local papers and periodicals, many of them short-lived, but most of them with a high standard of enthusiasm, ingenuity, and literary talent. Pamphlets were copious. The *comizietto in piazza*, a considerable vehicle in Italy for the diffusion of views, was a means of propaganda which required little control or encouragement. In all small Italian towns, most of the male population meets in the central *piazza* before a late lunch and again in the evening after working hours. In the big cities recognized places serve for this gathering; in Milan and Naples, the Galleria, a great covered arcade, in Rome, Piazza Colonna. *Comizietto* is the diminutive of *comizio*, a political meeting; it is

[1] See pages 109–15.

IKHAIL BAKUNIN

BENEDETTO CROCE
in 1944

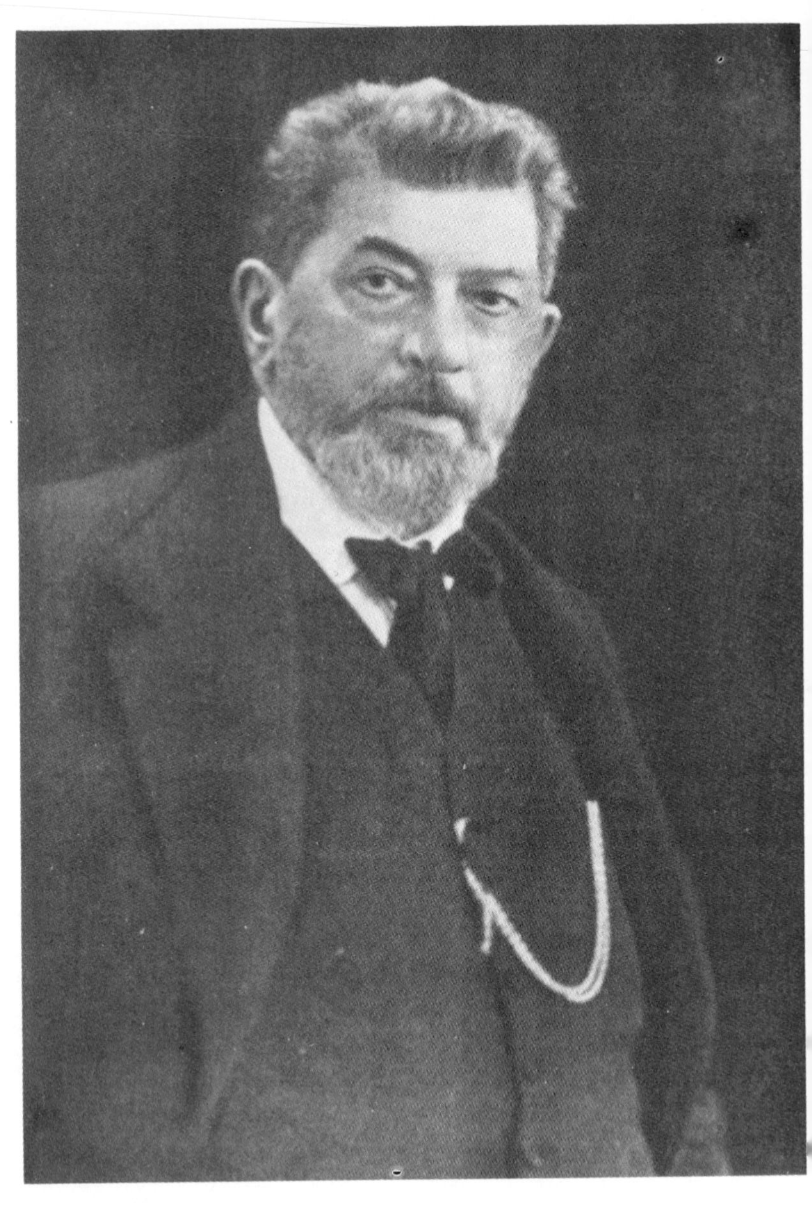

FILIPPO TURATI

the knot of promenading citizens which gathers for a political argument.[1] The expounding of political socialism in factories and in the Chambers of Labour was another aspect of propaganda that could be left to itself.

The speeches of socialist Deputies and the proceedings of Socialist Party Congresses were naturally widely reported in the national press, both of the left and of the right.

At the beginning of the century, the Socialist Party was not rich enough to undertake movements for the general education of the workers in addition to political propaganda, and indeed "cultural tea-parties" were occasionally censured by the Party Direction as a red herring and a dispersion of energies. There was never anything like the Workers' Educational Association in England.

The position of women in industry and in society in general occupied some attention; in particular Turati and Anna Kulishov devoted themselves to the question of prostitution and family life, with reference to the curious passage on these matters in the *Communist Manifesto.*

2. *The governments of Zanardelli,* 1901–3, *and of Giolitti and his lieutenants,* 1903–14

The last sad freak of violence was the assassination of King Umberto I in 1900 by an anarchist who had waited two years to take his revenge for the letter of congratulation which the King had written to the suppressor of the Milan riots. As a result of the assassination there was a move for the return of Pelloux, but the first action of the new King, young Victor Emmanuel III, was to call instead a liberal Prime Minister, who was quickly succeeded by one yet more liberal still, the very archetype and prophet of contemporary liberals, Zanardelli. He came to power in 1901 as the expression of a violent revulsion against all and every sort of repression.

[1] A characteristic account of a *comizietto* is given by Elizabeth Wiskemann in an appendix to her *Italy*; O.U.P., 1947.

The poet Gabriele d'Annunzio had been elected in 1897 as a Deputy of the right, and three years later he crossed the Chamber and sat on the benches of the extreme left exclaiming: "I go towards Life!" Whatever other political abilities he lacked d'Annunzio had, as we shall see, an unfailing sense of which way the wind was blowing. The exclamation was not merely a poetic eccentricity of the "Deputy for Beauty," it expressed a feeling that was general in the first year of the century, a feeling of release and of the beginning of a new age.

Zanardelli himself had been Minister of the Interior in 1889, and his resolute refusal to stop people doing just what they pleased had so compromised the work of his colleagues that three of them, the Foreign Minister and the two Service Ministers, had resigned.

While he was in office he passed the famous "Zanardelli Code," which was a revision of the old Piedmontese Legal Code. Code and revision together are still the basis of Italian law. His revisions included the abolition of the death penalty.[1]

Zanardelli's attitude to labour questions was well known because he had himself introduced the combination laws that were then in force in his Code of 1889. By the old Piedmontese Code of 1859, extended to cover all Italy, employers had been prevented from combining "unjustly to reduce wages," and workers from combining to "suspend or hinder production or to raise the price of production, without reasonable cause." The reasonableness of the cause was left to the magistrates. Every strike, therefore, should properly have been followed by a criminal action, if not necessarily by a conviction. With the growth of new industries this position was found impossible, and Crispi as Minister of the Interior, a still liberal Crispi, had set up a commission to inquire into strikes and combinations and the law concerning them. The commissioners, no Marxists, reported that "a return to the former concord between capital and labour is now impossible", and recommended that combination on both

[1] Restored by the fascists, and again abolished by the Republican Constitution, 1948.

sides should be freely permitted and that strikes, except those accompanied by violence, should be made legal. In 1883 Depretis introduced a bill based on these recommendations. It was defeated then by a narrow majority, but Zanardelli got it through with the rest of his Code in 1889. Between then and the end of the century Crispi and his successors overrode it so often with their emergency measures that the arrangement had little chance of a proper trial. In 1901 it was still on the statute book, and with the return to power of its promoter the socialists could be sure there would be no more repressions.

Zanardelli and Giolitti, his Minister of the Interior, the same Giolitti who had failed to suppress the Sicilian troubles when he was Prime Minister in 1893, proceeded systematically not to interfere. In 1900, the year of the general elections, there were 410 strikes and 89,000 strikers in the Po Valley. In 1901, when the Zanardelli-Giolitti policy was known and established, there were 1,671 and 420,000.[1] Pressed to use the Army to carry on with urgent work while the strikers were out, Giolitti replied that it would be "illegal, impolitic, and impossible." If a strike was accompanied by violence, he would suppress it by force. But he firmly refused to dissolve the organizations of the workers, thereby for the first time making the healthy distinction between workers in organizations with legal ends and the same workers exceeding the legal ends of their organizations.

It soon appeared that the motive force of the government was not the veteran Prime Minister but his lieutenant Giolitti, and in 1903 the latter was able to use the decline of Zanardelli's health and the opposition he aroused by proposing to legalize divorce in order to overthrow and succeed him. Giovanni Giolitti was a Piedmontese who turned to politics after a brilliant civil service career. His special capacities were for hard work, tact, and foresight. His long rule was of immense importance for Italy, since during it she emerged to the status of a modern nation. By a genius for inaction and soothing words he created an atmosphere in which the economic development of the

[1] Gentile, op. cit., p. 102.

country leaped ahead. But it is more with his politics than his economics that we must concern ourselves.

Luigi Sturzo, a dominating figure of a later time, said that "in the entire course of the half-century of Italian parliamentary government after 1870, two effective parliamentary parties confronted each other for the first and only time at the turn of the century, when Zanardelli took the place of Pelloux."[1] This is the key to the whole history of parliamentary rule in Italy. It was only then that the party struggle without which democracy is bound to misfire emerged, and for a year or two only. Before that time was *trasformismo* and after it was *trasformismo*, for Giolitti turned out to be the arch-transformist and to have a talent for the practice which made Depretis look like a bungling forerunner.

Giolitti quickly established a transformistic hegemony in parliament such that his incomings and outgoings depended not on the results of elections or of votes of confidence but on his own wish. Twice during his period of rule he voluntarily withdrew and installed a lieutenant as Prime Minister, and twice, dismissing his lieutenant with a brief speech, he took over from him again. This was a reversion to *trasformismo*, and its main cause was the personality of Giolitti. In other words, it was accidental; for it is not to be supposed that a Prime Minister can be chosen because he is known as a transformist, *trasformismo* being by its nature the business of Prime Ministers after their installation. But the willingness of another generation of politicians to accept *trasformismo*, and even in part Giolitti's own adoption of it, was probably due to the first appearance of sharply defined opposing blocs in parliament. Their appearance was provoked by violence and bloodshed in the country in such a way that the one parliamentary bloc was that of the repressors and the other that of the tolerators. Thus a nation whose politicians were without experience of party strife mistook the particular and accidental cause of its appearance for the only possible cause, and argued thus: "Civil strife and parliamentary strife are indissoluble; let us therefore have neither the one nor

[1] C. J. S. Sprigge, *The Making of Modern Italy*; Duckworth, 1943; p. 76.

the other." This attitude among the lesser politicians allowed Giolitti to develop his *trasformismo* until they were all bound to him either by definite bargains or by his skill in capturing their support for uncontentious measures with such sweet reasonableness that, when it came to the contentious ones, which were the very measures, sometimes, that they had been elected to oppose, they found that they were committed to support those measures as well. Giolitti's enemies both then and later made out that his *trasformismo* was all plain fraud and blackmail, with dead men at the polls, and such persuasive words as: "If you vote for this measure of mine you shall have running water laid on in that village where you had so small a majority at the elections." Those elements were not lacking. The solid block of supporters of this liberal minister which was returned by the backward south and the Islands throughout his terms of office was a standing joke. They were called the Askaris, and it was said that their parliamentary whip, though as dignified in appearance as could be wished, was illiterate. There are countless anecdotes about Giolitti's agents at elections, of which this is characteristic. Giolitti once met his agent for a group of constituencies which had a particularly fine record, and asked him how he did it. The agent answered: "I send out men secretly, at dead of night, to plant a number of white stones across the countryside in a straight line at intervals of a kilometre. Then I let it be known in the strictest confidence that they mark the line of an arterial road which will be built if Your Excellency is returned to power."

Nevertheless it is impossible to study Giolitti's actions with an open mind without arriving at the conclusion that sweet reasonableness had far more to do with his success than corruption. His most successful gambit of "sweet reasonableness" was to offer his adversaries places in the government. This he would do less with an air of "There, now, will *that* keep you quiet?" than of "I am so interested in your views on [say] rat-catching. There is a great deal in them. Would you care to take the Ministry of Pest-extirpation and try them out? You may be sure I shall give you every support." As soon as he came to power in 1903 he invited Turati and the radical leader Sacchi to join him in the government. For Turati to accept would have been as much as his head was worth; socialist Deputies might not even vote confidence in a government, let alone join one. He refused, and Sacchi could not well fail to refuse too. Nevertheless, within three years Sacchi was in the government and Giolitti, though he had failed to "transform" the *estrema en bloc*, had at least broken it up. But Turati stayed out. The frontal attack of sweet reasonableness having thus failed on the socialists, Giolitti resorted to the outflanking movement known in England as "dishing the Whigs," or choking the cat with cream. The history of the Italian socialists between 1903 and 1911 is that of their reaction to continuous, energetic, and accurate "dishing."

Among the measures passed by Giolitti which, if not actually the objects of the socialists' programme, did much to steal their thunder were these; a series of public health provisions; the regulation and co-ordination of charities by the state; regulations for preventing accidents in factories; the limiting of hours of work for women and children; a national insurance and pensions scheme; the regulating of night work for bakers; the compulsory observation of Sundays and some feast days in shops and offices; a subsidy for quinine and other measures against malaria; a treaty with France regulating the status of Italian *émigré* labourers there; the relief of poverty in the south; improvements in the conditions of elementary school-teachers; the establishment of subsidized technical schools; manhood suffrage; and, the most successful move of all, subsidies for the co-operatives.

Giolitti's attitude towards the socialists was indeed one of unanswerable reasonableness. Early in 1901, as Minister of the Interior, he made a famous speech in the Chamber of Deputies in which he said: "Now what is there illegal about these Chambers of Labour? . . . Their function is to work for the betterment of the working class. . . . As long as they do not break the law . . , the intervention of the state is unjustifiable. I think that at this juncture it would be a good thing to legislate about all this. The workers' organizations have a right to be represented in the same way as the industrialists and merchants. And since we have got legally recognized Chambers of Commerce, I do not see why the state cannot give legal recognition to the Chambers of Labour. Indeed I think it must. I believe we have got to make the capitalist and the worker equal before the law. . . . The friends of order have a duty to persuade the working class, and to persuade them with deeds, not words, that they have more to hope from the present order than from dreams of the future."[1]

When he came to power he invited the socialists, in the person of Turati, to co-operate with him in the programme suggested above. They refused, and he turned to implementing the programme by himself. He said: "You will not eat with me? Look, then, I will leave the food on the table, here!"

But it is not possible to dish a convinced revolutionary. Once the socialists had emerged from the narrow defile of persecution, they spread out and took up their positions to do battle, not against capitalism, but against each other. In 1900 Turati came out of prison and opened the National Congress of the Party at Rome with the words "*heri dicebamus*," "we were saying yesterday . . ." The phrase carries a suggestion of magnificent unity and dignity under the persecutions of petty spite, but, whatever the socialists had been saying in 1897 when adversity drove them together, no unanimous voice was to be heard in 1900 when they could disagree without suffering for it in the short run. The Congress was faced with two draft resolutions, one from the left and one from the right. That from the left called for continuous revolutionary propaganda, complete non-co-operation with the state, and finally revolution and the "dictatorship of the proletariat." That from the right called for reforms to be won through legal institutions, and it was not unlike the programme of the old Workers' Party. To vote one or the other would have threatened the party with disintegration, so the Congress agreed to vote them both and call them "maximum

[1] Gentile, op. cit., pp. 100–1.

and minimum programmes." Turati, in a fine attempt to make sense out of this procedure, said that they stood to each other in the relation of means (minimum programme) to end (maximum programme), and thereby brought the absurdity into full view. The maximum programme called for revolution and the minimum for reforms. It is bad enough to vote for a simultaneous pursuit of revolution and reforms, but to pursue reforms as a means to revolution is a truly remarkable decision for a supposedly Marxist Party. Whether one accepts Turati's assessment of the relation in which the two resolutions stood to each other, or whether one accepts that suggested by the words "minimum"—that which we cannot do without, and "maximum"—that which we hope for at the best, the situation remains an excellent demonstration of how the Party weakened both of two perfectly logical schools of thought in the attempt to keep them together.

The left wing of the Party was beginning to change its colour. The instinctive and emotional attitude of the revolutionaries was as passionate as ever, but their intellectual justifications were altering. We have seen how the philosophers examined Marx and reached varying conclusions about his teachings. The French journalist and political theorist, Georges Sorel, partly stimulated at first by Benedetto Croce's criticisms of Marx, went on to work out a revolutionary system of his own. His works were being published in Italy in the first years of the century at the instigation of Signor Croce. He has been described[1] as an armchair-revolutionary who put out his ideas mainly to see what effect they would have. His ideas were predominantly Marxist, but he differed from Marx in two important points. Firstly, he held that the revolution should be carried out not by the workers as workers, but by the workers organized in trade unions. Further, the revolution was not to be worked for as a revolution, but under the aspect, as it were, of a general strike. He set up the "Myth of the General Strike" as a sort of super-strike that

[1] By Ivanoe Bonomi, in *Le vie nuove del socialismo*; Rome, 1944. (First published in 1907.)

would come some day but which must above all be thought about all the time. The "myth" idea came from Bergson. The trade unions, therefore, were to exist primarily, indeed almost entirely, to work for the general strike, which was the revolution. Secondly, as to what was to happen after the revolution, Sorel openly taught that it was impossible to say what form of government the revolution should lead to, as it would be "the spontaneous production of history." From the first of these points his theory took the name of syndicalism. The importance of the second can hardly be exaggerated. A Marxist, on being questioned about just what the revolution was to be for, had two phrases to fall back on, "the dictatorship of the proletariat" and "the withering away of the state." He was not commonly able to explain how the proletariat was to exercise its dictatorship or what state it was that was to wither away. But a syndicalist was relieved of any need to think about these issues, for he could answer: "We cannot know beforehand what will be a spontaneous production of history." In other words, it will be quite all right if we just go ahead and see. Our generation, which has seen a successful proletarian revolution in Russia and the form of government that it led to, may be sceptical about the value of a Sorelian *tabula rasa* in the mind of a revolutionary leader. Lenin would never have got to Russia at all if he had been prepared to wait for spontaneous productions of history. But in 1900 there had been only an unsuccessful proletarian revolution, the Paris Commune of 1871, from which no conclusion could be drawn. Sorel gave comfort to those whose consciences were perhaps uneasy about the gaps in Marx. With syndicalism there came to the Italian Socialist Party an increasing flow of thoughtless revolutionaries who, because they did not need to bother their heads about what was to happen after the revolution, were all the more anxious to begin it. It was nearly anarchism again, and perhaps more dangerous from the point of view of responsible politicians than the old Bakuninism, because of its element of licensed thoughtlessness. The Bakuninists had been impulsive by instinct, but the syndicalists were impulsive by deliberation. There was in them a good deal of the calculated turbulence of Nietzsche, but in accordance with the Italian temperament the emphasis was slightly different. There is no current phrase in Italian for the Nietzschean *Will zur Macht*; it can be translated, of course, but the common word which most nearly corresponds is *volontarismo*, not the Will to Power, but just the Will. The German wills to power because he likes power, but the Italian wills simply for the pleasure of willing, it does not matter what. The increase of respect for the will itself and of indifference to the material it works on was one of the most important trends which led to fascism. For the moment it is enough to notice its appearance with the syndicalists.

The leader of the syndicalists was Arturo Labriola,[1] a tempestuous orator and supple journalist. Immediately to the right came the mass of old-fashioned proletarian revolutionaries, including the orthodox Marxists, for the most part under the leadership of the experienced and respected Costantino Lazzari. They wanted revolution, but not so much that they were not able to think about how to get on in the meantime. In the centre was another turbulent and unstable figure, Enrico Ferri. Ferri had been a distinguished disciple of Cesare Lombroso, much more distinguished than Turati, and was early converted to "scientific socialism." He was something of a transformist on the domestic stage of the Socialist Party. It was hard to say what he really was, for his personal vanity and rather portentous style of speech and writing concealed the outlines, or perhaps the absence, of his ideas. At heart he seems to have been a revolutionary, but he devoted his efforts above all to keeping the Party together, and together, it was to be understood, under his own leadership. To the right again were the reformists, led by Turati, whose personality and politics will become clearer in the rest of this narrative. There was also his red-haired Jewish lieutenant, Claudio Treves. Treves succeeded Turati as editor of *Critica Sociale*, and together they made a team formidable in honesty of purpose and persuasive argument. Treves' speciality was firm-

[1] Nothing to do with the Marxist professor, Antonio Labriola.

ness and outspokenness; Turati's was charm and wit. On the extreme right were those who quite frankly wanted to have nothing to do with revolution and wished that the Party would just get on with the business of politics like any other party. Their leaders were Bissolati, the first editor of *Avanti!* after it became the organ of the Party, and Ivanoe Bonomi, a man who was altogether too mild and peaceable for the Socialist Party.

The period 1900–4 was for the socialists one of expansion and development. Membership increased, new local sections were founded, and the Chambers of Labour increased their powers under legal recognition. But dissensions were beginning to appear at the Congresses which expressed the still obscure dissensions in the ranks of the Party. Its action was all at sixes and sevens now that it was no longer constrained to unity by persecution. The National Congress of 1902 at Imola was able to pass a motion in the name of Signor Bonomi which expressly allowed local sections to form alliances at local elections after the type of the alliance of the *estrema* at the general elections of 1900. And yet in 1904 some troubles in Sicily of the usual nature, strikes and minor clashes with the police, gave the syndicalist wing of the Party a chance to try out its policy of the national general strike. In spite of the opposition of the reformists, the syndicalists called such a strike. It was, as far as it went, a success; that is to say, it was nation-wide and general. For some days virtually no work was done in Italy. To the syndicalists the general strike was the revolution. The two were conterminous. The syndicalist leader Arturo Labriola said it had been "proved to the masses that five minutes of direct action are worth as many years of parliamentary chatter."[1] It was the first successful national general strike in the world, and there was profound alarm on one side and high jubilation on the other. But Giolitti had no intention of allowing a "spontaneous production of history." Clamorously the workers downed tools, and Giolitti waited. Exultantly they sat back and watched the disruption they had caused, and Giolitti waited. But for a day or two there was enough food in the

[1] Quoted in William Salomone, op. cit., p. 51.

kitchens for life to go on, and the high spirits of the workers and their syndicalist leaders began to evaporate. Giolitti waited. Finally, since there were no heroics and nothing seemed to have changed, the workers began to go back to work; and still Giolitti waited. At the height of the natural reaction, when everybody was asking: "Well, what *was* all that about?" Giolitti acted; he dissolved parliament and went to the polls. This was not only sweet reasonableness, it was a move of positive educational value. For the left it meant: "Was it really worth it? Here is your chance to answer"; and for the right: "You see, there is no need for states of siege and special tribunals; you just leave it to parliamentary methods, and if you don't like the socialists elect someone else." The number of socialist Deputies fell from 33 to 27.

The most lasting effect of the general strike of 1904 was a change in Vatican policy, perceptible even before the elections, and set forth in the encyclical *Il fermo proposito* of June 11th, 1905. The earlier encyclical *Non expedit*, in which at the time of the Union catholics had been ordered to abstain from national politics altogether, was superseded. Punctilious catholics might now vote and stand for parliament. There was however to be no Catholic Party; they were to vote and stand for any party whose programme did not conflict with the teachings of the Church.[1] Thus Giolitti, having failed to draw the socialists into the business of government, succeeded with that other group of rigid abstainers, the "black" catholics; their entry into politics was in answer to the rise of socialism.

The elections were fought mostly on the nationalization of the railways. Curiously enough it was the right which wanted nationalization in order to give the government power to forbid railway strikes, and the socialists who opposed it in order that the government should not have that power. The swing to the right was enough to make Giolitti think that nationalization would be justified, but not enough to make him feel like carrying it out himself. He went into tactical retirement and the project was

[1] The old formula had been: "*Nè eletti nè elettori*," the new one was: "*Non deputati cattolici, ma cattolici deputati.*"

carried through in a muddled and unsatisfactory way by his lieutenant Fortis. A short-lived government led by the conservative Sidney Sonnino led to even greater confusion. He tried to undo in a few weeks all the machinery of Giolitti's parliamentary alliances. He fell, and Giolitti returned with a reassuring smile.

The immediate effect of the syndicalist general strike on national politics was a perceptible swing to the right. In the internal politics of the Socialist Party, the first effect was perhaps the same. But when the socialists met in National Congress at Bologna a few weeks before the elections it was the passion for unity that prevailed once again. Enrico Ferri, by then editor of *Avanti!*, put down a centre motion which was designed to keep the revolutionaries and the reformists together. He presented himself and his motion as "integralist." His motion was voted, he became leader of the Party, and for four years "integralism" was its policy. It was, as the name implies, a negative policy, and worse than that it was a policy for the domestic affairs of the Party only. The Congress of Bologna was concerned not with the attitude of the Party in national politics, but with the attitude of certain schools of thought to other schools of thought within the Party. The whole question of Party policy for the year was settled when it was decided to "integrate" the two wings. In 1904 began the descent of the Party towards a mere debating society. Sorel, the inventor of syndicalism, wrote to his former collaborator Benedetto Croce: "*On me dit que Ferri obtient le plus grand succès; cela ne m'étonne pas outre mesure; c'est un signe que le socialisme devient partout un exercise de clown et qu'il perd son sérieux.*"[1] Later, for he believed nothing was to be gained by a fictitious unity, and wanted those of his school to be free of their opponents, he wrote: "*Turati ferait mieux de s'en aller avec ses groupes; et il en serait plus libre.*"[2]

Under all these manœuvres and acrobatics of the intellectuals, the workers were restless. In the same year of 1904 a group at

[1] Letter XCVII, of January 23rd, 1904; published in *Critica*, xxvi; Naples, 1928.

[2] Letter CI, of April 15th, 1904; published in the same number of *Critica*.

Milan called for a meeting to be attended only by genuine wage-earners, "without pastors and masters," and put out a manifesto calling for workers' control to begin at home.[1] At the Rome National Congress of 1906 the syndicalist leader Leone said that workers were not sent to stand for parliament because of their accents and their bad grammar. Turati replied that the ideal of a slave army liberating the world in skins and woad, more or less, was now out of date. At the same congress Ferri's henchman Oddino Morgari defined integralism as the belief that "there is no antithesis between the concept of violence as such and that of the gradual development of socialism within the very bosom of bourgeois society."[2] This is true, but there is a step missed out. There is no antithesis between the concept of man-eating as such and the concept of Androcles' lion. It is the "as such" that puts the argument wrong. There is an antithesis between the concept of the man-eating *of Androcles' lion* and the concept of the lion's behaviour as we know it, just as there is an antithesis between the concept of the violence *of the Socialist Party* and that of the gradual growth of the Party in the very bosom of bourgeois society.

Nevertheless from 1904 to 1908 the Party was "integralist," and was dominated both in parliament and in congress by Enrico Ferri. But in 1908 the scene changed suddenly. After five years of Giolitti's rule everything was going swimmingly. Italy, still the sleeping partner of the Triple Alliance, was advancing from strength to strength. Industrial development was vigorous. In 1901 coal imports had been five million tons, in 1912 they were ten million. In 1901 the production of hydro-electric power had been forty-eight million kilowatts; in 1912 it was three thousand million. However shady his methods, Giolitti was a parliamentary democrat, and under his liberal rule all Italians, including the socialists, learned to connect prosperity with liberal democracy. The workers were paid more, they were protected in many ways

[1] It is printed in Michels, *Sozialismus und Fascismus als politische Strömungen in Italien*; 2 vols., Munich, 1925; i, 356.

[2] Quoted in Salomone, *Italian Democracy in the Making*; 1945; p. 76.

by the state, and they were free to combine and to strike as they liked. Gradually socialist opinion swung to the reformists on the right. Turati's quiet but decisive charm pleased more than Ferri's bombast, and his fairly coherent position more than Ferri's exuberant eclecticism. In 1908 Ferri, acting in accordance with his fickle and unpredictable character, threw up parliament, party, press, and everything, and went on a lecture tour to America from which it was understood he would not return for some time. When the National Congress of that year met at Florence it was a foregone conclusion who would succeed him. Turati in his speech described syndicalism as the stone-age of socialism. Integralism was abandoned, and a motion was passed which said that syndicalism was incompatible with socialism. Groups of syndicalists had been leaving the Party since 1904. Those who were left were now expelled, and a reformist Direction was elected with Turati at its head. Treves became editor of *Avanti!*

In 1902 a National Union of the Chambers of Labour had been founded which became on the whole reformist in colour in 1904. In 1906 this union was expanded and became the General Confederation of Labour, *Confederazione Generale del Lavoro*. The new body was of comparable standing with the French *Confédération Générale du Travail*, that is to say, it was if anything more active and influential than the English Trades Union Congress. Leaders of all schools of thought in the labour movement struggled for supremacy in it, and the syndicalists perhaps most fiercely of all. Their doctrine of revolution centred on the trade unions and they held that the revolution was to be worked for by working for the general strike. Obviously then the General Confederation of Labour was of more importance to them than any political party. But the General Confederation of Labour had a democratic structure, and the workers, although they were as well prepared to strike under syndicalist leadership as under any other, tended to hold the more common-sense view that, when all is said and done, a strike is just a strike, and that between strikes one has to get on somehow. They were less impressed by the syndicalists than by the reformists, who were prepared to fight for their interests from day to day. So when in 1908 the National Congress of the Socialist Party at Florence voted for closer co-operation with the General Confederation of Labour it was in effect the political party which was coming into line with the labour organization.

It was the time of reformism in all the socialist movements of Europe, the time of Bernstein and Jaurès. For three years the Italian Socialist Party led a peaceable life amid increasing economic prosperity. It was still a small movement both politically and syndically. In 1910 out of eight million wage-earners only 843,811 were organized in trade unions, Chambers of Labour, Agrarian Leagues, and so forth.[1] This was above all because Italy was an overwhelmingly agricultural country. But there were also rival claimants to the workers' sympathies. Various catholic workers' unions had appeared before 1900, founded on the decorous corporativism of the famous encyclical *Rerum Novarum* of 1891, and before the outbreak of war in 1914 they had been welded into an organization rival to, but smaller than, the General Confederation of Labour. This was the Italian Labour Union, *Unione Italiana del Lavoro*. The catholic unions were not political, and even in the syndical field they were far less attractive than the socialist unions, since the attitude of the clergy towards the haves did not appeal to the have-nots as much as the attitude of the socialist leaders. The Socialist Party and the General Confederation of Labour avoided polemics with the catholic unions because a large number of workers, while accepting socialist politics, were very far from accepting socialist philosophy. The leaders could not afford, in an overwhelmingly catholic country, to antagonize their followers in religious matters.

Under moderate leadership the Socialist Party became less intransigent towards Giolitti and the state. They never allowed a socialist Deputy to become a minister, but when the Deputies began occasionally to vote for a government measure the outcry

[1] Salomone, op. cit., p. 51.

CLAUDIO TREVES

BENITO MUSSOLINI
before 1914

GIOVANNI GIOLITTI

ENRICO FERRI

was much less strong than it would have been ten years earlier. The right wing of the Party under Bissolati and Signor Bonomi was openly for a policy of collaboration. Why should they not join Giolitti and try to influence him a little? For ten years now they had deliberately renounced, for the sake of a revolution which might or might not come some day, any hope of helping the workers with their own hands. By despising governments to this extent they were forced to accept their charity. Turati, the leader of the Party, thought the same; but as long as the left wing thought differently he was not going to do anything that might endanger proletarian unity. On the left wing, now that the syndicalists had gone, Lazzari and his followers were as determinedly revolutionary as ever. Such was the position when in 1911 Italy declared war on Turkey.

In the days when Turkey had been the "sick man of Europe," and when the Powers had been agreeing how to divide his property when he died, it had been more or less admitted that Tripoli was to be Italy's share. Italian pioneers opened up the country with the full approval of Italian governments. Much Italian capital was invested there in the expectation that the country would shortly be acquired as a colony without effort and in the "fit of absence of mind" for which there was distinguished precedent. The Bank of Rome, which was under the influence of "friends of the Vatican," was heavily committed there. Then in 1908 the Young Turk movement began to regenerate Turkey from within and to strengthen her hold on Tripoli, the last Turkish Province in the Mediterranean. It became clear that the new rulers of Turkey would know how to counter "absence of mind," and that if Italian effort and outlay were not to be wasted a war would be necessary.

Giolitti was not a warlike man, but he was prepared to resort to war as readily as to any other device of government. From 1908 to 1911 he was under increasing pressure from many quarters to go to war with Turkey. The catholic conservatives urged it for a number of reasons, among which was certainly the appeal of a campaign which would be the last in the millennial war against Islam in the Mediterranean, and probably also the heavy commitments of the Bank of Rome in Tripolitania. The nationalists, a jingoistic party who had recently appeared as a political expression of overpopulation, urged it in order that the disaster of Adua might be avenged on African soil. Many of the radicals and republicans urged it because Germany was now Turkey's patron and protector. They saw in a war against Turkey a means of getting Italy out of the alliance with the autocratic Central Powers and into alliance with democratic France and England. D'Annunzio, now a "futurist" with nationalistic leanings, urged it as a first step towards a war against Austria for the redemption of Trieste and the Trentino. The overcrowded peasants of the south had been led to believe that the conquest of Tripoli would open up great areas of cultivable country to immigration; they would no longer have to go to America and learn English. Coming full circle from the nationalists, where right wing and left wing met, the syndicalists, still led by Arturo Labriola although he was now outside the Socialist Party, urged war because they believed defeat in war, or possibly even victory in war, to be the easiest way to revolution. The returning soldier was to keep his rifle and to use it against the bourgeois capitalist.

On September 9th, 1911, Giolitti declared war. In spite of the Turkish revival it was soon over, and Tripoli became an Italian colony. But the war lasted long enough to turn the whole Socialist Party upside down.

Just before the declaration of war Giolitti had finally announced that he would introduce an electoral reform amounting virtually to manhood-suffrage. Every man was to have the vote who had done military service or had reached the age of thirty, and the electorate would rise from three and a half million to eight million. Giolitti had publicly invited Bissolati to join him in the government. Bissolati refused, as Turati had in 1903. Nevertheless the socialist Deputies were more Giolittian than not. The reasonableness of parliamentary democracy had taken them to parliament, and the reasonableness of Giolitti, once they were there, took them, if not into office, at least into fairly continuous collaboration. And now they were landed in a war of imperialist expansion. The disconcertment and disunion were profound. It was no longer possible to gloss over the antithesis between the Party's Marxist theory and its daily actions, which differed little now from the actions of the most bourgeois and conventional of the other parties. At the National Congress of Modena in October, 1911, the embarrassment and inhibition were so complete that the Congress decided nothing. But during the months that followed it appeared once again that even such passive unity was reserved for congresses only; between whiles all was at sixes and sevens. In parliament the collaborationists, led by Bissolati and Signor Bonomi, declared that the Socialist Party must not disrupt national unity in the name of outworn revolutionary principles. But in the provinces, and particularly in those which were beginning to emerge as the Red Crescent, Emilia-Romagna, Umbria, and Tuscany, the rank and file thought otherwise. The most convenient target for manifestations of hostility to the war was the movement of troops and military supplies by rail. The socialists of the Romagna developed a technique for tearing up stretches of railway line, an operation which they carried out with enthusiasm in spite of strong police and military guards. Here and there they burnt down a railway station. Strikes became more numerous and more bitter. By the time the Party met in congress at Reggio Emilia in 1912 the incompatibility of revolution at the periphery with collaboration at the centre could no longer be ignored.

The second Congress of Reggio Emilia was a turning-point for Italian socialism and a turning-point thereby of Italian history in this century. Although the turbulent and "voluntaristic" syndicalists had been excluded, the extreme left of the Party differed little from them in its habits of thought and expression. It was on the issue of the war only that they fundamentally diverged. A revolutionary socialist might be glad to make use of disaffected troops and their arms, but he could never, as a revolutionary syndicalist could, bring himself to condone and encourage a war in order to spread disaffection. From this revolutionary pacifist wing of the Party an attack was expected at the Congress. But it came with a fury and a determination that were entirely new. The veteran Costantino Lazzari opened it, but he scarcely did more than introduce an unknown figure, Benito Mussolini. Still in his late 'twenties, Mussolini let loose an avalanche of oratory upon a Congress which, as we have seen, was uneasy and hesitant because of its divided policy about the war. He attacked Giolitti, he attacked the collaborationist Deputies, he attacked the war, he attacked the monarchy, the Church, the Masons, the aristocracy, almost everything. The main point of his speech was a demand for the expulsion of Bissolati and Signor Bonomi and their followers. He arraigned them on general grounds as imperialist war-mongers and traitors to the international proletarian cause, and he made a special attack on Bissolati for having gone in a party of Deputies to the Quirinal Palace in order to congratulate the King on his escape from an attempt on his life. He had earlier written: "Attempts are an inconvenience that goes with the profession of king"; and: "If Citizen Savoy were to fall by a pistol-shot, that would be justice."[1] Not only was Mussolini a particular advocate of bomb-throwing, but to be seen mounting the steps of the Quirinal had a symbolic significance for all republicans and revolutionaries. Those steps led to honours, to a fat belly, to all that the intransigents hated. When the vote came, Mussolini had his way. Bissolati and Signor Bonomi and all their kind were expelled. They founded an autonomous "Reformist Socialist Party" which because it had no following in the country quickly disappeared in the currents and cross-currents of ministerial parties. Turati and Treves and their followers were dominated once again by their concern for unity. They voted with the majority, and stayed on in baseless and uncomfortable association with the fire-eating revolutionaries. Lazzari became leader of the Party, and Mussolini shortly afterwards succeeded Treves as editor of *Avanti!* It was understood that he would be the power behind his veteran chief. The leadership of the General

[1] Pietro Nenni, *Sei anni di guerra civile*; Milan, 1945; p. 31.

Confederation of Labour was quickly changed in conformity with the revival of revolutionarism in the political party.

This was the most profound and sudden change which the Socialist Party had yet undergone. Ever since 1900, when it was first given time and space to debate its policy and freely to decide how to pursue its aims, it had been moving clearly to the right, towards collaboration with "bourgeois" governments, towards parliament, towards legislation, towards discussion and democracy. Between 1900 and 1904 the discrepancy between revolution and reform had not been clearly seen. Between 1904 and 1908 the integralist Direction, having seen the discrepancy, devoted itself to keeping the two wings together. Between 1908 and 1912 the long rule of a friendly ministry and increasing prosperity brought the reformist right wing into a position from which it could dominate the revolutionaries and hold them in check. In none of these three four-year periods had the revolutionaries been in control. Now the position was suddenly reversed.

What were the causes? First and most obvious was the war with Turkey. During the Abyssinian War of 1896 the Party had been tiny and harassed by government persecution. Its Deputies were an eccentric fraction of the left wing; they had enjoyed no favours from any government, nor had they asked them, and nobody cared much whether they were for or against the war. But in 1912 they were a considerable party, with forty Deputies and with the expectation of more when the new suffrage came into action. Giolitti had captured the partial support of many of them by sweet reasonableness and "dishing." But the Socialist Party was still the natural home of the turbulent, the intransigent, and the demagogues. A new generation had come. This new generation was fresh from the study of Marx and his annotators, whom perhaps the leaders had not read for twenty years. It saw the recent history of the Party stained by an opiate corruption, with Giolitti as Circe. The war gave this generation, headed by young Mussolini, an opportunity to tell the Bissolatis and the Turatis that they were no longer socialists but bourgeois dignitaries, no longer Marxist men but Giolittian swine. The personality of Mussolini himself had a lot to do with it. His speech would not have persuaded by its reasoning alone, but it was delivered, like all his speeches until 1939, at the critical moment for its matter, and not less for its manner. The tradition of red-hot tub-thumping had rather languished while Turati discoursed with moderation and charm and Treves with severe and equable logic, and while the left wing hardly touched on earthly matters before taking flight into an empyrean haze of myths and ideologies or of slogans and formulas. The sudden irruption of Mussolini was like a return to the good old days when you hated and shouted and didn't give a damn for anybody. It will soon be clear enough however that Mussolini was far from having the singleness of purpose of the old revolutionary demagogues.

The history of Benito Mussolini is written on a larger page, and his character has been submitted to many and diverse analyses. But we cannot follow the thread of our story without some account of him. His father was a blacksmith and an early anarchist agitator in the Romagnole town of Forlì, and his mother was a school-teacher. He grew up in the heyday of the apocalyptic prophecy and destructive ecstasy that still prevailed in the small cities of the Romagna long after modern socialism was under way in Milan. He took up his father's ideas with more determination and less unworldly idealism. His character in youth seems to have been morose, reserved, and ferocious. To avoid military service he went to Switzerland, where he lived for some time in great poverty, suffering a morbid dissatisfaction with himself, and frequenting international socialist circles. After a spell working on a socialist paper in the unredeemed Austrian province of the Trentino he returned to the Romagna and became editor of a weekly paper in his native town. In its columns he violently opposed the Libyan War, and with his friend the republican Pietro Nenni he organized and led many of the railway raids and other disturbances in which the turbulent working folk of that region expressed their dislike of it. When he took charge of the Socialist Party at Reggio Emilia in 1912 he had just come out from five months' imprisonment for such activities. In prison he and Signor Nenni had re-read Sorel together.

Turati's day was over by then. He remained in parliament and in the Party for many years yet and was always influential and respected, but he was a man of the first decade of the century, and a peace-time leader. When the class-war broke out afresh after the outbreak of the patriotic war, his moderation was no longer of any use. Years later, at a bitter turn in his fortunes, he said: "I know how to sacrifice my personal views, and that, which some ascribe to opportunism, is perhaps the greatest immolation one can make for the sake of one's ideal, for the cause of proletarian unity."[1] "Immolation" is a strong word and Turati's feelings on this point were strong. His whole political life was dominated by the struggle between two convictions. He thought that a workers' party should act through parliament and that it should achieve its end, the improvement of the lot of the working man, by reforms passed in parliament. But even more strongly he thought that the political unity of the proletariat must be at all costs maintained, whether it were for reforms or for revolution. Political unity of the proletariat however there had never been. A large majority of the working class, particularly the backward peasantry, were apathetic catholics; and on the other wing there were the followers of the expelled syndicalists. Particularly in 1912, when manhood suffrage was assured, it might have seemed that the enfranchised proletariat was big enough to support two socialist parties and that the one could have plunged untrammelled into the parliamentary game to pursue its ends with all the skill its leaders possessed, while the other held aloof and proclaimed the revolution as best it could. But at this time the attitude of Turati was common, and Turati, although his outlook was more positive than that of Ferri, was no less of an integralist. Unity in the face of the common enemy was still held essential.

[1] Speech in the Chamber of Deputies on November 24th, 1920; quoted in *Critica Sociale* of Milan; issue of December 1st–15th, 1920.

The Party was in the hands of Mussolini and the intransigents for two years before it was again turned upside down in 1914 by the European War. During these two years it was once again violent, terroristic, and above all "voluntaristic." Mussolini, having snatched the Party from the jaws of the corrupter Giolitti, began the new life, the clean page, through his editorship of *Avanti!*. The grave, conscientious discussions of Treves and his friends no longer appeared in its columns. Mussolini poured out instead red-hot manifestoes, full of the calculated turbulence which first appeared in Italy with the syndicalists at the beginning of the century. Mussolini himself, being on the extreme left wing of the Socialist Party, had been deeply influenced by syndicalism. But there were other schools of *volontarismo* which contributed to the popularity of his articles. Most notable was that of the philosopher Giovanni Gentile. Gentile had earlier been the collaborator of Benedetto Croce, but they had gradually moved apart and by 1912 were in sharp opposition to each other. The basis of Signor Croce's system was the distinction between Intuition, Thought, and Action. This trinity, under various names, has always been the epistemological and psychological basis of those systems of ethics which in their particular and political conclusions have been democratic, moderate, and peaceable. Gentile, on the other hand, denied the divisibility of the activity of the mind, and assimilated it all to the category of Pure Act. This is the underlying attitude, for they are commonly without real basis, of violent and authoritarian ethical systems. Gentile became the first fascist Minister of Education, and the philosophy of fascism became that of the Pure Act. The affinity on different levels between the minds of Mussolini and Gentile was by no means recognized in 1912, but both were preaching the value of action as opposed to that of ratiocination. Another "voluntaristic" school was that of the futurists. They were a group of Milanese intellectuals who were the first manifestation in Italy of that frame of mind which after 1918 blossomed into Dadaism and Surrealism. The most notable of them, Marinetti, had a project for flying over the Vatican, kidnapping the Pope, and dropping him into the Adriatic, and another for dragging the ministers out of the Parliament House to give an account of their stewardship to the true representatives of the people, the thieves, the prostitutes, and the murderers. The nationalists too, with their cult of Crispi as the Man of Destiny and their pre-occupation with national honour, were a voluntaristic party. Between the futurists and the nationalists stood at this time Gabriele d'Annunzio. His novel *Il trionfo della morte* told the story of a young aristocrat who threw himself and his mistress over a cliff from too much Nietzsche and Wagner. As befits those who care for the act of will alone and not for its antecedents or effects, these irresponsibles contemplated many ends, and Mussolini's end, the class-revolution, was only one among them.

But socialism was an older dissident force than nationalism or futurism, and the new prophet of the Will who had made himself master of the Socialist Party had a profound effect on the whole life of the nation. He disregarded any advantage which he might have drawn from the general elections of 1913, when fifty-three socialist Deputies were returned under the new franchise, and he sat at his desk in Milan and devoted himself to stirring up trouble in the provinces he knew well, in Emilia-Romagna and the Marches. The disturbances there were not much different in kind from the eruptions traditional to those parts, but they were the most ferocious yet experienced. They culminated in the Red Week of June 1914. A general strike, in which some railway workers were involved notwithstanding the nationalization of the railways, was accompanied by bloodshed, the locking of troops into their barracks, the hoisting of the Red Flag on the town hall of Bologna, and finally by the declaration of the Republic in the Romagna and the Marches. Socialist corporations paid their employees in credit notes on the local co-operative store, and here and there a local military commander took orders from a spontaneously arisen socialist dictator. Order had been more or less restored, but the dust had by no means settled, when the nations of Europe went to war in August.

In spite of the Libyan War, Italy was still in the Triple Alliance.

Giolitti, with his aptitude for letting sleeping dogs lie, had always refrained from upsetting the foreign alignments which he inherited from his predecessor. When war broke out he was in his third tactical retirement. After Mussolini had put his "clean page" policy across on the socialists, Giolitti had largely to write them off as supporters; it was the price of the Libyan War. Before the general elections of 1913 he had arranged for his "Askaris" and their agents to come to terms with the new masses of catholic electors. A certain Count Gentiloni negotiated secretly for the catholics and the agreement reached was known as the "Gentiloni Pact." In return for the support of the catholic Deputies, Giolitti agreed not to mention divorce, not to tamper with the Church schools, and to respect some other catholic susceptibilities. In the result he got his majority, but the possibility of an alliance between the forty socialists, seventy radicals, and twelve republicans on the one hand, and certain sea-green incorruptible conservatives on the other, although it could not have overthrown him, led him to think that the new parliament had better be entrusted at first to a lieutenant. He handed it over to Antonio Salandra, leaving him some of his ministers, and retreated to watch how the wind blew. Salandra was still in office in August 1914.

By the treaties of the Triple Alliance Italy was only required to join Germany and Austria in a defensive war, and Salandra let it be known in good time that he would not consider an attack on Serbia as a defensive war. In this he had the whole country behind him. Further, there was a provision that Italy should not be required to fight England. She was therefore doubly justified on paper in remaining neutral, and the belief of all Italians in neutrality was unshaken during the autumn of 1914. Her two neighbours, Austria and France, were unpopular, Austria because she was the traditional enemy of the days of the Risorgimento and because there were still a million Italians under Austrian rule in Trieste and the Trentino; France because she had snatched Tunisia, denigrated the Libyan enterprise, and obstructed Italy's Mediterranean expansion at every turn. But the more distant allies of the neighbours, Germany and England, were both popular; Germany because she had a fine army, fine universities, and a fine socialist party; England because Anglo-Italian co-operation in the Mediterranean was a natural protection against France. In popular sympathy therefore the position was neatly balanced. The political parties too were neutralist, Giolitti and the Giolittian bloc, including at first Salandra, because there seemed nothing to be gained by fighting that could not be gained by dexterous politics in the manner of Cavour, the Vatican Party because there was a great catholic power on each side, the nationalists because their exaltation of war was so indiscriminate that they were divided about which side to join, and the socialists and the other parties of the old *estrema* out of time-honoured pacifist principles.

But it was a fictitious lull.

CHAPTER III

WAR, REVOLUTION, AND COUNTER-REVOLUTION, 1914–25

1. *War*, 1914–18

THE movement of Italy towards war on the Allied side took place on two levels, the very secret and diplomatic and the very popular and enthusiastic, until the two levels finally merged in the crisis of May 1915. The story is too well known to need telling in detail. Very briefly: Salandra, having interpreted the initial unanimity for neutrality as showing the impossibility of going to war beside the Central Powers, made soundings to find out whether the Germans and Austrians would give him more for staying out of the war or the English and French for coming in on their side. The former offered him only a continuation *de jure* of the occupation *de facto* of Albania which Italy had exercised since 1912 when the Balkan Wars had thrown up as a separate state this last relic of the traditions of the Turkish Empire in Europe. The latter on the other hand offered him, supposing always a victory to which Italy should have contributed, not only Albania, but certain closely defined stretches of the Dalmatian coast and islands, and the acquisition of the Italian-speaking Austrian provinces of the Trentino and Trieste. Giolitti, and indeed everybody else, knew all about the negotiations with the Central Powers, but the negotiations with the Allies were carried on in the deepest secrecy. Eight months of bargaining in neutrality from which Giolitti was excluded weakened his hold on affairs and strengthened that of Salandra and even more that of the King, for courts come into their own at a time of secret transactions. In October 1914 the Foreign

Minister whom Salandra had inherited from Giolitti died, and the post was taken by Sidney Sonnino. The King now came even more to the front, since Sonnino, who had in the stormy days of 1899–1900 advocated a return to the letter of the old Piedmontese Constitution by which ministers were responsible to the King and not to parliament, was known still to favour such a change. In April 1915 the Salandra Government signed with the Allies the secret Treaty of London, whereby Italy agreed to declare war a month later on the terms set out above. Although the facts of the negotiation are not clear, it appears that some days later the Central Powers offered Giolitti a higher price for Italian neutrality than they had been prepared to offer Salandra, and at the beginning of May 1915 the neutralist Giolitti faced an interventionist government, each armed with a secret agreement.

Meanwhile popular opinion had swung definitely towards intervention on the side of the Allies. Both sides had strenuously wooed the favour of Italy with propaganda to the people no less than with prices to the government, and a French campaign of publicity to exhibit the Allies as democratic and progressive and the Central Powers as autocratic and reactionary was notably successful. The republicans and radicals were the first converts, and soon in popular estimation the interventionists were the shining Paladins of liberty and the neutralists the chicken-hearted and mercenary bulwark of reaction. In the early autumn of 1914, when attention was drawn away from the disorders in the Romagna, the Socialist Party found itself united again in supporting neutrality. They were all pacifists, Turati, Treves, Lazzari, and Mussolini. The promptitude with which the much respected German Socialist Party declared for the war gave them another basis for unity, pride in their faithfulness when others were unfaithful. But Mussolini's character was not such as to allow him to be happy in alliance not only with Turati and Treves but also with Giolitti and the Vatican. In such an alliance he was in effect a junior partner in a reactionary bloc, however different his inspiration might be from that of his partners. He found himself appearing on the side of prudence, of the eye on the profits, of what later became known in general as "*parecchio*."[1] So in October 1914 he proclaimed in *Avanti!* that while a socialist could not for a minute tolerate an imperialistic war, a "war to end war" was different. Socialists should support and join in this war with the Allies in order afterwards to overthrow for good and all those who promoted war. This was very near to the teaching of the expelled syndicalists who wanted war in order that the workers should be armed for the subsequent revolution. The reaction of the Party was immediate. Mussolini was summoned to explain himself at an improvised gathering. He was howled down, and only a few of his words were audible. He broke a glass and shouted: "You hate me because you still love me . . . if you think you're putting me out of politics, you're mistaken. You will find me always before you, proud and implacable."[2]

Within a month of his expulsion from the Party and the editorship of *Avanti!* he had founded his own daily in Milan, the *Popolo d'Italia* (*People of Italy*). It is said that the French Ambassador Barrère helped him with funds. For motto it bore Blanqui's "*Qui a fer a terre*." In the first number, Mussolini led off with these words:

"To you, to the youth of Italy, in the workshops and in the universities, to the young in years and in spirit, . . . to you I address my greeting, a word which in normal times I could never have uttered. But now I utter it loudly and clearly, without ambiguity and in sure confidence—the dreadful and fascinating word: War!" Later he turned to the socialist leaders who had expelled him: "It is not against the proletariat that I shall fight. The proletariat knows . . . that I have spent myself in an indomitable impulse to action, without caring for danger or counting my fatigue. But you, sirs, you who are the leaders of

[1] In early 1915 Giolitti caused an outcry by writing in an open letter that Italy would get *parecchio*—"quite a lot", or even "a pretty packet", by remaining neutral.

[2] Pietro Nenni, op. cit., p. 46.

the Party . . . you shall pass through the toils . . . I am here to spoil your game. The case of Mussolini is not finished as you think. It is beginning now: it is growing larger all the time."[1] The *Popolo d'Italia* was supposed to be a socialist paper, and Mussolini took with him from the Party a certain number of left-wing extremists who were in much the same position as the syndicalists; that is, they were so far to the left that they were almost indistinguishable from the extreme right, the common ground being the irresponsible impulse to domination, action, self-assertion, noise, and violence, and the revulsion from agreement, debate, compromise, procedure, and tactics. These followers he formed up into *Fasci di Combattimento*, Combatant Groups, who went about speaking and agitating for intervention. They still called themselves socialist; when Italy entered the war, their members joined up with the rest, but when the *Fasci di Combattimento* were re-formed after the war their composition and their programme were different. The change in their whole attitude was reflected in the changed significance of the word "fascist."

In April 1915 the young, the high-spirited, the big press, and the government were interventionist; the neutralists were Giolitti, the middle-aged, and some small weeklies, all the forces, indeed, of *parecchio*. May 24th was the day fixed in the Treaty of London for Italy's declaration of war, but Giolitti probably did not know this when early in May he decided that Salandra's time was up. When he had handed over to Salandra in 1913 he had not bothered even to expose himself in parliament to a vote of no confidence; he had merely advised the King to entrust the government to Salandra for a while. And Salandra, in power on the open understanding that he was only a *locum tenens*, showed signs of going against his absent master's wishes. Giolitti took a train to Rome. Parliament was in recess, but three hundred and twenty Deputies, an absolute majority, left their cards at his house. On May 11th Salandra resigned, and the King called Giolitti for consultations. But meanwhile another national figure

[1] Both quotations from Sprigge, op. cit., p. 121.

had arrived in Rome. On May 5th Gabriele d'Annunzio, that weathercock genius, had deployed his magnificent oratory in the interventionist cause at a Garibaldi celebration near Genoa, and he followed it up with a kind of personal march on Rome. Giolitti had been hissed at wayside stations; d'Annunzio was cheered. In the piazzas of Rome he raised the wildest enthusiasm by speaking of personal regeneration through heroism, exalting the military values and the poetry of war. A few days of processions and riots and disorderly exaltation were enough to convince the King that Giolitti should not return; on May 11th he overrode the parliamentary majority for the first time since the House of Savoy had been Kings of Italy and taking the Constitution at its word recalled Salandra to power. War was declared on the prearranged day. "Radiant May", d'Annunzio called it.

In Milan Mussolini noted how it was done.

Joining in a full-scale European war was the greatest test to which Italy had been subjected since she had been a nation, and she failed in the test. Her history from 1915 to 1925 is that of a too young nation undertaking too great an enterprise. Italy was not invaded, she was not attacked, she was in no way offended by the Central Powers. She went to war partly by the deliberate choice of her leaders after they had carefully weighed the advantages of intervention or neutrality, and that is a far more testing thing to do than resisting attack. But partly also she went to war as a result of popular agitation. The majority of the parliament, a parliament elected only two years earlier by manhood suffrage, had declared against war, and it was overruled by an alliance of King, minister, poet, and mob. It is no wonder that the state, only forty-five years old, disintegrated under the stress of a war so begun.

When war was declared Lazzari, as leader of the Socialist Party, sent a circular to all the local associations saying that the attitude of socialists to the war was to be "neither collaboration nor sabotage," "*né aderire né sabotare.*" At first this line was duly followed, but in the course of the long static trench-warfare of the high Alps a natural feeling of solidarity with their cousins and brothers at the front began to turn the majority of dutiful Party members towards collaboration. The extreme left wing of the Party however was moving the other way, and exploited in its propaganda the discomforts of mountain warfare and the rigours of the old-fashioned discipline to which the Italian soldier was still subjected. This propaganda was particularly effective among the share-croppers[1] of Central Italy where the absence of young men at the front made life hard for the farmer whose labourers were his family.

Some diehard pacifists in the Party still went to international socialist gatherings in Switzerland, at Zimmerwald in 1915 and at Kienthal in 1916, where they passed motions against the war and, far more important, met Lenin. But from 1915 to 1917 the movement of the country in general no less than of the Socialist Party in particular was towards a more wholehearted prosecution of the war. Salandra, in accordance with his Giolittian policy of refraining from more effort than was necessary to reach a desired end, had tried to confine the war to one against Austria, and in the Treaty of London had arranged to annex to Italy a territory inhabited by other enemies of Austria, the Southern Slavs of the Dalmatian coast. In August 1916 he was succeeded by Paolo Boselli, who formed a wider government and declared war on Germany. His government included the former socialist Bissolati and others of the school which held that, treaty or no treaty, Italy had no right to annex the coastline of a people who were struggling to win their independence from Italy's enemy. The former rift between interventionists and neutralists was closed over and a new one appeared, that between Renouncers, *Rinunciatori*, and those who held to the letter of the Treaty of London, which, though not yet published, was pretty generally known.

In March 1917 the Socialist Party, having largely swung back under the influence of Turati in consequence of the slow formation of a spirit of national cohesion, put out a very surprising programme. The Party's aims for after the war would be, said this programme, republican constitution, single-chamber govern-

[1] *Mezzadri*; French *métayers*.

ment with universal suffrage, election of magistrates and high officials, social insurance, and a wide programme of public works and land reclamations.[1] Even if Italy had emerged from the war unequivocally victorious and united, it is very doubtful if this moderate programme could have survived even a year of peace. As it turned out, it was overtaken and engulfed by two great events in the autumn of 1917, the defeat of Caporetto, and the Russian Revolution.

Before the events at Petrograd had been assimilated and understood by Italian socialist leaders, their effects made themselves felt indirectly in Italy through their influence on the Austrian war machine. For the first time the Austrian Army was able to turn its full strength southward to the Julian Alps. In May the Austrians and Germans attacked through fog with poison gas and caught the Italian forces in the middle of a major regrouping movement which had been postponed to the very eve of the fully expected attack by dissensions in the high command. Caporetto was a very ugly affair. The Italian Army was routed, and re-formed its positions sixty miles back. In his communiqué General Cadorna blamed the common soldier for the defeat. Deserters poured backwards in thousands, demoralizing the fresh units in the rear as they went, and many of them never returned. Cadorna took absolute power to himself all over Northern Italy, but was soon removed and replaced by the liberal and popular General Diaz who instituted a more humane discipline, and with the help of a stiffening of French and English units led the Italian Army in a series of victories that re-established its honour by the time of the Austrian collapse.

But the damage done by Caporetto was not to be repaired. It brought the first great wave of that disgust with the war which led to the revolutionary movements of 1919 and 1920. In the winter of 1917 Italy was very near to such a collapse as had overtaken Russia a few months earlier. But the energy of the new government of Signor Orlando and Signor Nitti, pledged to avenge Caporetto, and the wise humanity of General Diaz at

[1] Sprigge, op. cit., p. 159.

the front retrieved the situation. Turati, recognizing the danger, for once risked proletarian unity and proclaimed in the Chamber his unqualified support of the war. Speaking rather to the Socialist Party than for it, he said: "It is *our* Fatherland, too, that is fighting on the Grappa." The mere use of the word Fatherland, *Patria*, was a notable break with socialist tradition.

But the left wing of the Party was moved by Caporetto and the news of the October Revolution in Russia to a very different attitude. The man of the moment was the Romagnole Nicola Bombacci: his name ("nasty bombs") and his appearance, bulky, black bearded, red-tied, were found to suit his views. He and Lazzari, hearing what had been done in Russia, thought that at last the moment had come for the Italian Revolution. They saw in the disaster of Caporetto the opportunity for the Italian soldier to desert with his arms, as the Russian soldier had, and, organized in Soviets, to demolish the capitalist state. But there were no seeds of revolution in the Italian Army; the Caporetto deserters were filled not with bitterness against the whole social order so much as with boredom and disaffection from a gruelling static war and a useless code of discipline. Nor did the Orlando-Nitti cabinet play the part of Kerensky. So the Julian line was re-formed, and early in 1918 Bombacci and Lazzari were imprisoned.

During the war the Italian Socialist Party had in fact disintegrated. It was not possible in war-time to hold elaborate congresses, to thrash out a party line and expel the dissentients, and so when peace came the two wings of the Party had drifted apart to an extent which would not for a moment have been tolerated before. On the right were Turati and Treves, making resounding patriotic speeches in the Chamber and outlining great plans for social reform; on the left were Lazzari and Bombacci in prison for urging the troops to use their rifles not against the national enemy but against their own officers and government, and between the two was every possible gradation of opinion.

2. *Revolution*, 1918–20

At the end of the war the Treaty of London was the main political issue in the country. The Bolsheviks had found a copy in the archives of the Russian Foreign Ministry and had published it. The country and the government itself were sharply divided between the "renouncers" of the advantages due to a victorious Italy under the Treaty, and those who wished to extort their rights. Vittorio Emanuele Orlando, the Prime Minister, held to the letter of the Treaty; Francesco Saverio Nitti, his Finance Minister and ablest colleague, suspended judgment; and Bissolati, now in the government, was an enthusiastic renouncer. Early in 1918 the government had allowed and even encouraged the renouncer journalist Giovanni Amendola to gather in Rome a congress of the "oppressed nationalites" of the Balkans, where they made plans together for an age of peaceful collaboration between Italy and the Balkan States. When Wilson's Fourteen Points were published, it became clear that the renouncers were in the ascendant. Nevertheless, Signor Orlando's attitude seems to have stiffened, for in the very days when Wilson was touring Italy amid uproarious enthusiasm, Bissolati, the chief Wilsonian in the government, resigned. And so Signor Orlando and Sonnino, who was still Foreign Minister, went to the Peace Conference at Paris to claim Italy's pound of flesh. Naturally they were overruled by Wilson, Lloyd George, and Clemenceau, who held that the doctrine of National Determination set out in the Fourteen Points superseded the Treaty of London under which Italy had joined the war, and that therefore she might not have the Dalmatian Islands and coast.

This was the international background to the revolutionary year of 1919. The renouncers were delighted; Mussolini, still a "socialist" and therefore a renouncer, described Wilson as the "Prophet of the Peoples," and denounced the adherents of the Treaty of London as indistinguishable from the Austrian imperialists against whom the war had been won. But on the other hand a growing body of nationalist sentiment was embittered at Signor Orlando's failure to exact from the perfidious Allies what it regarded as Italy's due. It was widely remarked that, Fourteen Points or no Fourteen Points, England and France had pocketed the German colonies in Africa, while Italy had gained nothing from the victory to which she had contributed except the "unredeemed" provinces of Trieste and the Trentino, which it was believed that Austria had herself offered to Giolitti in 1915 as the price of Italian neutrality. A more serious and better-founded complaint against Signor Orlando and Sonnino was that they were so occupied with pressing Italy's territorial claims that they had not found time to consider her economic position. While the other victorious nations had been settling between themselves a very profitable structure of trade treaties, Signor Orlando had been walking out of the Peace Conference as a protest against not being given a stretch of somebody else's coast which was probably quite unprofitable in any case. Why had he not made economic agreements with the iron- and coal-exporting countries, with England, America, and the new Poland?

But the bitter sticklers for treaty rights were in a minority at home. The political scene had changed entirely since 1914, and it seemed that Giolitti and all his system had gone for ever. There were now two great parties with popular support—the "Mass Parties" they were called—the old Socialist Party and the new Popular Party. It was hoped that these two parties, in alliance or in healthy democratic opposition, would regenerate the political life of Italy.

The Popular Party, *Partito Popolare,* was something entirely new; it was the first appearance of a catholic political party in Italy. Very early in the century the idea that catholicism could provide a basis for conduct in democratic politics as well as for personal morals was introduced into Italy from the writings of various foreign authors, including Cardinal Manning. We have seen how for the first time Italian catholics were allowed to go to the polls in 1904, but not in a party of their own. They went as individual consciences making their individual choice from among the candidates before them. Two things stood at this time in the way of the formation of a popular catholic party; the first was the hostile attitude of the Vatican itself towards the lay Italian state which had usurped its realm, the second was the attitude of the Church in general to property. Even if the Pope had sponsored a political party in those years, it would not have got much support, because of the very stiff view taken by the clergy about property. Property was much discussed then; the socialists held that individual property was a principle of the oppressive capitalist state and was to be swept away by the revolution. This teaching was more attractive to the share-croppers of Central Italy and to the day-labourers[1] of the north than was that of the Church. But during the nineteen-hundreds two prelates at Pisa, Monsignori Bonomelli and Toniolo, expounded the doctrine that there is a distinction between the divine right (*jus naturale*) of property in general, and the human application of that right in particular cases; and that therefore, while the institution of property is not to be questioned, any particular form of property, such for example as the various forms of land-tenure in Italy, might be questioned as the product of human failings. This teaching converged with that of the new school that wanted to take catholic dogma in a symbolic sense only, and formed the Modernist Movement. The modernists, as was to be expected, made no political progress because of the very decided opposition of the Vatican to their theology.

But after the war the situation was different. Firstly, the Vatican had finally emerged from its half-century-long sulk about the Italian state and, while it did not actively participate in forming the Popular Party, it stood aside and did not obstruct. Secondly, whereas the old modernists had been preaching a spiritual revival during the full flush of Giolittian prosperity, the Popular Party was able to make the most of the pacifism of Christian teaching at a time when the memories of Caporetto and the present spectacle of Signor Orlando "losing the peace" had brought a great wave of reaction against the war and almost

[1] *Braccianti.*

of repentance for having fought it.[1] Thirdly, property was now a more burning question than ever. In 1916 a sheet signed by Salandra himself had been circulated in the trenches which promised that the peasants should "have the land" after the war. When the peasants came back and found no signs of any change being prepared they formed into processions behind Popular Party leaders, often bearing a crucifix, and occupied some big estates which seemed to be under-cultivated. The priests themselves sometimes exerted their influence to protect these peasant squatters. The peasants were naturally delighted with this new clerical approach to property, the socialists were sympathetic, and indeed nobody could find it possible to blame such peaceful *coups de main*, the effect of which was to raise the productivity of the land.

The founder and leader of the Popular Party was a Sicilian priest, Don Luigi Sturzo. Under the Italian Constitution a priest might not stand for parliament, nor yet hold office in the government. Don Sturzo was therefore a lobby man, a Party-Congress man, and a journalist. During the four years between the peace and the march on Rome he showed himself to be much the ablest politician in Italy except Mussolini. The basis of the Popular Party's programme, and its most potent attraction, was this same view that property itself is instituted of God, but that man can sometimes make a fearful travesty of it. In practice the Popular Party found it was good that a man should have his acre, his cow, his spade, or his bicycle, and bad that he should have a trust, a syndicate, a cartel, a holding company, a chain of estates, and so on. This put it squarely on the left and got it the title and standing of a "Mass Party." Its emblem was the Crusaders' Shield, inscribed "*Libertas*," which had been the emblem of the medieval communes, and it criticized the constitution of the time for over-centralization. It asked that bureaucratic Rome should give way to a sytem of regional semi-autonomy and multifarious enterprise, and it dramatized the

[1] See a most interesting article by Cesare Goretti in the *Critica Sociale* of January 16th–31st, 1920; Milan.

excellences of the centuries when the communes had been the biggest unit of government. Don Sturzo insisted that the Party should be "aconfessional," that it should not be confined to practising catholics, since the Vatican was not yet prepared to take charge of a political party coextensive with its strict religious adherents, nor would such a party have had much success at the polls. Aconfessional it was, though its leadership and inspiration remained Christian. It had two fairly distinct wings; on the right the orthodox "black" catholics, who saw in it a defence against advancing socialism, and on the left the hankerers after primitive Christianity, with "sell all that you have" and "the eye of a needle" for their mottoes. On the whole, the left wing prevailed.

The Party was formally constituted early in 1919 and grew rapidly in strength, detaching a new section of the syndical movement from socialism, and making its own central syndical organization out of the already existing Italian Labour Union, *Unione Italiana del Lavoro*.

As we have seen, the Socialist Party emerged from the war profoundly divided. Turati, patriotic but a renouncer, was widely canvassed as the next Prime Minister, since it was fully expected that the fifty socialist Deputies sent to parliament in 1913 would be very much increased at the next general elections. It seemed possible to hope that a Socialist-Popular coalition under Turati would carry out great democratic reforms and finally purge Italy of the paternal corruptions of Giolitti. But all such hopes depended on the outcome of the internal struggle between the left and right wings of the Socialist Party, between the defeatist ex-convicts Lazzari and Bombacci and the patriotic, liberal parliamentarians Turati and Treves. Long before battle was joined between them at the National Congress of the Party at Bologna in October 1919, it was becoming clear that the revolutionaries were once again in the ascendant.

It is hardly possible to overestimate the effect that news from abroad had on the Italian socialists in 1919. There was the fall of the Hapsburg and Hohenzollern monarchies, the Bolshevik

Revolution in Hungary, the formation of Soviets in Bavaria, the unsuccessful Spartacist Revolution in Berlin, and above all that continued trumpet-blast from the East of challenge, reproof, and assurance in one, the Bolshevik Government of Russia, defending the Revolution against the Armies of International Reaction. If the Italian Army had not actually been defeated in war it had been heavily beaten in one pitched battle, and the general spirit after the war was one of bitterness and revolt which seemed propitious for revolution. Best of all, 150,000 deserters were still in hiding, and more than a million cases, admittedly not all very serious, were awaiting trial by court-martial.. Now, thought the Italian revolutionaries, was the time for which they had been waiting. "The dictatorship of the proletariat through the peoples' Soviets" was the aim; possibly not all the revolutionary leaders clearly saw the difference between Russia, a defeated and backward autocracy, and Italy, a victorious and modern democracy.

But almost before revolutionary propaganda could get under way the General Confederation of Labour held its National Congress at Bologna in January 1919 and voted a programme. The main points were: republican constitution, abolition of the Senate, proportional representation, institution of popular initiative, veto and referendum in legislation, abolition of the political police, foreign politics to be controlled by the Chamber of Deputies, and, most interesting of all, the institution of "The Constituent." *Il Costituente*, the Constituent Assembly, was a continuous undercurrent of socialist propaganda at this time. Many socialists did not want it, and many who were not socialists did, but on the whole it was a socialist plank. It is hard to say what it meant. Some said it was to be a Chamber parallel to the Chamber of Deputies, a sort of producers' parliament, to which should be entrusted industrial and agricultural legislation. It would be the top of an elected pyramid of syndical bodies of which the base would be the Chambers of Labour. Others said it would not be quite like that. In any case it was the expression of the dissatisfaction with the legislative machine of those who were not full revolutionaries. It was an idea obviously influenced by the evolving structure of Workers', Peasants', and Soldiers' Soviets in Bolshevik Russia, and occupied much the same place in the socialist armoury as Regionalism did in that of the Popular Party.[1]

The programme of the General Confederation of Labour was voted down by the Parliamentary Group of the Party, who were mostly good Turatian reformists and thought it too far to the left. On the other hand the revolutionaries thought it too far to the right. It might have been acceptable if some comminations against the capitalist order had gone with it, but, stated baldly as a reform to be aimed at, it seemed to show that the authoritative syndical organ of the working classes was not wholeheartedly for the revolution.

Socialist action in the first eight months of 1919 was contradictory and inchoate. In March the Party Direction dissociated itself from the Second (Amsterdam) International and associated itself with the Third (Moscow) International, or Comintern. In April, during the parliamentary recess, the same Parliamentary Group which had voted down the programme of the General Confederation of Labour demanded the implementation of its most contentious point; in the name of the Wilsonian principle of "power to the peoples" they asked for the delegation of certain types of legislation to an organ of a reformed syndical system. Strikes were more widespread than ever before; during the summer even the state school-teachers struck. On July 20th and 21st was observed an international general strike in protest against intervention in Russia; the strike had been agreed on an Italian initiative at a socialist conference at Southport earlier in

[1] The agitation for the Constituent was strong enough for the very eclectic Nitti to take notice of it. Abbiate, the Minister of Labour in Nitti's third government (May 1920), worked out a scheme for the institution of a National Labour Council, which would be the elected peak of the syndical pyramid, and would have certain legislative powers itself and the right to delegate others down the pyramid. The Cabinet passed Abbiate's scheme, but Nitti fell the next day and it was pigeon-holed (*Critica Sociale*; July 16th–31st, 1920.) The Mussolinian corporative state was by no means a fascist invention.

the year. The French *Confédération Générale du Travail* had fallen away, and so had the Italian Railwaymen's Union; and the strike was more like a national holiday. In July also spontaneous and leaderless demonstrations against the rising cost of living which followed the war led to the appearance in the Romagna and Tuscany of "Soviets" for the distribution of food. Troops sent to put them down joined the amateur Bolsheviks. The General Confederation of Labour put out a manifesto in which it exhorted the "Soviets" not to believe that agitation could suspend economic laws, or that any amount of workers' control could force anyone to sell below the cost of production for long. But when invited by the government to send representatives to a commission on methods of stopping inflation, it refused. The General Confederation of Labour was known not to be revolutionary, but *Avanti!*, the organ of the supposedly Bolshevik Party Direction, said about these movements:[1] "The mob has every right to indulgence; but it is the duty of the Socialist Party to warn it not to fall into its own trap after it has suffered in the trap of profiteering commerce. . . . It is no good thinking that requisitioning goods will solve the complex national and international problem of a rising cost of living. What is more, this sort of sacred and resolute justice has a hidden danger of its own, because it sends up consumption and aggravates the trouble, and because it makes for feverish hoarding, another cause of shortages, which is besides unfair to those who have less to spend; because all in all it will bring about a very grave crisis after the hours of comfort it gives." Economically these are excellent sentiments, but politically they are surprising for an organ supposedly devoted to the violent overthrow of the existing order. It was the first appearance of another great inconsistency of the Socialist Party which became more and more evident as the revolutionary activity rose to its climax in the autumn of 1920, the unwillingness of the "revolutionary" leaders to exploit a really revolutionary situation when at last they had one.

[1] *Avanti!* July 3rd, 1919.

Meanwhile the disintegration of the state desired by the revolutionaries was undoubtedly in progress. The more spectacular symptoms of disintegration were rooted in economic factors which were not clearly visible at the time. First, and by far the most important, was inflation; at the end of 1918 the lira stood at 6·34 to the American dollar, in 1919 it fell first to 8·05 and then to 13·07, and at the beginning of 1920 it was down to 18·47. Allowing for the slight inflation of the dollar at that time, these figures show a rise in the cost of living of about 300 per cent in eighteen months.

There was also the usual crop of war-profiteers who, no wiser than their fellows in other countries, behaved in just that flashy way best calculated to draw down equalitarian vengeance. There was a grave housing shortage. The metal industry, to be discussed in more detail later, was in difficulties about reconciling the great increase which the war had brought to its productive capacity with the need to import almost all of its iron and coal. As demobilization went on, more and more returning soldiers found their pre-war jobs taken by younger men who, as often as not, were openly hostile to the war and its memory and laughed at them for having been such idealistic fools as to leave their jobs for it. Natural grievances, epitomized in the major who had to return to being a lift-boy, took on a political colour. Young men who had just or not quite finished their university training when they went to the front were unemployed, and their trained but inexperienced minds were as petrol to the flames of discord.

It would be hard to find a better short description of the nascent dissension between combatants and non-combatants than this, from the novel *Oggi domani e mai* by Riccardo Bacchelli.

"Then, when the war was wound up rather than won, when everyone was more or less discontented with the governments, both old and new, then it was as if all the expenses of promises and schemes and hopes had to bear fruit to the people. And the fruit it bore was wonderful fantasies, enchanted words, schemes of reform, and that need for something new which most often begins and ends in its own self, if indeed it does not end in shooting . . . and it bore too that need of doing something which made it seem that the world could not have laboured so much simply to achieve that which was achieved by the politicians at Versailles, the need which made Wilson a prophet for a year. It was born of the return of a generation, grown up and fortified in war, which found itself inexpert in civilian affairs, or even wholly ignorant of them. And then began the rancorous delusions, the vague hopes, and the multiplying contradictions which flourished among those who were relaxed and corrupted not so much by the social licence which naturally accompanies and follows a war, not so much by the life of an armchair-warrior in the civil service or war industry, as by a secret self-dissatisfaction which could not suffer the rebuke which the demobilized servicemen implied. The ex-servicemen, in their turn, were astonished to see how a whole world had gone on living, and painfully realized that they must themselves learn or relearn to live. They found faction and demagogy presenting the war to the people as a monstrous and bloody deception and the educated classes, with the characteristic insouciance of decadence, using an illusory prosperity to amuse themselves and, one may even say, making it a point of good breeding and *savoir-vivre* not to play the returned hero, not to afflict their neighbours with war stories. It was this spirit which called a whole literature 'Armistice Literature'."[1]

The hostility between those who had fought the war and those who had not did not reach its full intensity until the next year, but in 1919 it was already very noticeable. The issue was complicated by the presence of those, including the deserters, who had fought the war and wished they had not, and those who, because they were too young, had not fought the war and wished they had. The romantic heroes of these boys were the *Arditi*, the Daredevils, a kind of super-commandos who had been excused most of the discipline and all of the trench warfare, and had been kept in privileged comfort until they were needed for some hazardous exploit. When the *Arditi* were demobilized they had the habit of privilege and were filled with a dangerous

[1] Riccardo Bacchelli, *Oggi domani e mai*; Milan, Garzanti, 1940; pp. 29–30.

esprit de corps. Disappointed at missing the excitements of war, as many as liked of the generation that was adolescent in 1919 were able to console themselves with the thought that they too could have been *Arditi.* These second-hand daredevils, untroubled by any lack of the qualities which had been required of the original ones, aped their dangerous exemplars and went about looking for violence. There is in Italian politics and Italian affairs in general an unhealthy strain of respect for youth. A mediocre young poet is more esteemed than a good elderly one. He is esteemed not for the promise which he has, but for the achievement which he has not; and over and over again in the troubled history of modern Italy the high-hearted and useless gallantry of adolescence has been taken as inspiration, and the moderation and experience, not only of age but of young maturity, has been derided as pusillanimity. It was largely an adolescent mob that took Italy to war in 1915, and now after the war the adolescents were out again, jealous of their elder brothers, in search of "adventure," and saying inside themselves: "Me too! Me too!"

It was inevitable that d'Annunzio should come forward at this moment. He was by now a national hero; his exploits as an airman during the war had combined with the popularity of his poetry and his novels among the nationalists and all "voluntarists" to make him a figure worshipped, hated, or uneasily recognized, according to temperament. He was without any doubt a real poet and an effective, if undisciplined, novelist. The quality of his writing is torrential, oratorical, exuberant; it belongs, to quote Croce, to the Barrès tradition of "sadistic and luxurious"[1] literature. To live according to the moral implications of d'Annunzio's work would be rash; to act according to its political implications must be disastrous, and it was. In the late summer of 1919 he called to the standard of poetry and adventure a number of these bellicose adolescents, of demobilized *Arditi*, and of others who had failed, in Bacchelli's words, "to

[1] *Sadica e lussuriosa.* The Italian word has not travelled away from the medieval Latin *luxuria* as has the English.

learn or relearn to live," and even some mutinous units of the Army with their officers. These he formed into neo-Roman "legions" and, supported by some ships of the Italian Navy, marched on Fiume on September 12th.

The question of the Dalmatian coast had been left undecided at the Paris Peace Conference on the understanding that it was to be settled later by direct negotiations between the Italian and Yugoslav governments. The small port of Fiume had not been included in that strip of coast which by the discredited Treaty of London was to have gone to Italy, but shortly after the war the Italians in the population had seized power and declared Fiume to be part of Italy. The town had thereupon been made an international city and occupied by a mixed garrison of French, British, and Italian troops. The Italian contingent had been subsequently withdrawn because it could not be stopped brawling with the French contingent, and in September 1919 Fiume was in much the same position as Trieste in 1946; held away from both Italy and Yugoslavia by a mixed neutral garrison, it was a standing challenge to the nationalists of both countries. When d'Annunzio and his legionaries arrived, singing, excited, and determined on a gesture against the renouncers and those who dishonoured Italy's part in the war, the British and French garrisons, tired of holding the turbulent and unimportant little town, withdrew. D'Annunzio, finding a number of ships in the harbour conveniently loaded with food and other useful material, converted their crews to his cause, some by oratory and some by force, and having thus solved immediate economic problems he installed himself in the finest Renaissance palace and began to organize his government.

In June of the same year Signor Orlando, returning from Paris without having secured the implementation of the Treaty of London, which a large section of opinion did not in any case want to see implemented, had fallen, and had been succeeded by Francesco Saverio Nitti. Signor Nitti, like Signor Orlando, was a Southerner. He was an economist and political theorist of some standing, and his intention was to bring the two "mass parties," the socialists and the populars, into useful collaboration in the democratic state machine. There had as yet been no elections since the war, so he had not been able to show whether he could carry out his intention. D'Annunzio's march on Fiume was his first test, and his answer to it was conditioned by his determination that Italian politics were in future to be as free as the wind. Great new forces, nationalism no less than socialism and popular catholicism, were to sweep away the unsavoury wreckage of the Giolittian system, and any repressive gesture before the election was therefore out of the question. So instead of taking any action against the movement, which was based on mutiny in the armed forces and involved a direct violation of Italy's international agreements, he abrogated the rights that the Italian State had over the Renaissance palace where d'Annunzio had established himself.

In Milan Mussolini noted how it was done. In the middle of September he said in the *Popolo d'Italia*: "Our government is not at Rome, it is at Fiume."

Assured of no interruption from Rome, d'Annunzio promulgated the Statute of the Province of Fiume. This constitution was concerned more with the mystic whole and the poetic afflatus than with checks and balances. It "promised the completest liberties to all citizens, together with a maximum of hierarchic organization and authority."[1] The state was to be corporative, and the corporations were ten in number: first the labourers, second the managers and technicians, third the shopkeepers, and so on. The tenth "had no special trade or register or title." It was "reserved for the mysterious forces of progress and adventure." The Statute ends "In the pauses of music is heard the silence of the Tenth Corporation."[2]

The d'Annunzian state was held together by display and oratory. D'Annunzio introduced the "Roman salute," the outstretched arm and hand, and every morning would appear on the balcony of his palace and harangue his legionaries.

"What shall we do with the Deputies?" he would shout.

"Make sausages of them," came the legionaries' answer.

[1] C. J. Sprigge, op. cit., p. 175.

[2] Loc. cit.

"No, they'd poison us."

"Then we'll smack their bottoms in Piazza Colonna."

"That's better."[1]

He also invented the litany of nationalism:

LEADER: *A chi la vittoria?*
MOB: *A noi!*
LEADER: *A chi la gloria?*
MOB: *A noi!*
LEADER: *A chi l'Italia?*
MOB: *A noi!*
TOGETHER: *Eia! Eia! Alalà!*

and he gave his legionaries the motto "*Me ne frego!*", "What the hell!", or "*Je m'en fiche!*"

It seems that the smacking of the Deputies in Piazza Colonna was not only a daydream; d'Annunzio had plans of embarking his legionaries at Fiume, disembarking them at Ancona and other ports on the Adriatic coast, and marching on Rome. Even in 1919 the disintegration of Italy was such that this was not an impossible project.

In Milan Mussolini noted all these things.

Such was the state of the country; there were inflation, strikes, spontaneous "Soviets," mutiny, private armies erupting over the frontier, in short the incipient disintegration of the state, when the Socialist Party met in National Congress at Bologna in October. The general election was to take place on November 16th and it was to be for the first time by proportional representation. This was primarily Don Sturzo's idea, although the General Confederation of Labour and the Socialist Parliamentary Group had also declared for it, and its main purpose was to make impossible a reappearance of the Giolittian system of local bargains. If a Deputy had no constituency, he could not be offered a bridge in it. The principal matter for discussion at the Congress was therefore the composition of a national list of candidates for the election; it was unofficially called the "Congress of Candi-

[1] Pietro Nenni, op. cit., p. 73.

dates." The men who were put up would be an expression of the Party's policy.

It was of course the Russian Revolution which raised passions. All shades of opinion were expressed at the Congress, from those who were ashamed that two years had passed and Italy had not done likewise, to the old guard of gradualists who held that the savage upheavals of a half-Asiatic police-state were of no interest to a modern democracy like Italy. Italian socialists were already travelling in Russia, and their return and report were eagerly awaited by the left wing of the Party. Treves took a more independent line about these "Argonauts." "What? Are we to have a revolution or not according to whether they may decide by a majority vote that one is better or worse off in Russia?"[1] A fairly long extract from the acts of the Congress is worth quoting, since it shows the hair-trigger frame of mind that the mere word "Soviet" induced at this time, and also the attitude of Turati, who was still the most important man in the Party.

Turati is speaking:

"To-day everything is changed. Do you not hear? Thrones and dominations are crumbling on every side, and more or less social republics are taking their place; we are in a revolutionary phase. We have already got the dictatorship of the proletariat in Russia and Hungary. But I must say, Hungary doesn't seem to me a very encouraging example; and as to Russia, anybody who is not content with communism on paper would be wise to suspend all judgment until the experiment is a little better known. But, after all, in Russia they are holding fast. It may be that there is in Russia a sort of precocious, unforeseen maturity; I was just going to say a "premature maturity." And so, long live the universal Soviet!

The Soviet! There is a magic word which makes a great impression on the mob . . .

MARTELLI: Perhaps the Soviets are a laughing-matter?
A VOICE: Long live the Soviets! [Warm applause.]

[1] *Critica Sociale*; August 1st–15th, 1920.

LEONE:[1] Whoever said that knows what socialism is. Long live the Soviets! [Applause and vivacious noises.]

TURATI: My dear interrupter, I didn't say "long live the Soviets" nor "down with the Soviets." I was saying something else, with which your interruption had no logical connection.

[Leone shouts something from the back of the hall, but it is not understood because of the indescribable tumult which has been let loose. Brawling sets in on every side. The Chairman tries to restore order, but does not succeed. Serrati[2] and others descend from the platform in order to calm spirits. Shouts are heard such as: "We aren't at a cabaret!", "Enough witticisms!", "Long live Nitti!", "Long live Bolshevism!", "Long live the Soviets!", etc.]

CHAIRMAN: Let Turati speak, and he can explain the phrase which gave rise to this tumult.

A VOICE: And let him change his ideas. [Renewed and increased tumult.]

BORDIGA:[3] Well done the Unitarians![4]

RITA MAIEROTTI: Turati's a gentleman; he has always been coherent. It's the others who aren't gentlemen, because they haven't the courage to throw him out.

[The tumult calms down little by little. Serrati wants to speak from the middle of the hall, but the Chairman asks him to come up again onto the platform and then firmly calls on Turati to continue. During the uproar Turati has stayed at the rostrum.]

TURATI: Comrades: allow me to give a short and honest explanation, which will show you how absolutely unfounded this tumult is. [A little brawling sets in again, but is quickly subdued by the bellringing of the Chairman.[5]] Comrades of the other bank! . . . I had no intention . . . [Renewed tumult, provoked this time by the little group of the abstentionists.[6]

[1] A near-syndicalist of the pre-war type. See page 62.

[2] The Leader of the pacifists during the war.

[3] Extreme Left; later a founder of the Communist Party.

[4] The name under which the gradualist Turatian right went at this time. Proletarian unity again.

[5] Italian chairmen, including the Presidents of the two Houses of Parliament, have always been armed with bells.

[6] From the elections. See below.

The whole hall roars "Silence!"] I couldn't have had any intention of offending anybody at all. It's not in my interest and not in my nature to do so. . . . Frankly, can you seriously think that I don't feel a deep respect for the Russian Revolution? I should simply be an idiot if I didn't."[1]

There were three motions up for the vote, each calling for a change in the Genoa programme of 1892, and it was understood that the candidates for the election would be drawn mainly from the supporters of whichever motion was voted. On the left was the motion of the "communist-abstentionists," which called for complete revolutionary intransigence, the fusion of the Party in the International Communist Party, that its name as a national party should be changed to "Italian Communist Party", and, most important, that it should not fight the general elections at all. On the right was the motion of the "maximalist unitarians," maximalist from the "maximum programme" of 1900 and unitarian from proletarian unity, with whom Turati, as a "minimalist" by temperament, was rather unwillingly associated. They admitted the excellences of the Bolshevik Revolution but laid more emphasis on the internal democratic reform of the Party. The motion of the left got 3,417 votes, that of the right 14,880, and that of the centre 48,411. The motion of the centre therefore became the programme of the Party. It was put forward by the "maximalist electionists," and ran as follows:[2]

"The Congress of the Italian Socialist Party, met at Bologna on the 5th–8th of October 1919, recognizing that the Genoa programme is now outdated by events and by the international situation created by the world crisis which has arisen as a result of the war, proclaims that the Russian Revolution, the most propitious event in the history of the proletariat, has made it necessary, in all the countries of capitalist civilization, to work for its expansion. Given further that no ruling class has yet renounced its despotism unless constrained to do so by violence, and that the exploiting class itself has recourse to violence in

[1] *Critica Sociale*; October 16th–31st, 1920; pp. 255–6.

[2] Rinaldo Rigola, op. cit., pp. 440–2.

defending its own privileges and in stifling the attempts of the oppressed class to free itself, the Congress is convinced that the proletariat must resort to the use of violence to defend itself against bourgeois violence, to conquer power, and to consolidate revolutionary conquests. It also affirms the necessity of studying the means of spiritual and technical preparation. Considering further the present political situation with regard to the forthcoming elections, it determines to enter the lists in the electoral field and within the organs of the bourgeois state in order to carry out the most intensive propaganda for communist principles and to effect the overthrow of the said organs of bourgeois domination.

In view of the above considerations it determines to modify the programme of the Party so that it shall now run as follows:

Programme

[The first four heads are heads 1, 2, 4 and 5 of the 1892 programme; see p. 28. It continues thus:]

Recognizing further that capitalist society and its attendant imperialism has let loose and will let loose wars on an ever vaster and more deadly scale;

and that only the arrival of socialism can lead to civil and economic peace;

and that the ruin of the whole civilized world is an evident sign of the bankruptcy which threatens all countries, both victors and vanquished;

and that the manifest inability of the bourgeois class to repair the damage it has done shows that a revolutionary period has begun in which a profound transformation of society will lead from now on to the violent overthrow of bourgeois capitalist domination and to the conquest of political and economic power on the part of the proletariat;

and that the instruments of oppression and exploitation of the bourgeois domination (States, Communes, and Civil Services) cannot in any way be transformed into organs of the liberation of the proletariat;

and that against these organs must be set up new proletarian organs (Workers' and Peasants' Councils, Councils of Public Economy, etc.) which will function at first, during the bourgeois

domination, as instruments of the violent struggle for liberation, and later as organs of social and economic transformation and of reconstruction in the communist new order;
and that the violent conquest of power on the part of the workers will indicate the passing of power itself from the bourgeoisie to the proletariat, thus installing the transitory regime of the dictatorship of the whole proletariat;
and that in this regime of dictatorship the historical period of social transformation and the realization of communism must be hurried on, after which, with the disappearance of classes, will also disappear every domination of class, and the free development of each will be the condition of the free development of all;

DETERMINES

1. to inform the organization of the Italian Socialist Party with the above principles;

2. to adhere to the Third International, the world-wide proletarian organization which expounds and defends these principles;

3. to promote agreements with those syndical organizations which are engaged in the class-struggle in order that they should base their action on the deepest realization of the above principles."[1]

The second of these last three resolutions, adherence to the Third International, was carried by acclamation, the other two by the vote.

The new programme was a sharp repudiation of the old. The Russian Revolution had given a new life to phrases that had for twenty years been repeated with less and less meaning behind them, and more and more as a mere ritual. The main practical decision of the 1892 programme had been to work within the organs of the state and to try to convert them into "instruments of the economic and political expropriation of the ruling class"; which meant to pursue in them whatever might be socialist policy at the moment. The main practical decision of

[1] The fact that the verb "DETERMINES" has no subject is not due to the excision of the first four heads; it has none in the original. The English of this translation is probably no worse than the Italian.

the 1919 programme was to set up parallel organs of government, a state within the state, because it was now seen that the existing organs of government could not "in any way" be made use of to further socialist policy. Nevertheless, the Party was to contest elections as before. This was another compromise between revolutionaries and reformists. If it had adopted the left motion, withdrawn itself entirely from democratic politics, and concentrated entirely on building up the "new proletarian organs," the Soviets, the Party could have had a socialist revolution in Italy within a year of the Bologna Congress. Or if it had adopted the right motion, forgotten all about the state within the state, and concentrated entirely on democratic politics, it could within six weeks of the Bologna Congress have formed under Turati a government so strong as to tow the less experienced Popular Party with it and do more or less what it liked with the country. But to vote either the right or the left motion would have been to split the Party, and that was a possibility that no socialist could face any better in 1919 than he could in 1900.

The situation had not changed essentially since that date. The spectacular alarums and excursions of the strikers on the one hand and of the d'Annunzian legionaries on the other and all the signs of a coming break-up of the Italian State did not alter the choice before the Socialist Party. Before the war there had been no hope of a socialist revolution or of a socialist government. In 1919 there was every hope of one or the other, but not of both. The balance was the same, but the weights were larger. Before the war the Party had sacrificed coherence to unity; now it sacrificed to unity its certain success in either of two mutually exclusive courses, and it decided to follow them both.

The Party went to the polls under the Hammer and Sickle, and 156 of its candidates, drawn mostly from the centre and left of the Party, were returned. Next in number came the Popular Party with 100. Eight other groups, including the radicals and republicans, shared the remaining 252 seats. During the Speech from the Throne the majority of the socialist Deputies, each wearing a red flower in his buttonhole, walked out of the Chamber singing the "Red Flag." Those who remained shouted "Long live the Socialist Republic," and were forcibly silenced by the constitutional parties. Bombacci, now editor of *Avanti!*, proclaimed "revolutionary Italy is born," and published a draft Soviet constitution.

During the remaining six months of Signor Nitti's government the confusion of the country became almost indescribable. There was no civil war in the sense of campaigns and battles, because there was no clear issue to fight on. There was no revolution in the sense of the armed overthrow of government, because of the lack of leadership in the Socialist Party. There was instead a running series of useless violence and strikes, an ever-increasing bitterness between ill-defined factions, and a general demoralization. To give an adequate impression of the bitterness and demoralization would take pages of anecdotes and particular examples and it would not lead to any better understanding of the causes and issues. What the issues were it is impossible to say, so disorientated were the rioters and strikers, even the most determinedly violent of them. Of the causes it is only possible to be sure of one, the war. A very young country, hitherto on the boundary of the deadly game of European politics, had been drawn suddenly in, and while she had stood up fairly well to the war itself, she could not hold together in the unease and disruption that followed it.

It was at this time that the vilifiers of the war were most in the ascendant. Insults to officers in the streets reached such a pitch that the War Ministry ordered them not to go out in uniform, and a certain Misiano was elected to parliament on no other qualification than that of having been a deserter.[1] The natural reaction to this was an increase in the popularity of d'Annunzio; open appeals were addressed to him to come down and "liberate" Rome.

The Fiume enterprise had originally had all the classical

[1] He was physically expelled by the fascist Deputies in 1921.

characteristics of nationalism, and nationalism is usually to be found on the right. But we have seen how d'Annunzio tended to stay in the political antipodes where right and left meet, and no sooner had he established himself in Fiume than he sent ambassadors to Moscow, who exchanged compliments with Lenin.

The news from the East was for a time even more exciting for the socialists than it had been in 1917. The Red Army had defeated Kolchak and Denikin and was advancing into Poland; for a moment it seemed that it might be 1797 again, and that the Revolution would come sweeping across Europe with a victorious army. But there followed the campaigns in Poland, and the Italian socialists turned back to their impossible juggling with parliament and revolution.

They had already put themselves out of the running in parliament. They could have formed their own government, they could have controlled Signor Nitti, who was generous with offers of portfolios, they could have made themselves masters of the country in any number of ways. But no: bourgeois institutions could "in no way" be made to serve socialist ends; and therefore the Deputies reverted to a position very nearly as unco-operative as that which they had taken up in the brave old days of 1895. But this time nobody was going to arrest them or to pass repressive laws against them. In the winter of 1919–20 the general feeling among the non-socialists was: "You have shown us how powerful you are, and we have been much impressed by your strikes and your plans for reform. Will you now form a government and do what you like with us? We don't understand what you are demonstrating against. You are the biggest party in the country, and we are in your power." The socialist answer in parliament was to introduce a private measure to permit divorce.

Away in the cities and the fields, where the revolution was supposed to be in preparation, they were no more effective. Strikes were continuous, unopposed and almost always "successful." Wage increases followed rapidly upon each other and inflation therefore continued. But there was no strategy. One example will be enough. Early in 1920 the Post Office workers came out on strike. There were no second thoughts now about the illegality of government servants striking, and at the very moment when they went back the railwaymen, also government servants, came out. Over and over again there would be a general strike in one town followed by a general strike in another, when a little determined co-ordination by the Party through the General Confederation of Labour could have multiplied manifold the disruptive and revolutionary effect. But when faced at last with a real revolutionary situation, the socialist leaders remained somehow inhibited, fascinated by the theory of the thing. A certain Graziadei writing in *Avanti!* on February 20th[1] said: "There is nothing we can do except follow the course decided on at the Bologna Congress; that is, propaganda and parliamentary criticism, and provoking cabinet crises and the fall of governments, until there is born a conviction that only socialism in power can resolve the present political crisis." Speaking on May 20th at a meeting of the National Council of the Party, one of the organs whose proliferation contributed to the confusion, the same Graziadei said: "The general strike as an instrument of expropriation does not exist."[2] These two quotations admirably show two weaknesses of socialist leadership; the first a "never jam to-day" attitude; the second a blind dogmatism. In the second it is the words "does not exist" that are interesting. Graziadei might have said "a general strike has never yet been an instrument of expropriation," or even "it is vain to try and use a general strike as an instrument of expropriation," but to decide that a certain dynamic combination of events "does not exist" because it has never been tried is subtly indicative of the Marxist frame of mind, shown in both these quotations, that there is no need to hurry or take any active steps about the revolution because it is bound to come in any event.

[1] Quoted in Pietro Nenni, *Storia di quattro anni*; Rome, 1946; p. 73.
[2] "*Lo sciopero generale espropriatore non esiste.*"

In March 1920 came the first indication that, if the socialist leaders were content to let the strikes go on and on until somehow the revolution came about of itself, other sections of the community were not. In that month a congress of industrialists passed a resolution[1] calling for a stronger government which would insist on the efficiency of the state services. In the wording of the resolution, overtones are perceptible of a feeling of class solidarity against plebeian excess.

In Milan Mussolini noted it.

Among the celebrations on Labour Day, May 1st, was a football match at the Tuscan seaside town of Viareggio. A tendency to carry the class-struggle onto the football field gave rise to rioting and disorders in all Tuscany which were in turn reflected in the Chamber of Deputies, now in more or less permanent uproar. Signor Nitti resigned for the second time and at once proceeded to constitute his third cabinet. As a price for the support of the groups of the right, on which he had to rely in default of any glimmer of sympathy from the socialists, he agreed to lower the bread subsidy substantially. He promulgated the reduction by Royal Decree, since in the state of the Chamber he found it almost impossible to legislate by any other means. The consequent outcry in the country was aggravated by a go-slow movement on the part of the telephone and telegraph workers, and on June 8th Signor Nitti repealed the decree and resigned for the third and last time. Under him the state of the county had gone from bad to worse, and it is impossible to say that he had done much to stop it. He had arrived in power, an intellectual without party affiliation, hoping to preside over the healthy competition and development of the two mass parties. But they would not be presided over, and he was not strong enough to bring them to heel. He was forced back on the support of the right, and in consequence a standing complaint against him had been that he was afraid of dealing with a real grievance by taxing the rich or soaking up war profits. Almost his only positive act had been to confuse the police situation by putting alongside

[1] Printed in Nenni, *Storia di quattro anni*; p. 69.

the established corps of the *Carabinieri*, which had a tradition on the whole honourable, a new corps of Royal Guards, *Guardie Regie*, which quickly fell a prey to faction and resentment. The three great evils of Italy, inflation, strikes, and d'Annunzio, these he had left untouched.

There was little hesitation about his successor. A man was needed who knew the ropes, who could play off the parties against each other, who, if he could not inspire confidence, could buy it; better corruption than chaos, and above all anything for a familiar face in this stormy new world! The King called Giolitti. Giolitti was now seventy-eight; he had been seven years out of office, and it was five years since he had been hissed out of Rome by the "Radiant May" agitation. But he was still vigorous, and as reasonable as ever. He announced his programme: a treaty with Belgrade to settle the Adriatic question, with the liquidation of d'Annunzio to follow; parliamentary control of foreign affairs, balanced in internal affairs by a "return to the constitution" in the manner of Sonnino, which was to give the government a freer hand in dealing with disorder; the confiscation of war profits; and an inquiry into government expenditure during the war. His cabinet included the interventionist Signor Bonomi as War Minister, Count Carlo Sforza as Foreign Minister,[1] a professional diplomat with a passionately international outlook and a consequent impatience of disorderliness like d'Annunzio's, and Benedetto Croce as Minister of Education. Signor Croce was to enlist the sympathy of the Popular Party because, although no catholic himself, he had come to believe in catholicism as a social cement and he was to introduce religious teaching into the state schools.

This was a very reasonable programme, but the time for reasonableness had passed. The socialist Deputies greeted Giolitti with a new blast of defiance and Treves, who had been almost a Giolittian before the war, wrote in *Critica Sociale*:[2] "'Save us, Giolitti! Work the miracle! Save us, Giolitti!' Not that way

[1] The same who is again Foreign Minister now (1949).

[2] June 16th–30th, 1920.

lies salvation." Even the more moderate socialists had good cause to be disturbed at Giolitti's return, for, when between 1908 and 1912 they had come near to trusting him, he had brought the Libyan War upon them. The result of that had been the Congress of Reggio Emilia and the hegemony of Mussolini, and by now they did not like to be reminded that Mussolini had once been their leader.

With proportional representation, paternal corruption was no longer possible; but Giolitti had not lost his touch. During his last ministry he brought all the old skill to bear on calming the country down. He could not do it, but his ministry was certainly the best between 1918 and the end of parliamentary ministries.

Disorders continued. Giolitti's first act on coming to power was to announce Italy's withdrawal from the ill-defined protectorate in Albania; this was the first step in his policy of tidying up the Adriatic. Before the withdrawal could be carried out, there were some attacks by Albanians on Italian troops. The news of them, and the stories of malaria across the water, reached some *Bersaglieri* who were waiting to embark at Ancona. The *Bersaglieri*, a crack regiment with a great pride in their tradition, had been threatened some weeks earlier with dispersion among other regiments, and the detachments at Ancona mutinied and refused to embark. There was a sympathetic general strike and riots in the Marches and Umbria. Faced with another revolutionary situation the socialist leaders once again called for calm and discipline. Giolitti resolved the situation by evacuating Albania at once.

In September and October came the high-water mark of socialism in Italy, the Occupation of the Factories. The workers of a group of industries, tired of waiting for a lead from above, began the revolution for themselves. Their movement is usually called in Italian the "Metallurgical Occupation"; there is no one English word to cover the group of industries involved. This group included roughly everything to do with metal except shipbuilding. The shipyard workers had their own union, not affiliated to the General Confederation of Labour. The workers of the metal group, from smelting, rolling, pressing, and casting, down to turning and the minutest mechanical construction, were covered by the only great trade union in Italy, the Federation of Metallurgical Employees and Workers, *Federazione degli Impiegati e Operai Metallurgici,* or F.I.O.M. The F.I.O.M. was affiliated to the General Confederation of Labour, and influential in its counsels. It was an exception to the rule that in Italy it is the Chambers of Labour that count and not the trade unions; but it was not a nation-wide trade union, because the industries it covered were situated only in Piedmont and Lombardy, and particularly in and around Turin and Milan.

We have seen how the Italian iron and steel industries have to import from abroad almost all their raw materials; coal and iron. As far back as 1887 protective tariffs had been introduced in the form of a duty on imported finished products, and it was under the artificial shelter of this duty that the industries in pig-iron and raw steel had grown up. During the war the duties had been raised and the industry had rapidly expanded to meet the demands of war production. During the war too there had been some talk, particularly among the workers themselves, of international price-control of pig-iron and scrap-iron. This project had been half-heartedly mentioned by the Italian negotiators at Paris, and had met with little sympathy from the producing countries, the United States, England, and France. In 1920 there were many schools of thought among those concerned with the industry about how best to organize it, given the shortage of transport, world-wide in shipping and Italian in rolling-stock, and the need to import almost all the materials at one stage or another in their working. Some held that iron should be imported in ore, some in pig and scrap, some half-worked and in rolled steel, some even in finished products. The issues were further complicated by those who held that hardly any coal need be imported if Italy's water-power were fully developed for electric smelting. In the result there was unco-ordinated buying on an uncontrolled world market, and the financial structure of the industry was in a top-heavy condition indicated by the fact that wages were only 9 per cent of total expenses.[1]

It was in this unsettled industry that the particular phenomenon of constructive communism[2] grew up. Thirty-five thousand workers were employed in the foundries and rolling-mills, and more than three hundred thousand in engineering.[3] The nucleus of communism was in the great Fiat car-factory in Turin. It was a very different sort of communism from that of Bombacci, whose inspiration was more like the old destructive anhelitus of the anarchists. Torinese communism, associated particularly with Antonio Gramsci, the founder of the Italian Communist Party and its prophet and martyr, and Palmiro Togliatti, its leader from 1944 onwards, was essentially a constructive affair. Gramsci and Signor Togliatti, who were intellectuals, were its students and codifiers; but it was in the factories themselves that the new constructive communism grew up. The skilled and comparatively well-paid car workers had a structure of co-operative associations and union organs for various purposes, and these, reinforced by political debating circles, really did approach the Bologna ideal of the state within the state. Through this powerful machine, a machine of an enlightened sort by the standards of the class-struggle, the metal-workers of Turin had in 1919 and early 1920 carried out a series of strikes for well-defined ends which were praised for their determination by the Turin edition of *Avanti!* and blamed by the Milan edition, more closely under the control of the Socialist Party Direction, for setting too fast a pace for the "general strategy" to keep up with. At one point the Ministry of Labour put forward a scheme for increased tariff protection for the industry in order to allow the payment of the higher wages demanded by the F.I.O.M. The leaders of the F.I.O.M. answered that, whether they got the higher wages or not, increased protection which would raise the

[1] Article by Gino Luzatto in *Critica Sociale* of April 1st–15th, 1920.

[2] The communists were at this time still a group within the Socialist Party.

[3] Gino Luzatto, loc. cit.

price of metal products was against the interests of the whole community and they would not tolerate it.

In the summer of 1920 the leaders of the F.I.O.M., more revolutionary than their superiors of the General Confederation of Labour and more realistic than the "general strategists" at the Socialist Party, made the only large and organized revolutionary attempt of these years. By way of putting the screw on the managements during some normal wage negotiations, the "Agitation Committee," which was the spearhead of the strike organization, ordered no overtime to be worked in a group of factories. After some argument, on August 21st it ordered "obstruction" on a well-elaborated plan combining the advantages of the English methods of "going slow" and of "working to rule." An "obstructor" is just as useless as a striker, and more annoying to the management, because he stands about in the shop being openly useless instead of staying out of sight at home. The management of the Romeo factory at Milan lost its nerve first; on August 28th it proclaimed a lock-out and got the police to occupy its premises. This was where the process departed from the normal. The Committee of Agitation retaliated by ordering the workers to occupy upwards of three hundred plants, and to work them themselves. The order was carried out and the men began to work again. In some factories they held the management and the white collars down in their chairs, in some they tried to provide management and white collars from among themselves. The metal-workers' co-operatives guaranteed profits for as long as necessary. In some places "Red Centuries" were organized from among the workers, armed, and set to guard the factories against any attempt by the old managements to take control again. It was not clear at first what it was all about, but within a day or two those workers who were trying to run the managers' offices discovered the records of a kind of political espionage to which they had been subjected. This provoked the leaders of the F.I.O.M. to set forth their terms for treating with the expropriated employers. They were that the two sides should come together for discussions, on the understanding that organs should be set up which would give the workers a very substantial control over the management and policy of the industry. The proposals were not detailed.

The F.I.O.M. and the metal-workers themselves had now done all that they could; they had in effect carried out the revolution in their own sphere, and, what is more, they had carried it out swiftly, peacefully, and with determination. Either the thing had to go forward or it had to collapse, for the amateur workers' managements could not expect to win recognition and co-operation from the professional capitalist managements of the rest of the country's economy. Now if ever was the time for determined action by the Socialist Party. Instead of the demoralization of Caporetto or the vague turbulence of the bloody general strikes which had followed each other throughout the last year, they were presented with established workers' control in the country's most highly developed group of industries.

On September 5th the General Confederation of Labour made a pronouncement through its General Secretary. There were three possible courses: (1) to confine the movement to the metal industry and to consolidate the position gained there; (2) to promote movements of the same sort throughout the whole country; (3) to convert the movement into the revolution. It favoured the second course. Shortly afterwards came the reaction of the Socialist Party Direction; it offered to take charge of the movement. The movement was of course well in charge of itself, as far as it went. What was needed was either a swift follow-through to the proclaimed ends of the Party, or a frank recognition that it did not wish to pursue those ends. Parliament, that organ of bourgeois domination which could in no way be made to serve socialist purposes, was in recess, and the socialist Deputies asked that it should be convened.

But Giolitti did not intend to sit in Rome and listen to a hundred and fifty-six different versions and explanations of what was happening. He had been in daily contact with Socialist Party leaders for twenty-eight years, twelve of which he had spent manipulating them as Prime Minister, and he saw clearly that there was no danger of a real revolution. He himself in his *Memoirs* draws the parallel between the situation in 1920 and that of the general strike in 1904. As in 1904, he waited. "I was firmly convinced," he writes,[1] "that the government ought . . . to allow . . . the experiment to be carried out up to a certain point so that the workers should be able to see how unpractical were their proposals, and so that their leaders[2] should be left with no excuse to put the blame for failure on others. Besides, this long-term political expediency coincided with the short-term expediency of the police situation . . ." because, if he had put the police to keep the workers out of the factories, it would have taken all he had, and there would have been none left over to keep order in the piazzas, where the workers would then have gathered. In 1904 Giolitti had dissolved and gone to the country at the critical moment; the agitations of 1920 came less than a year after a general election, at a time when Giolitti had been in power for four months only and had hardly made a start on the programme which had been approved in parliament. So this time he did not dissolve, but, having completed his fortnight of educative inaction and sized up the inefficacy of the Socialist Party leadership, he went up to Turin. In Turin he held meetings all round and made reasonable speeches telling the workers that he recognized their claim to a part of the responsibility for direction. He convened a meeting of the employers and showed them an Order that he proposed to publish if they did not come together with the workers' representatives and reach an agreement. It ran:[3]

"A mixed commission is to be formed consisting of six members nominated by the General Confederation of Industry[4] and six by the General Confederation of Labour,

[1] Quoted in Nenni, *Storia di quattro anni*; p. 107.

[2] *Caporioni*: this means *Gauleiters* exactly, but since *Gauleiters* was not an English word in 1920, it will not do here.

[3] Nenni, *Storia di quattro anni*; p. 105.

[4] Corresponding to the Federation of British Industries.

including two technicians or employees on each side, and is to formulate proposals for the use of the Government in presenting a bill to reorganize Industry on a basis of the participation of the workers in the technical, financial, and administrative control of the concerns. . . . The workers are to return to their posts.

Giolitti

Turin, *September 15th*, 1920 President of the Council."[1]

The commission had to meet, and negotiations dragged on in irrelevant arguments about payment of wages during the Occupation. But by the time it was clear that no agreement would be reached and the government had proceeded to draft a bill by itself, there were other things for both workers and employers to think about.

Giolitti is not usually given much credit for anything he did in his last ministry; his conduct in the general elections of the following year has obscured all that he did earlier. But his handling of the occupation of the factories was undeniably satisfactory. By taking once more the risk of inaction he showed both sides in the dispute that the only reasonable course was to reach an agreement between themselves. If he had tried to deal with the crisis from Rome he could not have escaped offending one side or the other; by going in person to Turin he was able to convince both sides that the issue was both wider and less inflammable than they had thought and that thorough discussions were needed. When they had been held, something might be done about re-forming the whole structure of Italian industry. His soothing personal intervention gave the impression, in the words of the former socialist Signor Bonomi who was to succeed him as Prime Minister, that "liberty had killed rebellion, and, in full liberty, the rebels had to admit their failure."[2] That is one side of the matter; but the Giolittian speciality of smothering revolutions with liberty depended on the weakness of the revolutionary

[1] Prime Minister.

[2] Ivanoe Bonomi, *Dal socialismo al fascismo*; Rome, 1924; p. 37.

leadership. If once it had decided what it wanted to do, the Socialist Party could in 1920 have brushed Giolitti aside in parliament, or overthrown Giolitti, parliament, state, and all, in a revolution.

At this moment, when the socialist leaders were disheartened and divided among themselves, when the incompatibility of parliamentary and revolutionary activity had been shown once again, and when particularly the communists in the Party were complaining of the inadequacy of the Party Direction, there arrived from Moscow the famous Twenty-one Points. These were a statement of the conditions to be fulfilled by any party wishing to belong to the Third International, and were circulated to all the socialist parties. It is perhaps worth condensing them here.

To belong to the Third International, a socialist party had to: (1) conduct an entirely and coherently communist propaganda and expound the tenets of the International; (2) tolerate the presence of no bourgeois in its ranks, even if workers had at first to be used as experts; (3) form parallel, illegal organs of government; (4) conduct illegal propaganda in the army and (5) among the peasants; (6) systematically unmask patriotic socialists in the name of internationalism; (7) break with reformists and integralists (Turati, Modigliani, Kautsky, Hilferding, Hillquit, Longuet, and Ramsay MacDonald were mentioned); (8) conduct propaganda against colonies and protectorates; (9) organize communist cells in the trade unions; (10) conduct propaganda against the Second (Amsterdam) International; (11) if it must be represented in parliament have only truly communist representatives; (12) maintain an iron discipline and centralization in the Party itself; (13) purge the Party periodically; (14) do all it could to stop intervention in Russia; (15) abandon whatever programme it might have and draw up a new one which was to be approved by the Third International; (16) accept as binding the decisions of the Congress and Executive Committee of the Third International; (17) take the title of "Communist Party," in order that the workers might distinguish it from the old "yellow" socialist parties of the Second International; (18) see that any important pronouncements of the Executive Committee of the Third International were publicized in the Party's press; (19) call a National Congress within four months in order to have these things approved at which (20) a Party Direction was to be installed of which at least two-thirds should consist of those who had professed communism before the date of these Twenty-one Points, and at which (21) dissentients from these Points were to be expelled.

The matter of these points and the high-handed manner of their expression brought about a major crisis in the Italian Socialist Party. They were published in *Avanti!* on September 21st, accompanied by a leading article saying that whoever had compiled them, whatever his knowledge of other countries, did not know Italy. The Italian socialists, so they said, were different from those of other European countries because they had been officially pacifist throughout the war and because the reformists had been expelled in 1912. On the day after their publication the Party Direction had accepted the Twenty-one Points by a majority of seven to five, but an authoritative answer could only be given by a National Congress of the Party. It was arranged to hold a Congress at Leghorn in January, which was within the period of four months stipulated in the Points.

At the moment of the collapse of the revolutionary Occupation, the Bolshevik Government had struck a grave blow at the precarious unity of the Italian Socialist Party. We must now consider why, for the first time since 1900, unity was becoming necessary.

3. *Counter-revolution*, 1920–5

Mussolini's progress towards the right continued. At the end of the war he was still as bellicose a socialist as he had been in 1915, but he was also a "renouncer," as befitted a socialist. The next move towards the right was when he suddenly launched a fresh campaign against Bissolati, whom he had had expelled from the Socialist Party in 1912. After his resignation from the Orlando Government, Bissolati went about the country lecturing and speaking for the cause of renunciation. When he came to Milan, Mussolini heckled him in person and attacked him in the *Popolo d'Italia* for wanting to take the fruits of victory from the soldiers who had so heroically won them during the war. The circle was now complete and Mussolini had become a full-blown nationalist.

If he hated Bissolati, whom he had expelled, he hated still more the Socialist Party leaders, who had expelled him. It was primarily as an anti-Bolshevik movement that he founded fascism in 1919. The programme and inspiration of fascism do not concern us here in any detail, but there were two points in it relevant to the history of Italian socialism. First, it was as an alternative to bolshevism that Mussolini put the Fascist Party forward. The support he won came not only from the sadists and thugs, not only from the fanatical nationalists, but also from those who wanted a peaceable restoration of civil order and those who felt there was more in nationhood than was implied by the socialist who spat at a uniformed officer in the street. Mussolini caught Italian patriotism on the natural rebound from the injuries it had suffered. The second point is that Mussolini did not put himself forward as a dictator in 1919 and 1920. He did not offer to abolish parliament, civil liberties, or the press; he offered to discipline treacherous elements, those who needed disciplining, the enemies of the country. Few people will apply such phrases to themselves.

In the autumn of 1920, when the socialists were disconcerted by the failure of the Occupation and were threatened with a split about acceptance of the Russian ultimatum, the fascists were beginning to emerge from Milan and to raid and buccaneer round about Northern Italy. The castor-oil technique was being developed, and the phrase "punitive expedition" was becoming known: it described a gang of youths breaking up the offices of a Chamber of Labour, of a local section of the Socialist Party, or of a local socialist paper. In December d'Annunzio was finally called to order. Giolitti and Sforza had concluded the Treaty of Rapallo with Yugoslavia, abandoning the claims of the Treaty of London and making Fiume a Free City. Then they sent troops and a naval unit against it. The legionaries were at first disposed to resist, but a shell from one of the ships burst against the façade of d'Annunzio's palace and he surrendered, lamenting that death had spared him and thus prolonged the shame of being an Italian. The return of the legionaries brought colourful recruits to fascism, and Mussolini made use of their experience in the *mise-en-scène* of nationalistic adventure. The Fascist Party adopted the black shirts which had been the war-time uniform of the *Arditi,* learnt to chant the meaningless "*Eia! Eia! Alalà!*", and took "*Me ne frego*" as its motto. In November post-war demobilization ended, and the last returning soldiers found in the Fascist Party an organization that helped them to "learn or re-learn to live" by giving them a pseudo-military organization and a field for martial activity in civilian life. The next generation of adolescents, those disappointed not only of the war but also of the Fiume enterprise, found their release in fascism.

On November 19th, 1920, the fascists of Bologna staged a major "punitive raid" which bore much the same relation to earlier fascist agitations as did the Occupation to earlier socialist strikes. It was to be a show-down, a blatant gesture which could not be shuffled out of afterwards. On that day they posted the following notice in the streets of Bologna: "Women and all those who love peace and quiet are to stay at home on Sunday. If they wish to deserve well of their Fatherland, they should hang an Italian tricolour from their windows. Only fascists and bolsheviks are to be in the streets of Bologna on Sunday. It will be the test, the great test, in the name of Italy."[1] On the Sunday the fascists had everything their own way, and the town was given over for the day, not to fire and the sword, but to rubber truncheons and castor-oil.

From then on the fascists advanced as the socialists retreated. Against the disorderly violence of the socialists Mussolini brought an ordered and calculated violence. Turati called it "a revolution of blood against a revolution of words." It appears that the landowners and industrial employers were not averse from financing the fascist movement; they certainly became less and less averse from openly sympathizing with it. Mussolini himself was as much a moderating as an inflaming influence. At the end of 1920 he saw that the Occupation had been the high-water mark of bolshevism, and that it was now on the ebb. But his eclectic genius had learnt from Giolitti as well as from Sorel and d'Annunzio, and he gave bolshevism another two years to show its complete failure.

When the Socialist Party met in special Congress at Leghorn in January 1921 its members were getting used to the idea that they were now under physical as well as political attack, that to be a proclaimed socialist exposed one to bodily harm. Few local sections in North and Central Italy had not by the beginning of 1921 been beaten up or at least threatened by the blackshirts, and it was against this background that their representatives cast their collective votes for or against the acceptance of the Moscow Points. A letter had been received from Zinoviev, the President of the Comintern, in which he wrote: "The Congress of your Party meets at a moment when the proletarian revolution is knocking at the doors of Italy."[2] Zinoviev was late; the revolution had knocked in vain at a door which the socialist leaders themselves had failed to open, and insurgent fascism was now beginning to hold it shut. Another letter from Moscow was received at the Congress, saying: "The unity of the Party is an

[1] Panfilo Gentile, *50 anni di socialismo*; Milan, 1948; p. 147.

[2] Nenni, *Storia di quattro anni*; p. 121.

equivocal formula: it means the unity of communists with the enemies of communism. There is no place for this unity in the ranks of the Third International."[1] There were again three motions up for the vote: (1) that of the "pure communists" who whole-heartedly accepted the Twenty-one Points; (2) that of the "unitarian communists," who wished to adhere to the Third International but not at the cost of a split in the Party and not on dictated terms; and (3) that of the "concentrationists," the right wing, who held squarely that a party of the standing of the Italian Socialist Party accepted favours from no one, and frankly proclaimed that its policy should be decided in Italy and not at Moscow. The first motion got 54,783 votes, the second 92,028, the third 14,695. About 100,000 were not cast at all. The "pure communists" accordingly left the Party and founded the Italian Communist Party, while the supporters of the motions of the centre and right remained in uneasy unity for eighteen months more. At a subsequent congress of the General Confederation of Labour the casters of 432,564 votes split away to follow the Communist Party, while 1,435,873 remained attached to the Socialist Party. With the Communist Party went most of the wits and the guts of the socialist movement. The wits belonged to the Torinese tradition that brought about the Occupation, and whose most effective leaders were the two young intellectuals Gramsci and Signor Togliatti. Their different personal histories provide the link between the communism of the period after the 1915–18 War and that of the period after the 1940–5 War. The guts of the movement belonged as always to the Romagnole tradition, the tradition that produced Mussolini, whose leader was Nicola Bombacci. Bombacci later became a hierarch of the Fascist Party and ended his life in 1945 strung up with Mussolini in Milan.

It was in the summer of 1920 that Italian socialism reached its zenith. Then it had had a quarter of a million Party members, about three million workers organized in unions and Chambers of Labour who were more or less closely committed to socialist

[1] Ibid., p. 123.

politics, and of whom 2,320,163 were grouped under the socialist General Confederation of Labour, just ten times as many as in 1915. At the general elections of November 1919 the Party had polled 1,800,000 votes in an electorate of some eight million and had emerged the strongest party in parliament with 156 Deputies. At the local elections of November 1920, it won 26 provincial governments out of 69, and 2,162 communal governments out of a little less than twice that number. *Avanti!* in six editions had a circulation of 300,000.[1] But within six months, under the twin blows of the failure of the Occupation and the Twenty-one Points from Moscow, it had fallen apart; and the split which resulted from the Congress of Leghorn spread right down to the smallest local trade union group and to the Chamber of Labour of the smallest agricultural town. The rival communist and socialist organizations, both political and syndical, did not have time to crystallize during the four years of battering persecution to which they were subjected by the fascists, who profited by their division to seize power.

The period between the Congress of Leghorn in January and the second general election since the war in May showed how much enfeebled was the Socialist Party, in spite of the fact that this was the Party to which the great majority of the organized workers still adhered. After two years of its own hair-raising revolutionary propaganda and of action which, if not revolutionary, was undeniably violent and illegal, the Party decided that its best defence against the yet more violent and more illegal action of the fascists was to take refuge behind the laws which it had formerly despised. A catchword was launched by the new Secretary of the Party: "Back to the bosom of civilization!" The socialists appeared no longer as proud, unflinching rebels, but as decent law-abiding folk subjected to the brutal and unwarranted attacks of an illegal minority. This was a perfectly

[1] These figures are taken from Professor Gaetano Salvemini's introduction to *Italian Democracy in the Making*, by William Salomone; Philadelphia, 1945; p. ix; and from the article *Fascismo* in the *Enciclopedia Italiana*; 1936.

defensible position, but, as to law-abidingness, they had burnt their boats in the past two years. Their new humility at home was aggravated by a humiliation abroad. Although outflanked by the alacrity of the communists, the socialists still hoped to be allowed to join the Third International, and Costantino Lazzari went to Moscow to put their case. But even Lazzari, a foundation-member of the Workers' Party in 1882 and of the Socialist Party in 1892, the man who had introduced the purge of the reformists in 1912 and had been imprisoned for pacifism in 1918, always a revolutionary, always a proletarian, the spearhead of the class-struggle within the Party itself, even he returned empty-handed. The younger and more rigid Russians pointed out that the Party was still called Socialist, that it was riddled with yellow patriots like Turati, Treves, and Modigliani, the most whole-hearted "collaborationist" in the Parliamentary Group. So the Socialist Party continued to profess its allegiance to the Third International while the Third International would not have it as a member.

Giolitti thought that the time had now come for the country to pass judgment on the retreating socialists, and he announced a general election to be held on May 15th. In common with many other people he had mistaken the nature of fascism, or had perhaps overestimated his capacity to control it. He thought it would serve his purpose by leading the country away from turbulent socialism. The socialists had acted violently and illegally for too long for Giolitti to feel any scruples about turning their own methods against them. When a balance was reached between violent fascism and violent socialism there would be plenty of time for him or his successor to make the peace. It was this attitude on the part of the government that made possible the "Bologna happenings"[1] of the previous November. The attitude, moreover, fitted in very conveniently with the virtual impossibility of any other attitude, since an army which was liable to drop sections that would then follow a poet across the frontier was not of much use in suppressing disorders. It was

[1] "*Fatti di Bologna.*"

further a standing complaint of the socialists that the fascists were being supplied with arms by the police. A manifesto posted in the streets of Milan after an incident of socialist violence in May 1921 serves to show what degree of impartiality was observed by the Royal Guards that Signor Nitti had instituted.

> "Comrades and brothers in arms! The execrable misdeed wrought yesterday by the Socialists on our comrade has aroused a veritable shudder among the citizens, but from you it calls for implacable vengeance! And vengeance we shall have. The unfortunate mother of the victim implores us!
>
> "The Fatherland imposes it on us. Conscience demands it of us. Our lamented comrade wishes it!
>
> "Before this shameful and infamous crime, we feel that we must shake ourselves free of the duties which we have hitherto scrupulously carried out. We feel that the lament of our poor Sebastiano imposes on us the duty of prompt and bloody reaction.
>
> "Be brave and loyal and, while you feel flowering within you the '*nec devii nec retrogradi*,' cry out with one voice: 'Vengeance is ours!'
>
> "All good Italians have been, are, and will always be with us, as are with us the desolate comrades in arms who make you this appeal. The Fatherland will reward us; the poor desolate mother will be eternally grateful to you.
>
> "A Group of Royal Guards.
>
> "Milan, *May* 18*th*, 1921."[1]

Giolitti arranged that the fascists should fix the elections for him. He gathered round him a group which presented itself to the electors under the name of the National Bloc; it consisted of the Liberals, the moderate conservative party, with which Benedetto Croce was associated and in which were primarily the southern landowners and the liberal aristocracy, the Old Right, a little group which disliked everything that had happened since Depretis came to power, the democrats, a colourless central mass which found both socialism and the Popular Party too

[1] Nenni, *Storia di quattro anni*; p. 139.

demagogic for it, and the fascists. Now that proportional representation had made impossible the web of bargains which Giolitti had been used to spread out from the Ministry of the Interior, brutality was to take the place of bribes and the fascists were there to supply it. To be Giolitti's captain of mercenaries suited Mussolini well enough for the moment, who was now posing as the saviour of order, the man who would give form to the aspirations for national cohesion. He did his work well; there was more violence at the polls than had yet been seen in Italy and a number of socialist candidates were prevented from going to places where they were due to speak.

Giolitti's aim in the election was, as in 1904, to reduce the socialist representation. The Socialist Party, having voted down in National Council the usual motion to abstain from the elections altogether, got 128 seats, the new Communist Party 13, the Popular Party 106, and the National Bloc and Independent groups made up the total of 500. The Fascist Party got 33. If socialists and communists be taken together, socialist representation had therefore fallen only from 156 to 135. For a month Giolitti continued to govern uneasily without the support of either socialists or populars, for, notwithstanding Signor Croce's school-reform, the latter would not tolerate some of Giolitti's financial measures which affected the interests of the Vatican. They had earlier withdrawn from office his Minister of Finance, Meda, a man of their party. When therefore in June Mussolini withdrew fascist support, Giolitti fell. To succeed him the King sent for the former socialist Ivanoe Bonomi, who was able to command the support of the Populars. He too had been elected in the National Bloc.

When Mussolini went into opposition and Giolitti fell, government ceased to be exercised in Italy. The burning political question for the rest of 1921 was whether Signor Bonomi had done right in leading his cabinet to the Vatican in order to carry their condolences on the death of Pope Benedict XV. In the Chamber of Deputies Mussolini changed his tune now that he had kicked aside the ladder. He spoke sometimes like a sergeant to his troops, sometimes like a smug father to his children, claiming gratitude for having held back his champing Blackshirts, and sometimes he treated the Deputies to open threats of physical violence and grossly hectoring insults. He was a more thickset man now, and surer of himself; and his personality and the military cohesion and flexibility of his little minority seem to have exercised a kind of hypnosis on the disorganized legislators. It was in one of his smug fatherly moods that soon after the elections he signed the "Pact of Conciliation" with the socialists. He for the fascists and a certain Zaniboni for the socialists negotiated and signed under the eye of the President of the Chamber, Enrico de Nicola,[1] an agreement to the effect that the fascists in the country would stop beating the socialists up, and that the socialists would stop provoking the fascists to beat them up. When the terms of this curious treaty were broken by his followers, Mussolini took the opportunity to pose as a peaceful moderate by retiring from the Direction of the Fascist Party and becoming "a simple member of the Fascio of Milan." *Avanti!* said about the Pact: "This is not peace, for there can be no peace between the persecuted and the persecutor, between the dominated and the dominator." Needless to say, Mussolini was quickly reinstated and the Pact quickly forgotten.

Socialist action and propaganda now ceased to make any sense at all. The old struggle between reformists and revolutionaries went on in terms of Parliamentary Group and Party Direction. Turati was now sixty-five years old, and the active leader of the "collaborationists" in parliament was the lawyer Modigliani[2] to whom the Comintern had taken explicit exception in the Twenty-one Points. With varying success he tried to lead the socialist Deputies to an understanding of the situation. In the piazza and in the country in general the socialists had their backs to the wall, and only in parliament could they retrieve some freedom of action. Even without the communists they were still the largest party. If their superiors at the Party Direction would not let

[1] "Provisional Head of the State," i.e. acting President of the Republic, 1946–8.

[2] Brother of the artist.

them cast a vote at least from time to time in favour of some government, let them not renounce their only hope of saving not themselves alone but the country also. The Party Direction however was as convinced as ever that parliament was not the proper field for socialist action. At the National Congress at Milan in October 1921 Lazzari reported on his visit to Moscow, and the Congress, determined to show how unjustified was the Party's exclusion from the Third International, passed a resolution as intransigent and violent as ever, including a condemnation of "collaborationism" in parliament. Mussolini wrote in the *Popolo d'Italia*: "The result [of the Socialist Congress] will be an increase in the numerical and moral stature of the National Right.[1] It means that the National Right, in which the fascists are the majority, can be the arbiter of the life and death of governments, and that no government can govern without it. We therefore declare ourselves quite particularly pleased. Fascism now has before it a vast field of possibilities; it can do great things—things, not gestures, deeds, not words. . . ."[2] In the name of dogma, the Socialist Party Direction gave its 122 Deputies up to the mercy of the 33 fascists.

From now on the situation was in Mussolini's hands; he was merely waiting for parliament and parties to discredit themselves even more. A National Congress of the Fascist Party at Rome, also in October 1921, caused a general strike in the city; but the Congress was not interrupted. When there was a moment of quiet in the Chamber, Signor Bonomi could be heard saying: "I tell you the government holds socialist action and propaganda to be legitimate. They must be protected against all violence, and so must political fascism. But if groups and factions persist in violent methods, the government will have to apply the Penal Code."[3] After this debate on public order Signor Bonomi put a vote of confidence and the socialists, obedient to the Milan resolution, voted against him while the fascists abstained.

In January 1922 the collaborationists in the Socialist Parliamentary Group had the National Council of the Party called

[1] The fascists in parliament and their independent supporters.

[2] Nenni, *Storia di quattro anni*; p. 170.

[3] Ibid., p. 178.

together in a last attempt to get permission to take action in the Chamber. At the Council there was some impatience at the inaction of the Party Direction, but the Milan Resolution was confirmed. The Deputies were to go on sitting still while Mussolini did what he liked. At this Council Turati clung to the now non-existent proletarian unity as firmly as ever; he said he agreed with Kautsky that to collaborate with governments a Socialist Party needed a coherent and unanimous working class behind it, and that was something the Italian Socialist Party had not got. To collaborate without this unity would lay the collaborators open to the danger of becoming indistinguishable from the bourgeois parties. It is an indication of how much the socialists were out of touch with realities that even Turati should think there was still time to talk like this.

In February during the recess the Democrats, who had been the biggest unit in the National Bloc, declared that they would go into opposition. By doing so they hoped to effect Giolitti's return, and it is unlikely that they acted without his knowledge. Signor Bonomi resigned and there followed nine days of confusion, during which only one clear fact emerged; that Don Sturzo had vetoed the return of Giolitti. The Popular Party, in view of the socialists' continued abstention from supporting anyone, held the balance again now that the fascists were in opposition. Finally Signor Bonomi convened the Chamber and faced it again, saying that no one could be found to form a government. There were cries of "We want a dictator!" and "Down with parliament!" There followed a quite extraordinarily complicated episode which showed to what depths of inefficacy the Chamber had sunk. A motion was put consisting of three points: (1) the government was to work for the restoration of peace in the country; (2) the workers were to have some control over the management of industry and over the course of social legislation; (3) the economic unity of Europe was to be recognized and made the basis of Italy's foreign policy.[1] These

[1] F. G. Lo Bianco, *Un tentativo di Fronte Popolare in Italia*, 1921–1922; Rome, 1940; p. 67.

three points were acceptable to most shades of opinion, but there was complete confusion about which minister was to carry them out. The populars voted for the motion, thinking they were voting for Signor Bonomi; the democrats voted for it thinking they were voting for the return of Giolitti; and the socialists voted for it, not thinking they were voting for anybody, but because they agreed with the three points. At the last moment the fascists, having seen that everybody was interpreting the motion differently, voted for it too, and thereby discredited it in the eyes of the other parties. It was carried by 363 votes to 11. So then there had to be another vote explicitly to decide whether Signor Bonomi was to form a government. One hundred and twenty-seven votes expressed confidence in him, and two hundred and ninety-five, including fascists and of course socialists, expressed none. For a day or two nobody knew what was to happen. Then it was announced that Luigi Facta had formed a government in secret. This was treated at first as a joke; Facta was a Piedmontese Deputy, more or less a Giolittian, optimistic, equable, a nice little man, but with no more authority than hundreds of others. It was soon found that he really had formed a government, and that the fascists supported it. If any proof were yet needed of their attitude to parliamentary government, this cynical gesture gave it. It was pure *menefreghismo*. During his eight months' rule Facta became known as "Prime Minister I-cherish-the-hope" from his habit of beginning with these words his answers to all representations on the gravity of the internal situation. He fell in perfectly with the fascist thesis that nothing more was to be expected of parliamentary rule.

In the country the fascists continued to demonstrate their superiority by force. They undertook the forcible Italianization of the redeemed Trentino, and in March tried to emulate d'Annunzio by marching on Fiume. The enterprise failed. Organized labour, having seen how its political leaders had served it in the last three years, began to try to remedy the situation itself. The General Confederation of Labour remembered d'Annunzio's flirtation with Lenin at the time of his government of Fiume, and sent representatives to ask for his "protection." D'Annunzio went so far to meet them as to see d'Aragona, the General Secretary of the General Confederation of Labour, and Chicherin, the Soviet Foreign Commissar, when the latter was on his way to an international conference at Genoa. Later, d'Annunzio sent the General Confederation of Labour a bust of Dante, for which they thanked him profusely and thereby drew a rebuke from *Avanti!* More fruitful, if it had not been too late, would have been the defensive alliance of the General Confederation of Labour with the two great unions that did not belong to it, the dockers' and the railwaymen's. This "Triple Alliance of Labour"[1] was expanded in February to take in all the labour organizations in the country and became the "Labour Alliance."[2] The Labour Alliance was intended as a common defence against fascist violence and against the repressive measures of the increasing number of employers who supported and were supported by fascism. As the political movement split, so the syndical movement united. But trade unions do not govern a country.

While the socialist crow flapped clumsily about in parliament mobbed by the fascist starlings, the new Communist Party showed itself more concerned to attack that venerable bird than to defend it. The *raison d'être* of the Communist Party was primarily its quarrel with the socialists, not that with the bourgeois parties. During 1922 most of its polemics were designed to exploit the old, old division in the Socialist Party between "intransigents" and "collaborationists," and to trying to win over the former. Since the Socialist Party was still officially bolshevist, this was not unduly difficult. But the increasing domination of the fascists in parliament at last led the other wing, the collaborationists, to a decisive move, but a move which was three years too late. On June 15th Facta fell after one of the more or less continuous debates on public order, and the Socialist Parliamentary Group passed a resolution saying that it would "shrink before no action." The King called Turati for consultations. He cut away

[1] *Triplice del Lavoro.* [2] *Alleanza del Lavoro.*

his whole past and climbed up the Quirinal steps. Vera Modigliani, the wife of the reformist leader, has recorded[1] that Turati told her he said to the King: "At this moment the fate of Italy is in the balance. I may lose my place in parliament—a negligible detail for the records. You may lose your throne—an episode of small importance. But if we go on sliding down this slope, Italy will go to perdition, Italy will fall in ruins."

The reaction of the Party Direction was instantaneous; the next day *Avanti!* addressed Turati and the Deputies who had allowed him to go: "The political talks . . . you have held with the monarch, which are the beginning of your collaboration with the monarchy and the bourgeoisie, are also the end of your relations with us in the Party. We are not speaking of your good faith—that is beyond question; but we affirm that you yourselves, with your own hands, have shattered that unity of which until yesterday you would have had us believe you were the tenacious and ardent supporters."

So the King called Facta again.

Events now moved rapidly. In August the Labour Alliance called a last national general strike. Mussolini announced in the Chamber that he would give the government twenty-four hours to get the strikers back to work. Naturally Facta could do nothing of the sort, and at the end of that time Mussolini let loose his Blackshirts. Some worked the railways and postal services, but most devoted themselves to breaking up the strike with the now familiar weapons of the rubber truncheon and castor-oil. The offices of *Avanti!* were burnt out for the second time. The strikers returned, and shortly afterwards the railwaymen's union withdrew from the Labour Alliance. In October the Socialist Party in Congress at Rome formally expelled Turati and his followers. In the Chamber Enrico Ferri, back from his long absence in America, tried to form a group of "socialist" supporters of fascism. On October 24th the Fascist Party met in Congress at Naples and Mussolini at last openly declared himself a monarchist. On the 26th the fascists occupied the tele-

[1] *Esilio*; Garzanti, Milan, 1946; p. 483.

phone exchanges and columns of Blackshirts gathered in the towns round Rome. Facta prepared a proclamation of martial law throughout the country, but at the last moment the King refused to sign it. On the 28th a hundred thousand Blackshirts marched peacefully on Rome, filed for five hours before the King and the war-leader Marshal Diaz, camped in the Villa Borghese Gardens, and dispersed the next day. Mussolini accepted the King's invitation to form a government and arrived from Milan in a sleeping-car. He presented his cabinet to the Chamber with a brutally offensive and unconstitutional speech. When Giolitti was pressed to defend the parliament, he said: "I don't see any need; this chamber has the government it deserves."[1]

The first government of Mussolini consisted of fascists and non-party figures like the philosopher Giovanni Gentile, who went to the Ministry of Education, and the war-leader Diaz, and it enjoyed the precarious support of the Popular Party. It was not yet dictatorship, but it was understood to be a government that would not submit to the ordinary changes and chances of parliamentary democracy. Since 1918 the socialists had refused to accept any responsibility, and their four years' holiday had now allowed Italy to fall into the hands of Mussolini. The judgment of Pietro Nenni, the socialist leader of twenty years later, on the socialist policy of those years is particularly interesting, since it comes from one of the younger generation of socialists who watched their hopes being dashed by the sterile Marxist orthodoxy of their leaders. Here are three quotations from a book remarkable for its honest analysis of the failure of socialism to do anything with Italy after the 1915–18 War and for its determination to profit by the lessons of that time, his *Storia di quattro anni, 1919–1922*. The book was ready to come out in November 1926 when it was suppressed by the fascist government, by then fully totalitarian, and its author was forced into exile. It was finally printed in Italy in 1946.

[1] Gentile, *50 anni di socialismo*; Milan, 1948; p. 166.

"The Party was pleased to stand still and contemplate its own strength, to admire its own isolation, and did not perceive the absurdity of the watchword 'alone against the world' in a revolutionary period when success depends on absorbing or neutralizing neighbouring elements."[1]

"The Party did not discuss its action, it catalogued tendencies. . . . It was like the Doctors of the Church, arguing on the letter of the sacred texts while their world fell in ruins."[2]

"It was the time in which the fate of the socialists was decided, for a revolution announced every day and every day postponed ends by being a beaten revolution. And slavery awaits the beaten."[3]

Violence continued throughout 1923; some of Mussolini's more moderate fascist followers demanded that his "militia" be dissolved, but his answer was to make it a state, no longer a party, organization. In parliament he maintained his government by hypnosis and threats and induced the Deputies to give him full powers to govern by decree. The opposition parties, the labour organizations, and the press were still free on paper, but in practice they found castor-oil and the truncheon almost as hampering as legal suppression. Successive governments since 1919 had resorted to measures of control over industry, partly in defence of the socialists and partly as a defence against them; the control was now lifted and a disorderly business recovery resulted.

The socialist movement lay battered apart. On the left was the Communist Party, *Partito Comunista,* which was beginning to acquire the now familiar characteristics of a party under full control from Moscow; rock-like unanimity, an inconsistency that suggests time-serving, and an unwillingness to explain its motives. It also had that Olympian far-sightedness that comes with Faith; fascism was "an attempt to turn back the will of History," and was not therefore to be worried about. Its predominance, however long, would be as the morning watch in the sight of the

[1] Pietro Nenni, *Storia di quattro anni*; 1946; p. 55.
[2] Ibid., p. 196.
[3] Ibid., p. 55.

Proletariat. The Communist Party still turned most of its great journalistic talent against the heretics rather than the infidels, and strove to convert the socialists rather than to disconcert the fascists.

In the centre was the mass of the old Socialist Party, which was now called the Maximalist Socialist Party, *Partito Socialista Massimalista,* still from the "Maximum Programme" of 1900. Mistaking the nature of the Third International, this party still vainly proclaimed their adherence to it. In it gathered those who were faithful to the old ideal of intransigence and found comfort in the authority bestowed by the party's continued possession of *Avanti!* Its ranks were however thinned by defections to the communists.

On the right was the Italian Workers' Socialist Party, *Partito Socialista dei Lavoratori Italiani,* the party of that group which had at various times been known as legalitarian, gradualist, reformist, unitarian, and concentrationist. Turati was its leader and Treves and Modigliani were in it. The Secretary of the Party was a young Venetian of humble family, Giacomo Matteotti. He had since 1921 been the most able and determined of those parliamentary orators who especially devoted themselves to attacking fascism.

Late in 1923 Don Sturzo withdrew the ministers of the Popular Party from Mussolini's government. Mussolini was now forced to end the political breathing-space which their support had given him, for threats and hypnosis cannot be relied on for long. He accordingly used them for the last time to get through parliament the famous "Two-thirds Act." This altered the electoral law so that whatever party or bloc got the highest number of votes at a general election should automatically be allotted two-thirds of the seats in parliament. In the general elections of 1924 he presented himself at the head of a bloc of fascists and their entirely subservient supporters. Violence, intimidation, and fraud were on a far larger scale than in 1921; to vote otherwise than for the Big List, "*listone,*" of the fascist bloc called for a degree of courage and clear-headedness which not many electors possess even in a forward country. One socialist candidate, Piccinini, was called on as he was dining with his family by two fascists bearing forged membership-cards of his own party, taken outside his house, and murdered. It appears that he saw through the trick and went out with them to avoid violence in the presence of his wife and children.

The "*listone*" received the largest number of votes and accordingly the fascists and their stooges qualified under the new law for two-thirds of the places in parliament. Two and a half million votes went to the opposition parties, of which one million were for the three socialist parties. When the Chamber was convened in June, there was a feeling among the opposition that someone ought to make a formal accusation against Mussolini for his conduct of the elections. For some days no one dared, but finally on May 30th Matteotti, the young Secretary of the least intransigent of the socialist parties, stood up and extemporized. Here are some extracts from his speech.[1]

MATTEOTTI: We have the explicit declaration of the head of Fascism that his government did not consider itself bound by the result of the elections. Even if it was put in a minority, it would remain in power. . . .

FARINACCI: You've only got to have a revolution!

STARACE: That's right; we're in power and we're staying there.

[The whole Chamber is by now shouting uninterruptedly.]

A VOICE: We'll teach you to respect us with rifle butts in your backs.

ANOTHER VOICE: You're a cowardly scum!

. . . . .

MATTEOTTI: To uphold these views of the government there is an armed Militia . . .

VOICES ON THE RIGHT: Long live the Militia!

MATTEOTTI: . . . which is not at the service of the state, nor at the service of the country, but at the service of a party . . .

TERUZZI: That's enough! [The Right bang continuously on

[1] Taken from Pietro Nenni, *Sei anni di guerra civile*; p. 174 et seq.

their benches. For some minutes the speaker cannot make himself heard.]

. . . . .

MATTEOTTI: Perhaps in Mexico, where they have elections with bombs . . . [The Right begins banging again.] I apologize to Mexico for such an insulting comparison.

SHOUTS FROM THE RIGHT: That's enough! Throw him off the rostrum!

. . . . .

[Applause on the Left, uproar on the Right. The President takes the opportunity of calling on another Deputy to speak.]

MATTEOTTI: This is scandalous. I demand that my right to speak should be respected.

ON THE RIGHT: Shut up! We'll teach you the virtue of silence.

MATTEOTTI: One candidate, Piccinini, learned the cost of obeying his party. He was murdered in his own house for having agreed to stand. I salute his memory. . . .

A VOICE: You all deserve the same treatment!

ANOTHER VOICE: What you want is house-arrest, not Parliament.

. . . . .

And his peroration:

MATTEOTTI: You want to turn the country back towards absolutism; we are defending the sovereignty of the Italian people. We salute the people, and in the name of its dignity we demand that the government render account for its conduct of the elections.

[The Left is on its feet to applaud Matteotti.]

SHOUTS FROM THE RIGHT: Hireling! Traitor! Demagogue!

MATTEOTTI (to his colleagues): And now you can prepare my funeral oration.

Throughout Matteotti's speech both Mussolini and Giolitti sat silent and unmoved.

Ten days later, as he was walking along the Lungo Tevere from his house to the Chamber, Matteotti was kidnapped and murdered by five men in a car and his body was left in a ditch outside Rome where it was not found for two months. His disappearance and the accounts of various witnesses who had been on the Lungo Tevere gave rise to hysterical excitement throughout the country. Matteotti became a martyr and a saint; his mother, his young wife, and his two babies enjoyed open affection and sympathy. Flowers and wreaths were heaped on the pavement where he had been carried off.

Mussolini had to allow an ordinary criminal investigation to pursue its course. Five fascist thugs who had been in the car were arrested and later tried and condemned to nominal prison sentences. The name of their leader, Dumini, is still as much a part of the Italian language as Quisling is of the English. Following up the chain of orders received by Dumini, the judicial authorities stopped short only "at the door of Mussolini's private office." The Prime Minister dismissed his press officer, his private secretary, the administrative secretary of the Fascist Party, his Under-Secretary of State for Internal Affairs, and his Director-General of Public Security. The first three were arrested.

The unrest and excitement in the country remained intense for six months. The *comizietti* in Piazza Colonna at Rome and the Galleria at Milan were in more or less permanent session, and the news of the dismissal or arrest of each succeeding fascist hierarch was greeted with rejoicing there and in the opposition press, which was still free. Mussolini made few public appearances and spoke little in parliament; it was noticed that when he did he seemed distraught and tentative. It was widely believed in the country that the order for Matteotti's murder had come from Mussolini himself, or that it was at least a question of "Will no one rid me of this pestilent priest?" This belief took colour from Matteotti's youth and vigour; he would have been a greater nuisance to Mussolini than any of the old and established socialist leaders.

In this atmosphere the opposition parties made a last ill-co-ordinated attempt to overthrow the fascist government.

On June 27th, a hundred and fifty opposition Deputies gathered to hear Turati speak in memory of Matteotti. He spoke eloquently, referring to the last stand of Caius Gracchus and his supporters gathered round the Temple of Diana on the Aventine Hill. He said: "The only real representatives of the people are those who now stand on the Aventine of their own conscience, whence no wiles shall move them until the sun of freedom dawns once more, until the rule of law is given back, and until the representation of the people ceases to be the ghastly jest to which it has been reduced."

Turati's hearers, the communists excepted, decided to resort to the policy which had been found effective against the unconstitutional methods of Pelloux in 1900; they withdrew from the Chamber, and their withdrawal became known as the Aventine schism. But the modern Opimius had little trouble from these belated Gracchans.

The leadership of the Aventine fell on the southern liberal Giovanni Amendola, the same who as a journalist had gathered representatives of the Balkan nationalities in Rome in 1918 and explained to them the new policy of "renunciation." Amendola has been described[1] as a liberal too generalized to bring himself to bear on the particular need of the situation at this time, that of swift and decisive action. His habit of mind was all in terms of generations of democratic education; a less suitable leader in a crisis could hardly be imagined. Under the peaceable and overcautious guidance of Amendola, the Deputies who had seceded passed their days in enunciating sound constitutional principles and debating in which direction to develop their activity. Some were for invoking the help of the eighty-two-year-old Giolitti, some for dispersing to the communes and raising local disaffection, some for a press campaign, some for trying to win over the King, and some the judges. In the end nothing was done.

Mussolini's only danger was that the King should turn against him and this he was able to prevent by playing on the fact that

[1] By Piero Gobetti; article *Amendola* in the collection *Scritti attuali*; Capriotti, Rome, undated (but after 1944).

the Aventine parties were in the majority republican. As the months passed and he found that he was still in power, he turned again to the policy of Giolittian waiting that had served him so well in 1921–2; he lay low, in fact, for it was in his interest to raise no passions until the Aventine schism should have demonstrated its incapacity to do anything. At the end of December the opposition gave him the opportunity to act. It secured the publication in the press of the Rossi Memorandum. Rossi was one of the fascist hierarchs arrested soon after the murder of Matteotti, and his Memorandum gave an account of the antecedents of that murder and of many others committed by fascists during the preceding three years. The hope of the Aventine Deputies was that Mussolini could not now avoid a trial in which he himself would be involved. On January 2nd some of Mussolini's more moderate ministers resigned, and on January 3rd when he rose to speak in the Chamber it was already known that he would challenge the parliament to impeach him before the High Court of Justice. The constitutional machinery of impeachment demanded a majority of the parliament and this, thanks to the two-thirds law, the opposition could not muster; they did not therefore think it convenient to go to the Chamber and table a minority resolution. It was only a gesture they renounced, but it was the last opportunity they were given for so much as a gesture.

January 3rd, 1925, saw the end of democracy in Italy and the beginning of modern totalitarianism in the world. During his speech, Mussolini said:[1] "Article 47 of the constitution says 'The Chamber of Deputies has the right of impeaching the Ministers of the Crown before the High Court of Justice.' I solemnly ask whether there is anybody in this Chamber or out of it who wishes to avail himself of Article 47." He went on to deny personal and particular responsibility for the murder of Matteotti, but to accept general and political responsibility for all the violences carried out by fascists since the foundation of the Fascist Party, and ended his speech thus: "Finally, I here

[1] Quoted in Panfilo Gentile, op. cit., pp. 203–4.

declare before this Assembly and before the whole Italian people that I and I alone accept the political, moral, and historical responsibility for everything that has happened. If fascism has been nothing but castor-oil and truncheons, if it has not been the superb passion of all that is best in the youth of Italy, the fault is mine. If fascism has been a criminal club, then I am the head of that club and I am responsible for it. If all the violence has been the result of a certain historical, political, and moral climate, then I have created that climate with the propaganda I have carried on from the time of our intervention in the war up to this day. . . . There comes the moment when one says—enough! You may be certain that within forty-eight hours the situation will be cleared up in its every respect."

Mussolini's first move was to deprive the Aventine Deputies of their seats in parliament; they had forfeited their mandates by absenting themselves for six months from their parliamentary duties. There followed an amnesty for Rossi and all those of Mussolini's entourage who had been arrested after the Matteotti "accident," as it was finally called, and a spate of repressive legislation. The press was controlled, the opposition parties were suppressed, professional and ex-service organizations were taken over by the state, special political tribunals were instituted, and the new fascist labour organizations were given the exclusive right of negotiation on behalf of the workers. The light of liberty went out.

During 1923 and 1924 a generation of young men were asking the question—why has it happened? Whose fault is it? In those years it took a clear mind and perhaps a pessimistic temperament to realize what had indeed happened to Italy. Nearly a decade had passed since peace and order had been the natural condition of Italian life, and as far as violence went fascism was only distinguishable from its rival parties in the degree of it that it brought into politics. What distinguished it far more was its capacity for getting things done. Mussolini had for example as soon as he arrived in office personally seen to the building up of the shattered railway services. At a peaceful time a peaceful party that gets things done will win support. At a violent time a violent party that gets things done will win support, and it will be forgiven if it does so by being a little more violent than its opponents. The old men remembered the days when human life and human health were respected. But it was the young men on whose energy and violent passions Mussolini had relied in coming to power and on whose administrative ability and devotion to himself he had to rely to consolidate his régime, and the young men saw in fascism the most successful party in the political game as it was then played. Only a few, the thoughtful and honest by temperament, training, or background, had that political conviction which in a quarter of a century of attack and defence has become to us an automatic reaction and a commonplace, the conviction that democracy is better than dictatorship. It was from among these few that the rebuilders of democratic Italy arose.

The honour—and it is a great honour that all Italians have recognized—of being the first instinctive anti-fascist went to Count Carlo Sforza. Others had been anti-fascist as a matter of political tactics; the socialists in particular could claim no particular merit for their anti-fascism, because they had always been anti-everything. After the fall of Giolitti's government, in which he had been Foreign Secretary, Count Sforza became Ambassador in Paris. On the very day that Mussolini came to power after the March on Rome, Count Sforza sent an uncoded telegram resigning his post, and thereafter stubbornly refused either to countenance fascism or to keep quiet about it. It was an extreme gesture and seemed to many over-scrupulous, but it played its part in introducing young Italians to the idea of fascism as something not merely politically undesirable but morally intolerable. It was above all a disinterested gesture; an ambassador has everything to lose by resigning, whereas a politician may have everything to gain by opposition. The first act of militant anti-fascist propaganda was thus done by a middle-aged liberal aristocrat, not by any of the young left-wing bourgeois who became so active later. Another eminent figure to oppose fascism from the outset, although in a less precise and dramatic manner, was the former Prime Minister Signor Nitti, who was even prevented from standing at the elections of 1924. After the Matteotti murder Benedetto Croce brought his immense prestige to bear against fascism. It is interesting that he never went into exile and was never persecuted; his monthly *Critica* continued to attack Mussolini until the latter's overthrow in 1943, when Signor Croce suspended its publication because, he said, when there was no more fascism he felt like the man in the fable who lost his shadow. Probably Mussolini found it convenient to tolerate his most famous critic as an isolated proof of his clemency.

The renaissance of Italian socialism which came about in the years 1922–6 was primarily the work of three young men, Gramsci, Gobetti, and Rosselli, all of whom died at the hands of fascist thugs and became political martyrs. They were all attractive characters, and Gobetti and Rosselli had a blithe heterodoxy which the passive nature of the socialist resistance to fascism allowed for a time to appear something new and fruitful.

Antonio Gramsci was the most mysterious of the three, because at an early age he embraced orthodox communism; politically speaking, he took the veil. He was a Sardinian of very humble origin who worked his way to the university at Turin. Here it seems[1] that he was keenly aware of the differences between himself and the run of Italian students to whom poverty, if it is anything, is a temporary evil which can be set right at the beginning of the quarter. His body was frail and his intellectual temperament was increasingly attracted by the systematic rigidity of orthodox Marxism. He joined the Socialist Party and became an active journalist in the interest of pure communism, at the same time taking a leading part in the discussion-circles which were a feature of the Torinese communist movement, particularly in the great Fiat concern. In 1919, even before the breakaway of the Communist Party, he founded his own paper in Turin, the

[1] Gobetti, op. cit.; article *Gramsci.*

New Order (*Ordine Nuovo*), which was devoted to a clearing away of all preconceptions in a clean sweep and to beginning a fundamental re-examination of all the questions of the day from the communist point of view. In 1924 he was the leader of the Communist Party in and out of parliament. His gift of rigid analysis and a certain contained quality made him, young as he was, prevail over the older and more expansive revolutionaries Bombacci and Bordiga. In April 1924 Gobetti compared him with the other sort of revolutionary.[1] "He is in effect the revolution, the defeated revolution, going to parliament to predict woe for the victors. He is the first revolutionary to go to Montecitorio [the Parliament House]. No breaking of ballot-boxes, no arousing of scandalous scenes! Bombacci and Misiano [the deserter] were photographic reproductions of Enrico Ferri; theirs was a nice revolution fit for the chronicles of the *bons bourgeois*, and the style and ideological plan of those agitators were strangely like those of Mussolini." Gramsci introduced the new communism into Italy, the polite, rather sinister communism that, because it is controlled from abroad, is so surprising to Western ideas. In 1924 he went to Moscow for a short time, but returned, and in 1928 was sentenced to twenty years' imprisonment. He died in 1937 as a result of the hardships of political imprisonment under fascism. His voluminous notes on all manner of topics written in prison have recently been edited and published[2] and are now considered by Italian communists to be the most important Italian contribution to the Marxist literature of the world. The notes were preserved through the underground channels of the Communist Party.

On incidental matters Gramsci's writing shows an inquiring mind and a sense of humour; on Marxist theory itself it is dry, unoriginal, and humourless. The main interest of the book is in its attitude to Signor Croce. Gramsci is evidently unwilling to admit that so great a philosopher, so great an Italian, as Signor

[1] Gobetti, op. cit.; article *Gramsci*.

[2] Antonio Gramsci, *Il materialismo storico e la filosofia di Benedetto Croce*; Einaudi, 1948.

Croce should be entirely lost to Marxism. He plays with the idea of being to Signor Croce as Marx was to Hegel, and would like to carry the Marxist Dialectic one step further in its waltz through the philosophers by synthesizing Signor Croce and Marx.[1] Marx was presumably in his turn the synthesis of Feuerbach and Hegel. This, he said, would be the only "historically fecund way" of reviving Marxism. It would have been interesting to see how he drew Signor Croce into the Marxist Dialectic, in view of the stolid way in which Signor Croce had debunked it. In 1919 Gramsci had greeted Signor Nitti's arrival in power as the equivalent of Kerensky's in Russia; his mind was much influenced by the detailed precedent of the Russian Revolution, and even more by the prophecies of Marx.

Piero Gobetti[2] was the most remarkable of the three. He was something of an infant prodigy. Born in 1901, he was nineteen at the time of the Occupation of the Factories, twenty-one at the March on Rome, twenty-three at the imposition of the dictatorship, and twenty-four at his death. He was of well-to-do family, and the extraordinary merit of the pamphlets he wrote and the periodicals he edited while still at the university brought him to the notice of Gramsci, then in his late twenties. In 1921 Gobetti became dramatic critic on the *Ordine Nuovo* at Turin. His mind was then formed in contact with Gramsci and in the discussion-circles of the Turin communists. When *Ordine Nuovo* was burnt out by the fascists in 1922, he founded his own paper, the *Liberal Revolution* (*Rivoluzione liberale*), in which until its suppression in 1925 he poured out a series of criticisms of men and events which were by far the most lively and enlightening journalism of the time. He led a life of fantastic activity, conducting a voluminous correspondence, receiving politicians of three times his age who called on him for advice, learning Russian, and always reading and writing. He married and had a child. In 1926 Mussolini gave the famous order "make life difficult for him."

[1] Op. cit., p. 198.

[2] Besides the work quoted, an anthology of the *Rivoluzione liberale* was published at Turin in 1948, and contains a bibliography.

He was beaten up on his own doorstep but allowed to escape to Paris, where he died of his wounds some weeks later.

In sharp contrast with his friend Gramsci, Gobetti was profusely, gaily, wonderfully eclectic. He loved everything, except fascism, and tried to understand everything, including fascism. He was keenly aware of the responsibility of socialism for bringing Italy under a dictatorship, and he turned to the new communism as something which had no part in that responsibility; for the secession of the Communist Party in 1921 could be interpreted as a protest against the failure of the old planless insurrectionary propaganda. The Communist Party at that time had the appeal of being posterior to the old disorders of 1919–20, as the Popular Party had been to the war of 1915–18. But Gobetti was more struck by communist practice in the factories of Turin than by Marxist theory. He set himself the ideal of forming the "liberal conscience of communism," and the "liberal revolution" against fascism after which his paper was called was to have been a surge of open-mindedness to sweep away sects and dogmas. It was an attractive doctrine at the time, because it offered an alternative to the automatic, tradition-bound hatreds of socialist and nationalist, socialist and capitalist. From his association with Gramsci and the Torinese workers he had also acquired faith in the political wisdom of the common man; during the Aventine schism he was among those who urged a dispersion and a levying of resistance in the communes. But "liberal communism" has no great possibilities in this century, for communists, both workers and intellectuals, will not be liberals, and liberals will not be communists. Gobetti was for this reason without lasting influence in his generation or the next. What remains of value to-day in his work is his literary style, flexible, conscious, even a little *recherché*, his brilliant insight into the characters of politicians of 1920–5, and particularly the way in which his meteoric career stimulated and gathered the anti-fascists. He was a "marvellous boy," more aesthetic than political, more tentative than sincerely convinced, more a critic than an actor. He was above all very young. It was an incalculable loss that one so outstanding should die at a stage in his development when he still believed everything; if he had lived to learn that a belief only has a name of its own when it is incompatible with other beliefs, he might greatly have served Italy and the world.

Carlo Rosselli[1] was not nearly as well known in those years as Gramsci and Gobetti, but he must be mentioned with them because his more important activity in exile after 1929 developed out of the heart-searching of the young socialists in 1923 and 1924. He was a Jew of good family, one of several brothers.[2] After the war, as an ex-service student at the University of Florence, he fell in with Turati and Anna Kulishov and for a while accepted their kind of gradual socialism tempered by the overriding need for socialist unity. Later he passed under the influence of Professor Gaetano Salvemini, an unflinching hater of kings, priests, and capitalists, who had been in and out of the extreme parties for thirty years past. For Salvemini he wrote a thesis for his degree on reformist, almost labour-party, lines. In 1923 Serrati, another leader of the old Socialist Party, the Maximalist Socialist Party as it was now called, had gone to Moscow to plead for its admittance to the Third International and had returned with a proposal for its fusion with the Communist Party. The proposal was defeated largely by the exertions of Pietro Nenni, and Rosselli joined Signor Nenni on the latter's paper *The Fourth Estate* (*Quarto Stato*). We have noticed Signor Nenni twice before, first as a republican agitator collaborating with the socialist Mussolini in the Romagnole agitations of 1912, and again as the author of an honest book, the *Storia di quattro anni*. Signor Nenni had become a socialist after the war, and in 1919–21 had been the Paris correspondent of *Avanti!*. In 1923 he devoted all his energies to the possible refusion of the Maximalist Socialist Party and the Workers' Socialist Party, the Party of Turati and Matteotti. It was in the interest of this possibility

[1] See principally Aldo Garosci, *Vita di Carlo Rosselli*; 2 vols., Florence; undated (but after 1944).

[2] His brother Nello, who was murdered with him in 1937, is known for his study of Pisacane.

that Signor Nenni opposed Serrati's move to reunite with the communists, in the same interest that he later wrote the *Storia di quattro anni*, and in the same interest that he and Rosselli worked together on the *Quarto Stato*. Rosselli's grave and responsible character could not long tolerate association with the bombastic authors of Italy's ruin, and by the time of the Aventine schism he had gone over to the Workers' Socialist Party, while Signor Nenni, bent as always on unity, stayed with the Maximalists and became the editor of *Avanti!*

Rosselli's development was very much slower than Gobetti's, but in a graver, more solid, way he was moving towards Gobetti's position. As a thoughtful, educated young man who had lived through the upheavals of 1919–25, he too saw the need of a revived, purified socialism, and he too began to think that liberty in thought and liberalism in action might be the purifying agents.

CHAPTER IV

EXILE, 1925–43

WE have seen in the last chapter how in detail the political conduct of the Italian socialists opened the way to fascism, but their general spirit and outlook also bear a responsibility. In every healthy movement there are weak spots that may degenerate into a disease which affects the whole body politic; in Italian socialism the weak spot was demagogic violence. Uncontrolled, it spread and ran riot until it was finally gathered up and disciplined by Mussolini. The formation of the political character of Mussolini himself is perhaps in the last resort the gravest charge that can be brought against the socialist movement in Italy, for he was in effect no more than a bundle of socialist attitudes slightly rearranged and informed with a powerful and brutal character. He had from socialism class-hatred, corporativism, the will to revolution, a contempt of democracy, and intolerance of political ideas other than his own; he showed how easy it was for a socialist to fall over the edge, to go bad. He was able to turn into nationalist hatred the technique of class-hatred which he had learnt from the Socialist Party. He openly taught his followers that it was not they who were exploited by the capitalists, but Italy which was exploited by the other Allies after the war. The will to revolution which he learnt from the Socialist Party he was able to bring to bear against his former teachers when their own revolution had failed. It was one of the fascist yells that they wanted a revolution, not a bolshevik revolution, but a "*rivoluzione I-TA-LIA-NA*." The disciplined violence of the fascists in 1921–4 was rather more of a revolution than the diffuse violence of the socialists in 1919–22.

Where Mussolini learnt his contempt for democracy will be obvious enough from the past chapters; he too took his followers to parliament to work for its overthrow, but once there he worked for it with a will instead of sitting back and trusting to "intransigence." It was a difference of technique; the fascists succeeded in blowing up parliament, whereas the socialists had failed to kill it by constipation. As a shadowy alternative to centralized democratic rule, the socialists had put forward various forms of corporativism;[1] we have noticed the agitation for "the Constituent" and the draft bill of Abbiate, Signor Nitti's Minister of Labour. The Soviets were of course a form of corporativism; take away the Communist Party from the Russian Constitution of 1936, and there remains a beautifully balanced idea of a corporate or plural state. Mussolini took over socialist corporativism and turned it upside down; the socialist pyramid was to work upwards by mandates and elections, the fascist pyramid worked downwards by orders from the top. In fact in Italy, as in Russia, the parallel pyramid of the single party did more and more of the work of governing, as is indicated by the ever less frequent meetings of the Fascist Grand Council, the peak of the corporative pyramid. The political intolerance which he had learnt from the old Marxist Party came out in Mussolini ever more clearly as his government hardened into a dictatorship; not only had he expelled the reformists Bissolati and Signor Bonomi from the Socialist Party in 1912, but in 1914 he also expelled the Freemasons, claiming that their lodges were hives of fraternization in the class-struggle and cells of corruption. At the formation of the Fascist Party, he put away this intolerance and launched the slogan "A membership-card and nothing else" ("*Una tessera personale e poi basta*").[2] As the movement gathered force however the Masons were expelled from it and later from Italy, and after Giovanni Gentile had constructed a fascist ideology—with special accommodation for catholics—fascism was as well

[1] Cf. the "pluralism" of G. D. H. Cole and Harold Laski in the same period.

[2] *Enciclopedia Italiana*; article *Fascismo.*

equipped for intolerance as ever Marxism had been. The basis of the fascist ideology, the "Myth of the Nation," was itself taken from Bergson through Sorel, but we have seen how on the syndicalist left wing of the Socialist Party, Mussolini's wing, Sorel was a stronger influence than Marx.

Having noted the double contribution of Italian socialism to fascism, directly through mistaken politics and indirectly through the creation of a headstrong and violent atmosphere, we shall concern ourselves no further with the latter.

Socialism lived on in exile and underground in Italy, and took on the natural character of those two conditions. The socialists and other anti-fascists in exile carried on what is called in Italian "tadpole politics," that is, the politics of leaders without followers, all head and no tail. They had no elections to fight, no daily political situation to cope with, and above all the great socialist organization of the General Confederation of Labour was no longer there to be placated, coerced, ignored, or deferred to. The exiles watched European politics from the outside, dined together, and waited.

The resistance in Italy was until 1943 a shadowy business, and it will probably never be possible to determine how much of it there really was. To begin with, as with every underground political movement, no member of it knew what another was doing, and its leaders, when there were any, were apt to make unverifiable and probably exaggerated claims. The organization of resistance among the workers in Italy was the speciality of the communists; they had a number of clandestine papers, including one for children, and agitation was carried at any rate far enough for the later communist leader Pietro Secchia to devise a system whereby the agitators of the Party should not all be in prison at the same time; they took it in rotation.[1] The communist resistance was popularized in the novels of the exile Ignazio Silone, who became a democratic socialist after the war of 1940–5.

The story of the exile is briefly told. The emigration fell

[1] Leo Valiani, *Tutte le strade conducono a Roma*; Florence, 1947; p. 60.

roughly into three periods; between 1921 and 1924 went the small men, the local socialist organizers, the labour leaders, those who were not protected by some constitutional office such as that of Deputy. Between 1924 and 1927 went the big men, when fame and eminence were no longer any protection against persecution. Very early Count Sforza retired to Brussels; Signor Nitti went with his family to Paris, and so did Modigliani and his wife. Palmiro Togliatti, Gramsci's colleague, went to Moscow. A young leader of the Popular Party, Alcide de Gasperi, became a librarian in the Vatican. In 1925 the Aventine leader Giovanni Amendola was beaten up by thugs and, like Gobetti, allowed to escape. At Cannes some months later he died, like Gobetti, from his wounds. In 1926 Bruno Buozzi arrived in Paris, the last Secretary of the General Confederation of Labour, come to keep alive a skeleton of his great organization with the help of the French *Confédération Générale du Travail.* In 1943 he returned to Italy to refound the General Confederation of Labour, and was captured and shot by the Germans the next year. Treves, over fifty, walked over the high Alps with Giuseppe Saragat, the democratic socialist leader of after the war of 1940–5. They avoided the fascist patrols and came to Paris. Signor Nenni too escaped over the Alps. In 1927 Turati, now seventy, was smuggled out of Savona in a motor-boat by Carlo Rosselli and Ferruccio Parri, the Prime Minister of Italy in 1945. After ten days' house-to-house evasion of the fascist police, Rosselli called out the code phrase to the fishermen at the harbour-mouth: "The big fish is out of the net." Turati landed in Corsica and came to Paris. Anna Kulishov had been dead for five years. Rosselli and Signor Parri went back. Don Sturzo came first to Paris and then to London. The Freemasons came; the liberals, the democratic catholics, the dissident and extremist fascists came; after them came the *agents provocateurs* and the spies, and a *Fascio* was formed in Paris.

At first the exiles lacked confidence; Vera Modigliani describes[1] how the arrival of Turati quieted their consciences. If Turati

[1] V. Modigliani op. cit., p. 74.

had come out, then they were right to have come out. In those early days they would sit in the canteen they had established in Paris and sing the song of an anarchist group which had been expelled from Switzerland in 1898:[1]

Addio Lugano bella,	Farewell beautiful Lugano,
O dolce terra pia,	O sweet and friendly land;
Cacciati senza colpa	Driven out for no fault,
Gli anarchici van via.	The anarchists go away.
E partono cantando	And they leave singing,
Con la speranza in cuor,	With hope in their hearts,
E partono cantando	And they leave singing,
Con la speranza in cuor;	With hope in their hearts;
Eppur la nostra idea	And yet our idea
Non è che idea d'amor.	Is only the idea of love.

In 1929 came the third and most spectacular group of exiles, only three of them. For organizing the escape of Turati, Rosselli and Signor Parri had been tried and sentenced, after making resounding speeches, to *confino* on the island of Lipari—something between banishment and imprisonment. Here they met Emilio Lussu,[2] a democratic Sardinian Deputy who had opposed the late imposition of fascism on his native island, and Francesco Fausto Nitti, a son of the former Prime Minister. Signor Parri determined to stay in Italy; after his release he went to work in the Edison business in Milan, where he stayed until 1942. There his political character slowly matured, through silence and inner freedom, in a life that outwardly conformed to the order he hated; we shall see him later as surely one of the most remarkable Prime Ministers who ever governed a modern state. Rosselli, Signor Lussu, and Fausto Nitti talked of "Escape with variations, in all tenses, past, present, future, conditional; escape, escape, escape. Escape by rowing-boat, by motor-boat, by steamer, by aeroplane, by dirigible."[3] Their first attempt

[1] V. Modigliani, op. cit., pp. 64–5.

[2] In 1948 Signor Lussu became a Senator. A book of his is translated into English: *Enter Mussolini*; Methuen, 1936. It contains his account of the escape from Lipari.

[3] From Rosselli's lively account *Fuga in quattro tempi*, reprinted in Aldo Garosci's life.

failed, but a second succeeded by the help of a companion of the earlier attempt who had finished his time and had brought a motor-boat from Tunisia to pick them up off a rock within swimming distance of the island.

There were two distinct sides to the activity of the anti-fascist emigration; the spectacular propagandist side, and the quiet serious business of keeping alive the democratic politics of Italy without any democracy to work in. The escape from Lipari makes a convenient starting-place for an account of the first side. In the same year, 1929, a young maximalist socialist, Ferdinando de Rosa, fired on the Prince of Piedmont, the heir to Victor Emmanuel III, in Brussels. He had acted on his own judgment; at his trial, where, incidentally, he was defended by a young socialist lawyer called Paul Henri Spaak, he said: "When I was in prison I read in some books that in the common criminal his reason holds him back while his instinct urges him towards the crime. In my case, my instinct revolted from the bloody act while my reason imposed it on me as a supreme work of justice."[1] Another young maximalist, Sandro Pertini, a lawyer who was a leader of the partisans in 1944–5 and after the war one of the leaders of the Italian Socialist Party, took work as a plasterer at Nice. In 1929 he went clandestinely into Italy trying to raise revolt, was captured and tried, and made resoundingly defiant speeches in court. In 1930 some members of "Justice and Liberty," Rosselli's group which we shall shortly discuss, planned a bomb attack on all the Inland Revenue Offices throughout Italy as a prelude to a general rising; the plot was given away and the leaders were arrested. Attempts on Mussolini were frequent. In 1930 an otherwise worthless character, Mario Bassanesi, flew low over Milan dropping anti-fascist leaflets. He and Rosselli as an accomplice were tried by a Swiss court; Turati and Count Sforza gave evidence and the trial became a sounding-board of anti-fascist propaganda. Bassanesi was sentenced to four months' imprisonment; Rosselli was acquitted. In 1931 Lauro de Bosis carried out his more famous flight over Rome.

[1] V. Modigliani, op. cit., p. 194.

De Bosis had taught himself to fly in his spare time while working as a *concierge* in a Paris hotel. He was a young man of wide culture and some poetic achievement. He translated into Italian some Greek plays and Frazer's shorter *Golden Bough*, and wrote a remarkable verse tragedy, *Icaro*, in which he showed his early preoccupation with the element where he was to meet his death. The night before he flew over Rome he wrote a *Story of My Death* which he gave to a newspaper for publication if he should not return from his flight. In fact he did not return; he was seen flying "almost up the Spanish Steps" in Rome, dropping leaflets, and later flying out to sea. He may have been shot down by fascist fighters, but it is more likely that he ran out of petrol. In 1936 the Spanish Civil War at last gave the exiles their chance to take up physical arms against fascism. Rosselli, de Rosa, and Signor Nenni went to Spain; so did Randolfo Pacciardi, later the leader of the Republican Party in Italy, and Signor di Vittorio, later the Communist General Secretary of the Italian General Confederation of Labour.

The first political move of the exiles was the foundation at Nérac in 1927 of the Anti-Fascist Concentration, *Concentrazione Antifascista*. This was a gesture of unity between the principal parties and organizations, excluding the communists, of the anti-fascist emigration. There adhered to it the two socialist parties, the Republican Party, the General Confederation of Labour, and the Rights of Man League, which was the Italian wing of a predominantly French organization of enthusiastic left-wing tendencies. The Concentration started its own paper in Paris, *Libertà*, of which Treves was virtually the editor. In 1928, when the Fascist Grand Council took to itself the right to decide the succession to the Italian throne, the Concentration became officially republican. It had little direct communication with the underground movement in Italy, but, besides journalism, it conducted some propaganda among Italian tourists in France. Rosselli later called it a "continuation of the Aventine abroad."[1]

[1] Garosci, op. cit., ii, 66.

The "Justice and Liberty" group, "*Giustizia e Libertà,*" was the creation of Carlo Rosselli. He brought with him from Lipari via Tunis not only the romance of his escape, but also a book written in *confino*, his *Socialismo liberale*."[1] In it he propounded a liberal socialism, based on the same principles as Gobetti's liberal communism, but more fully worked out. He was particularly concerned by the way the young intellectuals had deserted socialism since 1908 and gone to revolutionary bellicose syndicalism, to d'Annunzian paganizing nationalism, to *laisser-faire* liberalism, and finally to fascism. The answer, he held, was less dogma and more morality. The book treats little of economics, but with this reservation it is imbued with a careful and high morality of the "look-before-you-leap" sort. There is no class-hatred in it. Treves disliked the book; Gobetti had called him the Jew born with a knowledge of the class-struggle.[2] He was faithful to the old ideas of labour and capital.

In Paris, Rosselli, Signor Lussu, his companion of the escape, and the liberal Signor Tarchiani[3] founded the "Justice and Liberty" group. It was consciously a group and not a party. This might seem a hair-splitting distinction for exiles to make, but it is in fact an indication of their basic idea. The parties were there, socialists of three colours, republicans, liberals, and so forth. Rosselli's idea was to gather all those who could meet on his wide ground and to create the germ of the future political life of Italy. His motto was: "Let us pigeon-hole our party membership cards for the moment." "Justice and Liberty" was to be the new Italy in miniature, government, opposition, civil service, and all. "If we had to define 'Justice and Liberty' in one sentence, we should say that it is, or would like to be, the anticipation in miniature of the new and wholly liberal state of to-morrow, of the new world of justice and liberty that will emerge from the revolution. It is the explosive cell of future society existing in present society."[4] As time went on and party

[1] Edizioni "U," 1945. [2] *Scritti attuali*; article *Treves*.

[3] Italian Ambassador in Washington after the war of 1940–5.

[4] *Quaderni di Giustizia e Libertà*; bimonthly, Paris; No. 8, August 1933; p. 9.

life in exile remained vigorous, "Justice and Liberty" got to look more and more like a party. In 1931 it joined the Anti-Fascist Concentration beside the other parties. It framed a programme which automatically narrowed the range of opinions that could subsist in it: armed revolution against fascism, and the foundation of a lay republic on a basis of small-proprietor socialism. Afterwards a constituent assembly was to be called to "consecrate the work of the revolution." While on the one hand "Justice and Liberty" became more and more like a party in relation to Italian politics, in relation to European politics in general it became more and more like an international centre of anti-fascism. It polemicized against Hitler nearly as much as against Mussolini, and we have seen how Rosselli went to fight for the republicans in Spain. In the end it showed itself too eclectic to have a permanent influence on Italian life; its adherents formed in 1943 and 1944 the "Party of Action" inside Italy. This party ceased to exist in 1946 and its members went mostly to the republicans and the democratic socialists.

The natural tendency of a number of party leaders with no followers and no day-to-day politics must be carefully to recognize their differences and then to ignore them. The two socialist parties in particular found themselves united in hating fascism and not in practice divided on the old question of revolution or reform, because they had no country in which to make the revolution and no parliament through which to work for reforms. Turati, the leader of the Unitarian Socialist Party as the Workers' Socialist Party was called after its reconstitution abroad, was as always a firm believer in socialist unity, and in the Maximalist Party too there was an increasing opinion that dissension was not becoming in the desert. The Maximalist Party had never secured recognition by the Communist International, whereas the Unitarian Party was firmly established in the Socialist International; fusion would allow the Maximalist Party to re-enter the "European socialist family" from which the old leaders had rashly withdrawn it in 1918. The champions of unity were, for the maximalists, Pietro Nenni; for the unitarians, Giuseppe Saragat, a young reformist who had come to socialism through a knowledge of capitalism gained in a responsible banking post, and who had escaped with Treves across the Alps. Not all the maximalists were for fusion; at a Congress of the Party held to discuss it at Grenoble in 1930 the left wing got to the hall first and barred the doors against the fusionists. But at a more orderly and valid congress in Paris later in the same year Signor Nenni swayed the majority and the two parties were reunited. There was now once more a single Italian Socialist Party attached to the Socialist International. Nevertheless, a little group of those who still hankered after the Communist International continued to publish *Avanti!* at Lugano, and the paper edited by Signor Nenni for the reunited party at Paris had to take the name of *Nuovo Avanti!* (*New Forwards*). Signor Nenni and Modigliani represented the Party at the Socialist International—one from each of the old parties.

The adherence in 1931 of the eclectic but predominantly socialist group "Justice and Liberty" to the Anti-Fascist Concentration brought the socialists in the latter into so strong a majority that the Republican Party withdrew in 1932. Turati died the same year and Treves, the motive force of the Concentration, died in 1933; the Concentration then broke up. The Republican Party remained active in journalism until 1940; the General Confederation of Labour under Buozzi continued to organize Italian *émigré* workers under the auspices of the *Confédération Générale du Travail*, and the Rights of Man League continued its work of assistance to *émigrés* of all classes.

In 1934, the year of the murder of Dollfuss, the Italian Socialist Party and the Italian Communist Party concluded an agreement for "Unity of Action"; it was in no sense a fusion, but only a declaration of common hostility to fascism. Both parties took part in the Congress of the "Single Front" at Brussels in October 1935 when communists, socialists, radicals, and Christian Democrats of many nationalities came together to protest against Mussolini's war against Abyssinia and to demand sanctions against Italy.

In 1937 Carlo Rosselli, convalescing from a phlebitis contracted in the Spanish Civil War, was found murdered with his brother Nello beside their car on a lonely road in Normandy. It was generally accepted that the murderers were fascist agents, and since the war it has been proved. In 1938 the French government for the first time allowed the *émigrés* to broadcast to Italy.

At the outbreak of war in 1939 the Italian socialists had been fifteen years in exile, and their leaders had all changed. The death of Filippo Turati in 1932 was to those who were present and to those who came after one of those symbolic deaths through which the passing of a period is made visible in the passing of one man. Turati was more nearly a real statesman than any other leader of Italian socialism. Others, such as Bissolati and Signor Bonomi, had been more moderate and more humane. But none had succeeded as well as Turati in influencing the great body of small socialists towards moderation and humanity. Bissolati and Signor Bonomi had been expelled from the Party, but Turati had clung to it even when at every hour of every day it was acting against his dearest principles. He was a remarkable man in the Italy of that time who could be at once wise, humane, and a socialist, and Turati was a remarkable man. But it would have taken a superman in the Italy of that time to lead the socialists conclusively to wisdom and moderation, and Turati was not a superman. If wisdom and socialism clashed, Turati went with socialism. During the Four Days of Milan in 1898 he once found himself before a mob which he judged would shed blood if it was not at once assured that its wishes would be granted. Turati took it on himself as their acknowledged leader to tell them that their wishes had already been granted, which they had not, and were not thereafter. His life was such that he was continually being forced to choose between two conflicting desires. In the small incident he chose peace and rejected truth, and in his whole political career he chose socialism and rejected peace. But he did violence to himself in associating himself with violence. He died in physical exile to which he had been driven by fascism, but his spiritual exile had begun in 1912 when the Socialist Party was taken from him by Mussolini and plunged into turmoil and bloodshed.

Turati, Treves, and Rosselli were dead, and the revolutionary leaders too had all changed. Serrati had gone to the communists; Arturo Labriola, an interventionist in 1915, had come into exile for a while but had later gone over to fascism. The new leader was Pietro Nenni, and his most distinguished lieutenant was Giuseppe Saragat. Neither had been a power in Italian politics before 1922; their experience was all of exile. We are so familiar with political leaders who have a million or so votes behind them and who are fighting day by day for their ideas against opponents with other ideas that we cannot easily imagine the effect of fifteen years' politics on a man with no votes behind him, who is quite out of contact with his opponents, and whose only company is that of his allies. But such was the position of Signor Nenni and Signor Saragat, and since it was they who carried socialism back into Italy after the war we should do well to examine it. Politically, exile is a leisured life; there are no parliamentary debates, no elections, no serious party congresses. It is moreover a peaceful life for a politician, since the essence of exile is to have been beaten by one's opponents. The anti-fascist exiles were all agreed on being anti-fascist. They had therefore plenty of time to think out exactly what they wanted and no need to compromise before attack. In fact they carried out endless theoretical examinations of the bases of their positions, they read, they learned from the examples of France, of England, of Germany, and of Belgium as well as from their past experience of Italy, they discussed, and they learned not to rest content with anything short of a formulation of their principles that was both complete and polished to the last detail. They tended to become in fact political theorists more than politicians. "Justice and Liberty" were the best documented, but the socialists were not far behind. The communists of the Diaspora, being of course in touch with developments at the Temple, had no need of revising the Scriptures. But the corner-stone of Italian socialism, Signor Nenni, had come into exile with a conviction that stood firm amid the atmosphere of "getting things absolutely straight from the beginning," the conviction that the ruin of Italy was in the first place due to the splits in the Socialist Party. In Italy before 1926 and in France from 1926 to 1940, he devoted his talents first to reuniting the divided forces and then to keeping them united. We have seen how in 1930 he fused together the two socialist parties and how in 1934 he arranged as close an agreement with the communists as was possible, given the fusion with the reformists.

Signor Saragat, on the other hand, had not this conviction. He had not seen working-class politics close at hand, he had not been brought up among the Chambers of Labour and factory committees. Coming from the world of high finance he tended to see socialism more as an economic trend than as an expression of the hatred of classes, nor had he experienced the daily politics of the revolutionary period of 1918–25. In exile he examined the theoretical basis of his position with the best, and he deeply studied the history of English socialism.

It will be plain by now to the reader that Italian and English socialism have almost nothing in common. The one grew out of the confident manipulation of a rudimentary trade union movement by a little band of vigorous and politically minded intellectuals; the other grew slowly and massively out of a highly developed trade union movement which threw up its own political leaders, working-class men who learnt not from books but from their own mistakes. The one was predominantly revolutionary, the other entirely reformist. Nevertheless Signor Saragat decided that Italy had much to learn from England about socialism, and in the freedom and fantasy-breeding leisure of exile he determined on a campaign of anglicization. When fascism had fallen, the socialists were to forget revolution, forget Russia, and to go into parliamentary politics with a steady determination there to achieve an economy controlled in the interests of the majority. The result of the training which exile gave these men and their colleagues was that Signor Nenni knew to the last detail where he differed from Signor Saragat, and Signor

COSTANTINO
LAZZARI

BENITO MUSSOLINI
after 1918

CARLO ROSSELLI

FERRUCCIO PARRI

Saragat where he differed from Signor Nenni, and so with all the gradations of opinion between the two, and so with the many to the right of Signor Saragat and with the few to the left of Signor Nenni; but none of them knew in any detail at all where they differed from any of the opinions which were not represented among them, or indeed from the fascist dictatorship itself. The absence of practical problems made them theoretical and the absence of political opposition made them introspective. For fifteen years they had been defining their positions *vis-à-vis* each other alone.

When the war began there was at first little for the exiles to do; the younger of them took service in volunteer corps with the French Army to fight against Germany but not, if she should join the war, against Italy. It is interesting that it was Signor Nenni who for the socialists insisted on this stipulation,[1] so far had maximalism travelled since 1919. In August 1939 came the first great change in the static condition of Europe which had favoured the reunion of the Italian socialists in exile; on the 23rd of that month the agreement was announced between Soviet Russia and Nazi Germany for the partition of Poland, and the Western Communist Parties obediently applauded. The next day Signor Nenni denounced the agreement in the *Nuovo Avanti!* and shortly afterwards the Socialist Party severed all relations with the Italian Communist Party. Signor Nenni, as the protagonist of the "unitary" policy of friendship with the communists, resigned from the editorship of the *Nuovo Avanti!*, from the secretaryship of the Socialist Party, and finally from all influence in the Direction of the Party. The Russo-German agreement of 1939 was the beginning of a new problem for Western socialism, the problem of how to work with a party which, while professing the same socialist ideals, and at times working nobly for them, was yet fully subservient to the policy of a Great Power that was engaged no longer in fostering the international revolution but in pursuing, as yet by defence, its own nationalistic ends. It was in 1939 a problem which affected

[1] V. Modigliani, op. cit., p. 284.

many countries, and particularly France, but it did not yet affect Italy. The Italian exiles were disconcerted, but the simple millions of Italy hardly knew of it.

The German occupation of Paris in 1940 scattered the exiles and the Allied landing in Sicily in 1943 carried the new problem with it. As the Allied armies blasted their slow way up the Italian peninsula, behind them grew the seed of dissension. Into the industrial plains of the north the underground fighters came secretly, over the high Alps, floating down on parachutes, and clambering out of the lavatory windows of fascist prisons. They carried the same seed of dissension with them, the dissension between totalitarian communism and democratic socialism. The dissension was symbolized by the eclipse of Signor Nenni in Paris in 1939.

CHAPTER V

INTERNATIONAL POLITICS, 1943–8

The governments of Marshal Badoglio, July 1943–May 1944; Signor Bonomi, May 1944–June 1945; Signor Parri, June 1945–December 1945; Signor de Gasperi, December 1945–

ON July 25th, 1943, the military disasters suffered by Italy led to a palace revolution and Mussolini was overthrown. King Victor Emmanuel III called on Marshal Pietro Badoglio to form a government. Badoglio was a soldier of the entourage of Mussolini, and he announced at once that the war beside Germany would continue. For a week there was sudden and disordered political freedom; then military law and censorship reasserted themselves. But on September 8th Marshal Badoglio accepted the secret armistice terms of the Allies and fled with the King from Rome across the lines to Brindisi in the heel of Italy; free Italian politics began again after twenty years.

Marshal Badoglio's government at Brindisi included no politicians. It was one of soldiers and sailors and technicians, governing the small but expanding territory behind the lines in such measure as the Allies allowed. But within a few days of the armistice Sorrento was liberated, and Benedetto Croce, who was there, was able to devote himself to politics. Signor Croce was now seventy-eight, but he became at once the focus of such politicians as were not still behind the German lines. With Count Sforza, who had returned to Italy from the United States, and Enrico de Nicola, who had been President of the Chamber of Deputies in 1922, he began to canvass for a real government of the parties. The parties were in practice six and remained six for two years. Already at this time they fell into two groups, the left and the right.

On the right were the Liberals, the Christian Democrats, and the Democratic Labour Party; on the left the Action Party, the Socialists, and the Communists. The Liberals were, as always, Signor Croce's own party and were at that time entirely under his control, following meticulously some of the remoter quirks of that great mind, such as that a political party ought not to formulate an economic programme.[1] They cast back to the pure liberalism of Cavour. The Democratic Labour Party, *Democrazia del Lavoro,* was a shadowy body which existed in Naples only on the strength of its reputation as the party of Signor Bonomi, who was still in Rome. Signor Bonomi did in fact favour it, but it had very little character and soon died. The Christian Democrats, *Democristiani,* were the old Popular Party under a new name. Behind this party were the masses of the catholic peasantry; it had as yet no clear programme, but it was understood that when the time for a programme came, it would be much like the traditional popular programme, or possibly a little to the left of it. The Action Party had no roots in pre-fascist politics. It was in Italy what Rosselli's "Justice and Liberty" had been in exile; the party of those who were determined to build a new and firmly democratic Italy and who were convinced that none of the old parties was worthy of their support. It was, as "Justice and Liberty" had been, exuberantly eclectic, taking pleasure in "reconciling liberalism and Marxism." Its leader in the liberated south was the Crocean professor Omodeo, and many Croceans who were too equalitarian or simply too young to tolerate the old Liberal Party found an outlet for their energies in the Action Party. Its mainspring then and later was the hope of a rationally ordered society with equal opportunity and equal responsibility combined with free enterprise. In the practice of politics it showed itself headstrong and undisciplined, although as rich in talent as "tadpole parties" usually are. Signor Croce himself, who was in continuous contact with the actionist leaders

[1] Croce, *Quando l'Italia era tagliata in due*; Laterza, Bari, 1948; p. 94.

at this time, says in his diary:[1] "Only when the Action Party has provided itself with a coherent programme will it be possible to determine the situation of that party; perhaps then the socialist and positively communist elements in it will go to socialism and communism, and the liberal elements to liberalism, for the whole question is one of method; anyone who wants the method of discussions, elections, assemblies, and majority votes, and who does not want dictatorship in any form, however slight it may appear or however heavily disguised it may present itself, he ought to be in the Liberal Party; and anyone who believes in the other method and talks of 'having an economic revolution and then installing true freedom,' he does not know what freedom is; he leans towards dictatorship, whether it be fascist or communist." This was the antithesis which later caused the Action Party to break up and the Socialist Party to split in three. The socialists and communists were present in 1943 at Naples and Sorrento and Salerno, where the powerless and preparatory politics of that year centred, but they were not influential. Their leaders were still either in exile or away to the north in German-held Italy.

Signor Croce, Count Sforza, Signor de Nicola, and the party leaders turned their energies to getting rid of the two most obvious relics of fascist rule, the non-political and military cabinet, and the person of King Victor Emmanuel III. Marshal Badoglio was not at all unsympathetic to their attitude, but his concern was to extricate Italy with as little bloodshed and upheaval as possible from the disastrous situation into which Mussolini had led it. In demanding agreement between the parties before cabinet changes he was in a strong position because he had in fact brought Italy across to the Allied side; it was with him that the Allies had signed the armistice and he was entitled to demand that they should not be faced with a prolonged cabinet crisis within a few months of it. The person of the King was another matter. The Allied authorities at this time were adamant not only against changing the monarchical form of government

[1] Ibid., p. 53.

but also against changing the person of the monarch until the whole Italian people could be consulted. Here there seemed to be a deadlock; the Allies would allow no change, the King would not take the matter into his own hands by abdicating, and the six parties and the eminent independents would have nothing to do with a government swearing allegiance to the man who had been Mussolini's patron for twenty years. In October 1943, Signor Croce and Count Sforza met Marshal Badoglio and the three agreed to try to induce the King to abdicate in favour of his son or grandson. But for the moment they achieved nothing and all the political leaders refused to collaborate with the King, while those of the extreme left refused even to collaborate with Marshal Badoglio, King or no King. Count Sforza exacerbated the situation by continuous railing at Mr. Churchill ("featherbrain")[1] for what appeared to an Italian to be stubborn royalism. But to the Allies the most important matter was to get and keep the fleet, which was monarchist, out of the ports of German-occupied Italy.

In January 1944 a number of representatives of all the parties and various independents gathered in congress at Bari. Before the sittings opened the three left parties, actionist, socialist and communist, agreed to put up a motion saying that the Congress itself was the legal government of Italy and that the Allies must now treat with it and no longer with Marshal Badoglio. This misplaced initiative was quashed largely by Signor Croce, who dramatically walked out of the room when they came to tell him of it, and in the end the Congress decided to set up a "*junta*," or committee with a watching-brief, formed of representatives of the six parties. This was the germ of the six-party coalition of 1944–5.

In February Signor de Nicola persuaded the King to accept the principle of abdication or "retirement" in favour of his son, the Prince of Piedmont. But there was no *détente* yet, for this Prince had been Commander-in-Chief of the Italian forces at the time of the attack on France in 1940 and was always the obedient

[1] Croce, *Quando l'Italia era tagliata in due*; p. 108. ("*Testa di passerotto*.")

military figurehead of the fascist régime. To the left-wing parties he was little better than his father. Moreover the Allies were as strongly opposed as ever to any change without a referendum.

But on April 1st, 1944, the whole situation changed dramatically. On that day the exile communist Palmiro Togliatti arrived in Naples from Moscow. Straight from the fountainhead of authority, he swung the communist leaders right round overnight; the communists would henceforth be prepared to collaborate in the government with anybody at all, with the King, with Badoglio, with black catholics, with *laisser-faire* liberals. Now was no time for sterile gestures of disapproval; the war must be won in collaboration with anyone who was prepared to win it. At the same time communist propaganda in Naples suddenly increased and demonstrations became more businesslike. The socialists and actionists could not allow themselves to be outflanked by the presence of communists in a government from which they were excluded, and they too agreed to support Marshal Badoglio at once. The three right parties on the other hand remained firm in their objections to the person of the King. The Allies were therefore faced with the possibility of a government of the left, of communists, socialists, and actionists. They gave way and agreed that the King should retire. The representatives of the six parties were informed; the left agreed that they would serve equally willingly with the Prince of Piedmont as Regent, and the right that they could now support Marshal Badoglio. The regency was proclaimed and, after the Action Party had been restrained from an attempt at the last minute to stay out of the government and to prepare an opposition, a six-party cabinet was formed on April 20th. Marshal Badoglio was Prime Minister and Signor Croce, Count Sforza, and Signor Togliatti were ministers without portfolio.

Such was the first effect on Italy of the arrival of the new communism. For seven months the democratic parties had striven decorously to carry out their unexceptionable purpose of removing the King and had been decorously blocked by the Allies, while the socialist parties seemed ready to fall back into the old "intransigence" of 1918–22. Within three weeks of Signor Togliatti's injection into Italy from Moscow, the King was gone and there was a coalition in which Signor Togliatti held a position of equal standing to that of the two veteran ministers, Signor Croce and Count Sforza. Politics were not at that time much more than a parlour-game; there was nothing immediately at stake, for power was still in the hands of the Allies. But habits were forming, and the arrival of Signor Togliatti gave the answer to those who wondered what the post-war communism was going to be like. There was evidently going to be no more of the Bombacci-Bordiga tradition of intransigent political virginity, but a determination to get into the government at all costs. For the communists, the most implacable, incorruptible and gallant of the anti-fascists, to lead the way in co-operating with a monarch who was compromised even in the eyes of a convinced monarchist like Signor Croce was a break with tradition that showed how far above other aims did they rate the getting of places in the government. They did not thereafter revise this rating.

Marshal Badoglio's six-party government had neither the power nor the time to do anything, for within a few weeks of its formation the Allies overran Rome and the situation was again changed overnight. With the liberation of Rome the first influx of leaders of the resistance came into Italian politics. Resistance to fascism had, as we have seen, existed inside Italy all along, but it was not, naturally enough, until the Allied troops were on Italian soil and there was the certainty both of being of some use and of not having to keep it up indefinitely that it became a shooting matter. On the fall of Mussolini in 1943 the resistance grew suddenly from a matter of tiny clandestine cells into a mass movement. After September of that year the fighters of the resistance were left face to face with the power of the German Army. When Marshal Badoglio and the King left Rome, the only Italian authority left was that of the kidnapped Mussolini and his republican fascists, who were allowed by the Germans to form a nominal government at Salò on the Swiss frontier. The issue was therefore clarified and the struggle became an international one, comparable with that of the *Maquis* in France and of Tito's partisans in Yugoslavia. The movement was both wider spread and more spectacular in the North, but at Rome were gathered most of the well-known politicians of pre-fascist days. Under the chairmanship of Ivanoe Bonomi they formed the Rome Committee of National Liberation. In theory this was the senior unit of a network of such Committees throughout the country; in practice it had great prestige and a power which varied in accordance with the state of communications. The function of the Committees was primarily to act as political liaison between the partisan bands, which were all of some definite political conviction, communist, socialist, actionist, or democristian. The Committee was also to watch over the military command of the bands within its area from the point of view of the parties. Needless to say, the functions of the Committees varied from place to place and from time to time, particularly according to how far the communists would collaborate in them. The Rome Committee of National Liberation included representatives of the same six parties as formed the government of Marshal Badoglio at Naples; but when communications were restored, the parties in Rome withdrew their support from the government formed by the same parties in Naples. Three dominating personalities emerged from clandestinity; Signor Bonomi himself, a former Prime Minister and now the chairman of the Rome Committee of National Liberation, the socialist leader Signor Nenni, and a little-known catholic from the Alps, Alcide de Gasperi, who came out from the Vatican City to take command of the democristians. The result was a foregone conclusion; Marshal Badoglio fell, and a government of the same six parties was formed under Signor Bonomi.

During the rest of 1944 the political situation became rather more stable. The Allied advance was slow, often halting for weeks on end. Little new was to be expected until the next wave of dominating resistance fighters should be freed by the capture of Milan. The territory behind the advancing Allied lines was handed over bit by bit to the Bonomi government. The greatest difficulty with which the government had to deal was that of administering these territories without offending the zeal of the left parties for purging all the fascists. A spurious harmony reigned between the parties, for all were united in prosecuting the war and in wanting to rebuild a democratic Italy. Neither closer definitions of a democratic Italy nor the struggles that would follow upon them commended themselves to politicians who had before them the example of the Civil War in Greece and of the Allies' reaction to it; nor was there a parliament in which to thrash out such definitions. The parties in Rome kept much the same character as they had had in Naples. The liberals were now squarely on the right wing, the democristians were cautious for the present but promised great reforms for the future, the Democratic Labour Party still rested entirely on the prestige of Signor Bonomi, the Action Party was brilliant and high-intentioned but lacked both stability and followers. The socialists were now under the unquestioned leadership of Signor Nenni, with Signor Saragat as his lieutenant. Their breach with the Communists over the Russo-German treaty of 1939 had been closed in 1943 by another "Unity of Action Pact," concluded in clandestinity in Italy. The Pact provided for a joint standing committee to formulate the united action in question, for the unification of the reviving communist and socialist labour organizations, and for a common effort to see that the responsibility for the fascist régime should not "fall upon the people." It "recognized the Soviet Union . . . as the surest friend of the peoples in their struggle for independence and freedom against reactionary and imperialistic forces, and placed the confidence of the two parties in the solidarity of the British Labour Party."[1] After the capture of Rome, a further "Pact of Alliance" was agreed between the two parties on August 8th, 1944, by Signor Nenni and Signor Togliatti.[2] It was Signor Nenni's proclaimed and passionate conviction now as always that the ills of Italy were due to the splits in the Socialist Party in 1921 and 1922, and

[1] Published in *Orientamenti*; January 19th, 1948, Rome; p. 5.
[2] Ibid., p. 6.

that the best way to avoid their repetition was for the two proletarian parties of 1944 to behave as much as possible as though they were one. If there was any difference between the two parties at this time it was perhaps that the communists laid more emphasis on the personal purge of all fascists, and the socialists on a purge of institutions to be brought about by a republic. For the republicanism of the Socialist Party was different now from what it had been before fascism. There was to be no more boycotting of institutions from outside; the socialists were to fight their way into them and to put their ideas into practice through the existing machinery. Signor Nenni himself said in a speech in September 1944:[1] "Socialism is no longer stuff for propaganda; it is not the sun of the future that Garibaldi talked of. Socialism in Italy is a day-to-day problem, in the most concrete and positive sense." In the same way, their republicanism was no longer a matter of not walking up the Quirinal steps, but was part of their wish for the total abolition of the old Italy that should precede the building of the new. An old saying of Turati's was much quoted at this time; in Italy tobacco is a government monopoly, and Turati had said that the republic was not to be merely a matter of changing the crest over the tobacconists' doors.

The three left parties were explicitly republican; the three right parties tended to leave the matter officially to the consciences of individual members, though naturally there was no way of stopping the opinions of party leaders from being taken as party pronouncements. Throughout 1944 an uneasy truce was kept on the "Institutional Question" as it came to be called for short, for the Allies from time to time issued reminders that there was to be no question of a change before a plebiscite. Count Sforza on the whole kept the peace, but it was well known that he was *persona non grata* with the Allied authority for the views which he had formerly expressed at Naples. But Signor Nenni could not contain himself and often expressed his republican sentiments forcefully and unequivocally.

It was in the nature of Signor Bonomi's six-party government

[1] Nenni, *Una battaglia vinta*; Rome, 1946; p. 16.

not to be able to follow any definite line of action. For one thing, it was an all-round-the-compass coalition; for another, it had to keep on good terms with an Allied Military Administration which was not over-solicitous about Italian political aspirations except in so far as they affected the supply lines of the armies; but more important still, the north with its resources and its men was still in the hands of the Germans. News reached Rome of the exploits of the resistance; a resistance plane even managed to drop leaflets on the capital. There was a feeling that it was at Milan that the new Italy was coming to birth, and a disinclination to do anything that might later be disowned by the men whose present deeds were realized to be fitting them for the future leadership of the nation. In the absence of any legislative assembly, government was still by Royal Decree, and there was among those who hoped to build a new democracy a natural antipathy from going too far with the present unavoidably autocratic methods. The communists however did not share this antipathy. They were for "revolution by royal decree." In the absence of any industry to socialize, their activity was mostly limited to the purge. In Signor Bonomi's government they had secured the post of "High Commissioner for Epuration" for their man, Signor Scocimarro. He purged so many officials that ministers with executive responsibilities threatened to resign. The crisis came when the Minister of the Navy finally did so. The issue was quickly seen to be the general difficulty of co-operation between those ministers who interpreted their duties as holding on without precipitating issues until general elections could be held, and those, the communists and socialists, who interpreted them as getting down at once to the creation of the new democratic Italy. Signor Bonomi saw this and resigned. But here another difficulty arose, for he handed his resignation to the Lieutenant of the Realm, or Regent, the Prince of Piedmont. Now it was a plank of socialist policy that the Committees of National Liberation should be kept in being as the nucleus of the new Italy, as something between an Old Antifascists' Club and a Second Chamber to act as a check and balance in the yet unwritten constitution. Signor Nenni had for some months been using the slogan "All power to the Committees of National Liberation." So far did he carry this exaltation of the Committees' functions that he found it an offence on Signor Bonomi's part to have handed his resignation to the Regent and not to the Rome Committee. The constitutional paradox in the idea of Signor Bonomi as Prime Minister handing his resignation to Signor Bonomi as Chairman of the Rome Committee of National Liberation, that is of one man fulfilling the functions of both Prime Minister and President, did not deter Signor Nenni from putting out a truculent manifesto saying that the socialists would not serve under the reactionary monarchist if he should form another government, nor with the reactionary liberals in any government whatsoever. For twelve days the crisis continued in a confusion natural to the negotiations of inexperienced politicians with no parliament, with a monarchy under sentence of plebiscite, and with a fighting line only two hundred miles away. One fact emerged clearly from the series of interviews, visits, telephone calls, meetings, cabals, and rival cabals; that a delegation had called on the British Political Representative, Sir Noel Charles, to ask whether Count Sforza would be acceptable as Prime Minister or even as Foreign Minister. They were told he would not. It was a natural decision; Count Sforza had compromised himself hopelessly by his fiery republican speeches at a time when the only sane policy on the institutional question was the one imposed by the Allies, to wait for a plebiscite. Against that was to be set his unequalled reputation and prestige as an anti-fascist, his passionate and famous hatred of all nationalisms, a relevant quality when it comes to bringing a fascist power back into the fold, and above all the grave consequences which can be expected to follow when one country overrides the free process of politics in another. The blackballing of Count Sforza in November 1944 was the last gesture of the monarchic policy followed by the Allies since they arrived in Italy sixteen months before. The policy won the Italian Navy over, but it earned the Anglo-Saxons, and particularly England, a quite predictable odium which the left-wing parties in particular were quick to exploit. England came in for the major part of this odium because Mr. Churchill was rightly or wrongly believed by all Italians to be the source of the policy.[1] During the crisis of November 1944, the first rumblings of anti-occidental propaganda came from the volcanic Signor Nenni when the news of the interview with Sir Noel Charles became known.

When Signor Nenni defied Signor Bonomi the intellectuals of the Action Party, unskilled in demagogy, hastened to associate themselves with him for fear of being outdone. The division that later killed the Party was beginning to appear, and its actions during this crisis were already hampered by the conflicting ideas of the "quasi-socialists" under Signor Emilio Lussu, the same Lussu who escaped from Lipari with Rosselli, and the "liberaloids" under a brilliant young politician, Signor Ugo La Malfa. The decision to back up the socialists strained but did not break the unity of the Party. The issue now seemed to be between a government of the three right parties under Signor Bonomi again, or of the three left parties, probably under Signor Nenni. In view of the presence of the Allies and the memories of the socialists' part in the events of twenty years before, there was little doubt that the right would have it. As a last correct gesture to clear the field before forming a ministry of the Democratic Labour Party, the Liberals, and the Democristians, Signor Bonomi invited Signor de Gasperi, Signor Nenni, and Signor Togliatti to join him. Signor Nenni replied once again that Signor Bonomi should present himself to the Committee of National Liberation for the solution of the crisis. Signor de Gasperi agreed to join a government. All this was expected. But to the general surprise Signor Togliatti agreed too. It is said[2] that he sought Signor

[1] This belief was heightened in February 1946, when, during the campaigns which preceded the referendum on the monarchy, Mr. Randolph Churchill contributed two articles in the monarchist interest to the daily paper *Buonsenso*, the organ of the neo-fascist "Common Man" party. (See p. 183.)

[2] "*Giulio Romano*"; *Dodici giorni di crisi*; Rome, Ed. "La Vita"; undated (1945).

Nenni's assurance that his acceptance would not be considered a breach of the Pacts of 1943 and August 1944, and received it. Be that as it may, the Pacts were not terminated and proletarian unity continued to be the slogan even when the communists were in the government and the socialists were in opposition.

Here was another indication that the ruling passion of the new type of communism was government office. Signor Scocimarro, who had precipitated the crisis, was moved from the Purge Commission to the less crucial post of Minister for Occupied Italy, that is to say of liaison with the resistance men in the north, and Signor Bonomi formed his second government with the four parties. On the showing of their public pronouncements, therefore, the socialists and actionists found Signor Bonomi too reactionary and monarchistic to inspire their confidence, while the liberals, democristians, democratic labour men, and communists did not. What presumably happened was that Signor Nenni, more impatient than his communist colleague, thought the time had come to try and form a government of the left. To understand why he was wrong, one must remember not only the presence of the American and British Armies and their political advisers, but also that the socialists and communists were discredited parties in the eyes of all those who remembered or had studied the politics of 1918–24, and that the Action Party was an untried body of intellectuals.

Signor Bonomi's second government was a little more lively than his first, for the communists, having decided that for the moment collaboration was the right course, proved easier to get on with than had the socialists. Signor Togliatti is a more equable man than Signor Nenni. In January 1945, the government decreed universal franchise for the next elections; it was the first time the principle of the women's vote had been allowed. In February the Allied authorities revoked their right to veto decrees and appointments, and handed over to the Foreign Minister, Signor de Gasperi, full control over Italy's foreign affairs within the terms of the still unpublished armistice. In March, stimulated by a riot in which the people of Rome expressed their dissatisfaction at the way in which the purge was being administered, the government pledged itself to call a consultative assembly which would advise it until elections could be held.

The socialists were of course in no position to develop a strong line in opposition, for their sister party was committed to support Signor Bonomi. It was therefore a quiet time for Signor Nenni. The communists continued to show themselves pliant in practice although rigid in theory. A shade passed across their honeymoon with the socialists when Signor Nenni, in London for a meeting of the World Federation of Trade Unions in March, agreed that his party should join in studying the possibility of refounding the Second (Amsterdam) International, the body which had broken up in 1914 and in 1939. Faithful to the old contempt for the "Yellow International," the communist daily *Unità* admonished Signor Nenni. In the government, however, Signor Togliatti followed his declared policy of collaboration with the Regent and the forces of reaction "for the moment"—"*per adesso.*" He lost some popularity as the chief propagandist and defender of the call-up of classes for the Royal Army, an army which was admittedly fighting the Germans but was for all that no less under the command of the House of Savoy than had been that of Mussolini. Thus the first three months of 1945 passed in waiting, purging, and the keeping of tempers, as had 1944.

In April the Allied offensive against the Gothic Line, postponed since the autumn before by the necessity of finding troops for the invasion of Southern France, was finally launched. There followed the Rising of the North. This long-prepared insurrection, the justification of twenty years' underground opposition to fascism by a few, and many months' partisan warfare by numerous bands, has been called the "Second Risorgimento." In a sense the comparison is not far-fetched; for a month the people of Northern Italy were united as they had not been since the great days of 1848 and 1861. But in its result it must be admitted that the second Risorgimento gave birth to no new nation but rather for a time to passions and revenges comparable to those of 1918–22.

ALCIDE
DE GASPERI

PALMIRO
TOGLIATTI

PIETRO NENNI

GIUSEPPE
SARAGAT

The military history of the Italian Partisan Movement is outside the purpose of this study, but its political origins lie more in the history of socialism than elsewhere and its political effects still dominate Italy and Italian socialism. In 1942 and 1943, Allied bombing of the great cities of the north, Milan, Turin, and Genoa, brought a wave of disaffection against the fascist war which gave their chance to the experienced leaders of the Communist and Socialist Parties and of the "Justice and Liberty" groups, later the Action Party; and they began to organize resistance on a large scale. Bands of youths, avoiding the call-up for the Fascist Army, took to the hills and there found leaders who turned them into something many of them had never thought of being, fighters for a political ideal. The communists started "Garibaldi Brigades," the socialists "Matteotti Brigades," the actionists "Rosselli Brigades," and the democristians "Green Flame Brigades." When the fascist régime fell and resistance became resistance to the Germans only, these bands grew enormously. Committees of National Liberation sprang up in the principal cities. The Allies began to drop supplies, arms, and liaison officers with wireless sets, at first mainly to help in passing escaped prisoners through the German lines, but later in recognition of the direct military value of the guerillas. A central command for the bands was finally achieved early in 1945 after a series of obscure manœuvres wherein two financial supplies were gathered in the hands of one body, the Committee of National Liberation of Milan. An officer of the Fascist Army, General Operti, got away in the confusion with a hundred and eighty million lire of Army funds. Proclaiming himself a patriot, he began to pay out this money to those bands he considered most patriotic; since he was a keen monarchist, the communist bands did not receive any. But after long negotiations, General Operti made over the money to the Committee of National Liberation of Piedmont. This Committee, in charge of the resistance in the ancient communist stronghold of Turin, asked the authority of the Rome Committee to administer the funds in the interest of the movement throughout the north. An arrangement was at last made whereby the money was handed over to the Milan Committee, and the Rome Committee was to send a further monthly sum through Signor Pizzoni of the Credito Italiano.[1] With Signor Pizzoni as financial organizer Feruccio Parri as Chairman of the Committee and political leader, and an iron communist, Luigi Longo, as military co-ordinator and commander, the Milan Committee of Liberation organized the great uprising of April 1945.

Again, the detailed history of the uprising does not concern us, but a word about the scale of it is necessary to an understanding of post-war Italy. Between two and three hundred thousand men were under arms in the north at the best moment. At certain places, and particularly in the Val d'Ossola—familiar to English tourists who pass in the train through the Simplon tunnel and Domodossola—the Germans and fascists were entirely expelled for long enough to allow the setting up of free republics with the full mechanism of government, municipal elections, and even formally organized prisoner-of-war camps for captured German soldiers.[2] Field-Marshal Alexander called the Italian Partisan Movement the best in Europe after Tito's. After the end of the war, Signor Bonomi gave the following figures for

[1] Leo Valiani, *Tutte le strade conducono a Roma*; Florence, 1947; p. 104 et seq.

The way in which Valiani, who is of the generation which grew up under fascism, became an anti-fascist is interesting. On pp. 52 et seq. of his book he tells how he lived as a boy near Trieste. The port area was forbidden to those who did not have special military passes, and it became the pursuit of Valiani, second in excitement only to attending the bicycle races, to smuggle himself in and out of the port area in the luggage vans of trains. In time he got so good at it that he was given the job of taking in clandestinely printed anti-fascist propaganda. Naturally it was not long before he began to read it. He was filled with such enthusiasm that he went off to seek the Olympian Carlo Rosselli, and from then on devoted his life to subversive agitation. In 1947 he became a member of Signor Saragat's democratic socialist concentration.

Signor Pizzoni is now (1948) the head of the Credito Italiano.

[2] The capture of Germans was relatively easy once the German-speaking guerillas from the Trentino had possessed themselves of a few German tanks and uniforms.

the losses suffered in the resistance: dead, 8,760; wounded, 20,000; houses destroyed as reprisals, 10,000; dead in prison, often after torture, 1,090. The dead of the "co-belligerent" army which fought beside the Allies on the other side of the line he gave as 18,000.[1]

The young Italians who died as guerillas did not die for the same cause as that for which young Englishmen and Americans died in the regular armies. They died not for a new Europe, but for a new Italy; not even to "win the war," but to get rid of fascism and to place their brothers well for political reconstruction. For the moment the aims of the Anglo-Saxon and, it must not be forgotten, the Russian governments converged with those of Italian patriots and democrats. The rising was political, and if the main aim of its leaders was to get rid of the Germans quickly, a subsidiary aim was to be in charge when the Allies arrived. In this they succeeded, but at the cost of a terrible slaughter of their own people, as yet and probably to be left for ever unreckoned. For in the few days between the final collapse of the German and neo-fascist power and the arrival of the Allies in Milan, many thousands of fascists and others "whose faces," in a current phrase of right and centre journalism, "were not found sympathetic," were butchered by the former guerillas. Even when the Allies took control it was found impossible for some weeks to stop a run of murders in Milan, estimated at thirty a night. The new Italy appeared knee-deep in the mingled blood of Germans and Italians.

At the same time the first impingement of Slavonic communism came at Trieste. The troops of Tito took the city, and the first news of them that Italy had was when the Germans refused to surrender to them but fought on waiting for the New Zealanders to arrive. When the confident and sometimes turbulent methods of the Yugoslav partisans in absorbing the redeemed city of *Trst* to the Slavonic world became known, there was criticism in those Italian circles and papers to whom it seemed that, whatever the situation in the hinterland, the Italian majority in the city itself

[1] *Manchester Guardian*; January 10th, 1946.

was entitled to some say in its own affairs. The reply of the communists in their press was an attack on the French government for some episodes in the Val d'Aosta where French officials, more or less exceeding their functions, had tried to annex a small Italian territory inhabited by French-speaking peasants. It was the first appearance of what has since been a regular line of communist propaganda, that whatever the Slav nations might do, the Western nations were always doing something just as bad if not worse.

Such was the end of Italy's war. The American, British, and Dominions Armies were victoriously installed in the Po Valley, the Yugoslav Partisan Army was victoriously installed at Trieste, the defeated German Army was present in disorder, and Polish and Indian units were scattered about. Deserters from all these armies were at large. The situation in 1945 was very different from that in 1918. Then the war had ended with a victorious Italian Army and its allies encamped on the Julian Alps. In 1918 Italy had won. In 1945 Italy as a whole had neither won nor lost. Fascist Italy had lost and democratic Italy and communist Italy, in fortuitous alliance, had won. Her position was in some ways like that of Russia in 1918; she had surrendered and had then been rent by dissension and civil strife. But Russia in 1917 surrendered to the losing side, Italy in 1943 to the winning side. And if in the years following the war of 1940–5 Italy was further from revolution than she had been in the years following the war of 1915–18, it was because of the presence and might of victorious armies on her soil. When democratic politics started once more in the reunited Italy, they were subject to the unlimited control of those armies. Signor Nenni told the Socialist Party Congress of 1948 that at that time he or any other politician could have been arrested at the orders of a British sergeant. This is an exaggeration, but it describes the feelings of Italian politicians in 1945 and 1946.

Back from exile and out of clandestinity, the political leaders were acquiring free followers for the first time in twenty years. But because there had been no elections their followers were as yet unnumbered. The leaders were working no longer as it were in a vacuum, but in a dark room.

The liberation of Milan and the north had the same effect on central politics as had the liberation of Rome a year earlier, but on a larger scale. Just as the Badoglio government had fallen to Signor Bonomi and his resistance men, so the Bonomi government fell to the yet more active resistance men of the north. For fifty days Italy was without a government. The Allies allowed at first no freedom of communications between Rome and Milan; the first Italian who was allowed to cross the *cordon sanitaire* was the Regent, who toured the north making speeches and met with an equivocal reception. Later the politicians from one side of the line and from the other were allowed to fly to meetings in Rome and in Milan, and after various leaders of the big parties had failed in private meetings to find support among the other politicians, for there was still no Assembly, Signor Parri formed a government.

Signor Parri was the leader of the Action Party which, though as far as anyone could guess it was not nearly as big as the Communist, Socialist, or Democristian Parties, stood so high in popular estimation and popular hopes that its leader was able to command the confidence of the leaders of the traditional parties. More even than the good name of the Party the personal reputation of Signor Parri was responsible for this remarkable turn of events. His power was based almost entirely on the devotion he had inspired in the resistance leaders of the north. He was a man of great organizing ability, absolute rectitude and freedom from spite, and of a positively eccentric modesty—even humility. His personal unassumingness, famous in many stories of his displeasure when anyone offered to help him off with his coat and so on, was matched by a political unassumingness that, attractive or not, ill became a democratic politician. While in prison in Switzerland early in 1945, a temporary inconvenience to which the resistance men of the north were always open, he expounded to a friend his ambitions for the Action Party. If he could, he said, he would prevent the Party from taking part in ordinary politics and from holding office and would encourage it to give its best men to the civil service and to the non-political organs of reconstruction which, it was to be expected, would be doing the detailed and useful work of administration after the war.[1] This conception of Signor Parri's makes an interesting contrast with that of Signor Nenni. Both men had seen the failure of democratic politics after the war of 1915–18, both had suffered under the totalitarianism to which the country had turned, and both had now returned to build a new Italy that should be safe from a recurrence of fascism and of the sort of politics which had led to it. Signor Nenni's slogan was "*politique d'abord,*" Signor Parri's attitude, though he never voiced it as crudely as this, was "*pas de politique.*" Signor Nenni was convinced that it was not democratic politics as a system which were to blame for fascism, but a mistaken working of the system; the mistake, of course, being the splits in the Socialist Party in 1921 and 1922. Signor Parri on the other hand, while not denying that someone must carry on with democratic politics, hoped that it would not have to be the Action Party. As we have seen, he wanted this high-minded and intelligent *élite*, largely his own creation, to devote itself to administration and to shun all polemics and demagogy. Nevertheless, in June 1945, Signor Parri found himself carried willy-nilly into office.

The Action Party had been in opposition for the last four months of Signor Bonomi's government, and when its leader formed a government the socialists joined with him so that there was again an all-round-the-compass coalition of the six parties. Signor Parri inaugurated his government with a broadcast in which he said: "Enough murders and reprisals; let us roll up our sleeves." Order was in fact restored to the North, but new troubles appeared in the form of inflation, with food-prices soaring to fantastic heights, the black market almost driving the white out of existence, and salaries lagging behind the cost of living so that a civil servant or a school-teacher was on paper condemned to living on one loaf and two cups of coffee a week.

[1] Leo Valiani, op. cit., p. 119.

Wages on the other hand followed prices up, or pushed them up. Twenty-five thousand Allied deserters were at large, and armed communist, fascist, or undisguisedly criminal bands roamed the country. The armistice terms were not published until November, and Italy was not invited to send even observers to the San Francisco conference. The communists led a series of riots in protest against the slowness of the purge, and there were other disorders in which those of the right protested against its speed. A neo-fascist party appeared, the Common Man, *Uomo Qualunque,* which took as its motto the "*me ne frego*" of d'Annunzio and the fascists. Its leader, Signor Giannini, proposed in serio-comic terms a nation-wide sit-down strike of patriots against too much politics. It was suddenly remembered that Signor Nenni had started his political career as the henchman of Mussolini in the Romagna riots of 1912, and Signor Togliatti lost popularity for having addressed a message to the people of Trieste bidding them welcome the Yugoslav partisans. The more trouble there was in Trieste, the more the Communist Party fell in public estimation. In November the Pope appealed to the government to allow no more death-sentences to be passed at the trials of fascists, and the government refused. Over this scene of mounting passions Signor Parri presided with too much goodness; in November he fell.

The crisis was opened by the liberals, still under the leadership of Signor Croce, even though he had not been a minister since the liberation of Rome and the fall of Marshal Badoglio. The cumulative impatience of the liberals at serving with the communists and socialists came to a head on the particular issue of the purge. Signor Togliatti was Signor Parri's Minister of Justice; and as an insurance against the imprisonment without trial which was a common feature of "defascistization" under his administration, the liberals demanded that Signor Parri should take into his cabinet some elder statesmen who had nothing to do with the Committees of National Liberation and who opposed the continuation of the purge on its present scale, particularly Vittorio Emmanuele Orlando. Signor Parri refused and the liberal ministers resigned. For the democristians, Signor de Gasperi called for the continuation of the six-party coalition; in other words, since he knew the liberals would not withdraw their resignation, he associated his Party with them. Then Signor Parri resigned, not omitting to make a set speech to the Rome Committee of National Liberation and to representatives of the northern Committees who had been flown down for the occasion; he was not going to fall into Signor Bonomi's error of handing his resignation to the Regent only. During the days of negotiations for a new government the three octogenarians Orlando, Nitti, and Bonomi were so much in and out of the Quirinal Palace for consultations with the Regent that they came to be known as "O.N.B.," which were also the initial letters of *Opera Nazionale Balilla,* the fascist youth-movement. As a *tertium quid* between the candidate of the three right parties, Signor Orlando, whose age failed to inspire confidence, and the candidate of the three left parties, Count Sforza, whose position *vis-à-vis* the still present Allies was found too equivocal, Signor de Gasperi was able to form a government and became more surely established in control of the country's destinies than any democratic politician since Giolitti.[1]

Alcide de Gasperi has been in and out of this narrative once or twice. A native of the Trentino, his first experience of politics was as a Deputy for the Italian-speaking people of that former Austrian province in the parliament at Vienna before and during the war of 1915–18.[2] When the Trentino was ceded to Italy he continued to represent it at Rome, and became one of the young leaders of the Popular Party. Gobetti saw him at a Popular Party Congress and set down his impressions in one of his supremely intelligent articles.[3] "As a good organizer," Gobetti wrote, "he puts administration higher than culture or criticism."

[1] He remains Prime Minister at the time of writing (1949).

[2] When at the elections of 1948 Signor Togliatti found himself branded as "Comrade Togliatov," the communists made much of "von der Gaspern's" position at this time as *Schriftführer,* or translator, to the Italian Deputies at Vienna.

[3] *Antologia della Rivoluzione Liberale*; Turin, 1948; p. 491.

Though this might not appear very high praise, it is in fact still the key to Signor de Gasperi's success in a country where politics are usually a matter less of getting things done than of expounding the theoretical bases of the things one would like to do. Signor de Gasperi is almost alone among Italian politicians in not being an intellectual. He was an ardent supporter of the Aventine schism and after its failure was in prison for a time. On his release he went into the Vatican, where he was a librarian until the resurgence of free Italian politics in 1943 and 1944. The tenacity that once found expression in fighting for the interests of a dissident national minority within the Austrian Empire and in resisting fascism as long as that was possible is to-day turned to upholding a number of causes that have been thrown together by communist pressure in Italy. Order, democratic methods, freedom of opinion and of the press, to a certain extent the privilege of the propertied class, all these are behind his stand against the communists; but principally it is as a Roman Catholic that he governs Italy. After twenty years in the Vatican he takes every opportunity of being photographed at religious ceremonies. One of his daughters is a nun. Signor de Gasperi is the expression of that which Italy has in particular to oppose to communism, and it is not as in some other countries democracy, but catholicism.

The Liberal Party could not stand the strain imposed on it by bringing down Signor Parri; it split into two and quickly ceased to be an effective force in Italian politics. Signor de Gasperi therefore formed a five-party coalition. The Democratic Labour Party soon vanished when its inspirer Signor Bonomi was no longer an active power and the Action Party, as Signor Croce had predicted, fell into two halves, the "quasi-socialists" going to the Socialist Party and the "liberaloids" going not, as Signor Croce had hoped, to the now discredited Liberal Party, but joining with the remains of the old Republican Party to give new life to that. Count Sforza became loosely associated with the new Republican Party. The issues were now clarified, and the Action Party and the Democratic Labour Party, which had sprung up as an expression of high hopes but were without any foundation in the life of the nation, were out of the way. Signor de Gasperi therefore faced the first elections for twenty years with a coalition of the three great parties, the democristians, the socialists, and the communists. With food-prices still soaring and full-scale battles in progress against separatists in Sicily, the government went forward with arrangements for elections and a referendum on the monarchy. In January 1946, the new electoral law was promulgated—still, of course, by decree, for there was as yet only a nominated consultative Chamber. In places of under thirty thousand inhabitants voting was to be by simple majority; in places of over thirty thousand inhabitants, it was to be by a complex form of proportional representation which favoured the small parties, though not to the same extent as that introduced into France after the war. There was also a proposal that voting should be compulsory. The proposal came from the parties which thought they could count on the votes of those who were not in the habit of voting, notably the democristians, and it was of course opposed by the communists, whose well-organized followers would go through fire and flood to get to the polls. Signor Togliatti announced to the Annual Congress of his Party that he would resign if compulsory voting was passed. It was in fact passed, but Signor Togliatti did not have to resign, as the decree was accompanied by no sanction other than the publication of the names of those who did not vote.

In April the Socialist Party met in National Congress at Florence. The issue was that of relations with the communists. A motion for outright fusion was defeated, and there were appointed to the new Party Direction seven members who favoured close ties and seven who favoured independence. Signor Nenni, whose attitude on this question he defined as "unity of action for political, not ideological, reasons," was made Chairman. The issue was, in fact, shelved.

The referendum and the elections were fixed for June 2nd. It seemed fairly certain that the monarchy would go. In the last few weeks there was indeed a sudden recrudescence of monarchist feeling and agitation, and on May 8th King Victor Emmanuel III abdicated and left the country surreptitiously for Egypt. The final disappearance of the offending person did something to make the institution more popular, and the supporters of the former Regent, now King Umberto II, were quick to take advantage of the change. The referendum and elections passed off smoothly enough. When the results began to come in, it appeared that the democristians had come out top in the elections, and that Italy was to be a republic. It was then that things began to go wrong. The first error was Signor Nenni's; as a deputy Prime Minister without portfolio, he had the figures for the referendum announced before they were complete, in order to let the world know on the anniversary of Matteotti's murder that Italy was a republic. There was naturally a sudden and violent outcry from the monarchists, which was not calmed even when on examination of the incomplete figures it was found that they were in fact conclusive; that is to say that the republic already had its majority. The monarchists' next line of defence was that all the spoiled papers ought to be taken as monarchist votes, presumably because it was generally admitted that the majority of the illiterate southern peasants were for the monarchy. Against furious opposition from the King's advisers the government made the Prime Minister, Signor de Gasperi, "Head of the State," an arrangement which had been previously agreed upon to avoid a possible gap between the voting of the Republic and the election of a President by the new Assembly. The Palace did not recognize Signor de Gasperi, and for some days a very ugly situation continued, with a King and an acting President disputing the supreme position in the Italian state; there were some riots and many fiery manifestoes on each side. The socialist Minister of the Interior, Signor Romita, earned respect for his tactful handling of a difficult situation which had been created by his political master, Signor Nenni, although there were not lacking monarchists to say that he cooked the figures. The situation was resolved when, before the final figures had been published, the new King drove surreptitiously out of Rome in a fast car and left the country by air. Thus the House of Savoy left Italy without waiting either for the official verdict on its fate or for the ceremony that had been prepared by the government of the day. On June 18th, the authoritative figures were published and showed very little difference from the disputed ones. They were: for the Republic—12,717,923; for the Monarchy—10,719,284.[1]

It was not primarily the institution of monarchy that the Italian people rejected in 1946, but the persons of two princes who had been the agents of a system of government whose every trace it was now desired to wipe away. The King who had refused to sign Facta's proclamation of martial law in October 1922, and the Prince who had grown to middle age in a seclusion conditioned by the fascist rulers, would, if they had remained, have been a continuous reminder of a shameful time. It might perhaps have been possible to make a regency for the infant son of King Umberto II, the former Prince of Piedmont, or to turn to a junior branch of the House; but that would have led to all the strains and complications of an heir by right of birth living in exile. For an epitaph on the dynasty Signor Croce's words at the Congress of Bari in 1944 may serve: "Faith is no longer placed in the person of a sovereign of the dynasty which made its own the cause of the Italian Risorgimento and governed us for the first sixty years of our national unity. This is, alas, an irreparable misfortune, one of the countless corruptions and destructions of fascism, the corrupter and destroyer."[2]

The uproar over the referendum figures rather distracted attention from those of the general elections. The democristians polled 8,080,664 votes, the socialists 4,758,192, and the communists 4,356,686. The communists and socialists presented themselves to the people in a loose electoral alliance called the

[1] *Elezioni per l'Assemblea Costituente e Referendum Istituzionale*; published by the *Istituto Centrale di Statistica* and the Ministry of the Interior, Rome, 1948; p. lxiv.

[2] *Gli Atti del Congresso di Bari*; Ed. "Messagerie Meridionali"; Bari, 1944; p. 20.

People's Bloc, though they did not go so far as to have a single list. In the new Constituent Assembly, the democristians had 207 seats out of a total of 547, the socialists 115, and the communists 104. The two left-wing parties were thus able to vote down the democristians, but not to vote down the democristians when they were supported by the votes of various right and centre groups, which they always were. The revived Republican Party had 23 seats, and Signor Giannini's quasi-fascist Common Man Party 30.[1] Signor de Gasperi accordingly continued with his wide coalition.

It was not yet a legislative assembly that had been elected. This Constituent Assembly of 1946–8 functioned only in two committees, one for framing a constitution, and one for watching the framing of the Peace Treaty which was being worked out by the Four Great Powers, and later for ratifying it. Legislation was still by decree, and decrees were now signed and promulgated by the President. The veteran politician and professor of constitutional law Enrico de Nicola was elected to this office by the Assembly; but he was styled "Provisional Head of the State," leaving the election of the first real President to the first real legislative Assembly.

For two years the Assembly worked on the new constitution. In the final form agreed upon and published early in 1948 it was an unexceptionable document instituting government by a Chamber of Deputies and a Senate, as before fascism, and by a President, a functionary to be elected as in France by the parliament and not as in the United States by the people. The violent conflict of ideas between the parties concerned in framing it was resolved by general phrases about the right to work and to strike, and even more by the constant use of the phrase "in accordance with the dispositions of the Law," a wording which left open to argument most of the disputed matter. There are chapters of the Constitution which read more like an index of the subjects covered by the Legal Code than a lasting enshrinement of the principles of human society as conceived in Western Europe.

[1] Figures from the statistical survey quoted above, p. lii.

There was only one moment of dramatic political interest during the framing of the Constitution. In April 1947, an article was under discussion in draft to regulate the relations of the Italian state with the Roman Church. The communists joined with the democristians in voting the inclusion in the Constitution of the Lateran Treaties concluded by Mussolini with the Vatican in 1929, which defined relations on terms very acceptable to the Church. It was a clear indication that catholic votes were, for the moment, more important to the Communist Party leader than consistency with the time-honoured tenets of his ideology.

Until the publication of the draft Peace Treaty, Signor de Gasperi was his own Foreign Minister. He then handed over the Foreign Ministry to Signor Nenni, whose duty it thus became to reconcile the Italian people with the terms in the Treaty which were widely felt not to be consistent with the part played in driving out the Germans by the resistance movement of the north. After the political changes to be dealt with in a moment, the Foreign Ministry passed to Count Sforza, who, in mitigating those terms, achieved a success to which events on a wider scene have contributed since the beginning of 1947.

At the end of 1946, the unity of the Italian socialist movement began to break up again. The right wing of the Socialist Party was now led by Signor Saragat, who was Chairman of the Constituent Assembly after his return from Paris. In December it opened an attack on Signor Nenni. The difference was about co-operation with the communists and the matter which brought the issue to a head was the comparative failure of the socialist-communist alliance in some recent local elections. Signor Saragat and his reformist colleagues had joined with the old maximalists in exile, and in exile and in clandestinity they had accepted the pact with the communists. But in open democratic politics they became restive and found that socialism and communism were two different things. Signor Togliatti and Signor Nenni were taking part with fair orthodoxy in democratic politics but they both showed a disquieting reluctance from proclaiming their faith in the basic principles of democracy.

There was often a riot or a light-hearted strike to suggest to the suspicious that the tractability and "transigence" of the left-wing parties was very much "*per adesso*."

The general political situation appeared in clearer detail in the syndical movement. The exile Bruno Buozzi had returned to Italy during the war and, before he was caught and executed by the Germans and the neo-fascists in 1944, he had succeeded in restarting the General Confederation of Labour, of which he had been the last Secretary General before it was suppressed by the fascists. In the form in which he started it and the form in which it emerged into the light of day in April 1945, it was a fusion of the old socialist General Confederation of Labour with the old catholic Italian Labour Union, a fusion symbolized by adding the word "Italian" to its title. It was now called the Italian General Confederation of Labour, *Confederazione Generale Italiana del Lavoro*, or C.G.I.L., as it is generally abbreviated. Its structure was altered to keep pace with the inclusion of several political opinions; it was provided with a Secretary General, and three Assistant Secretaries General of equal standing, a communist, a socialist, and a democristian. The chief post of Secretary General fell to Signor di Vittorio, a communist. In this arrangement the familiar conviction of the left-wing politicians that there must at all costs be unity in anything to do with the working class combined with the natural feeling of the workers themselves that a single all-embracing syndical organization would be able to bring greater pressure to bear on a hostile government, and perhaps also on a friendly one. It was this feeling which kept the C.G.I.L. together for eighteen months after the socialist movement in politics had split.

Far more important in determining Signor Saragat's revolt than the general internal political situation or the friction of three parties lumped together in one syndical body, was the situation of the world. It is not necessary here to go into the deterioration of relations between Russia and the Western Powers since the end of the war; but one matter needs emphasis, that American loans and grants for European reconstruction did not begin with Mr. Marshall's Harvard speech in 1947. Already at the turn of 1946–7 Signor de Gasperi himself and other negotiators were back and forth from Washington seeking loans. As loans were made, so communist propaganda against American imperialism mounted, and as communist propaganda mounted, so the American government poured in money and favours to check the rise of communism, for "poverty breeds communism." This was the real issue on which Signor Saragat differed from Signor Nenni, and it was an issue which went far deeper than traditional party loyalties. Signor Saragat was for immediate wealth and a slow, thoughtful reform of society. Signor Nenni and the communists were for an immediate reform of society and wealth afterwards. In these terms it must be admitted that Signor de Gasperi's objective was simpler; he was just for immediate wealth.

In January 1947, an extraordinary National Congress of the Socialist Party met in Rome to decide on Signor Saragat's demand for a break with the communists. Already before the Congress came together things had gone so far that Signor Saragat and his followers met in one hall and Signor Nenni and his in another. Signor Saragat made much of the loss of middle-class votes to the Common Man Party, and accused Signor Nenni of packing the party administration with those who favoured fusion with the communists whereas, he said, a balance should have been established between them and those who favoured an independent policy. At his Congress, Signor Nenni showed himself pacificatory, even going so far as to say that Russia was sometimes wrong; she had been wrong, for instance, to come to terms with Hitler in 1939. Polemics continued between one end of Rome and the other until on the fifth day Signor Saragat appeared on Signor Nenni's platform and attacked the subservience of the Party Direction in following the communists in strikes about trifles. Later on the same day he retired again to his own hall and announced the formation of a new party, to be called by the name of the old party of Turati and Matteotti, the Italian Workers' Socialist Party. With him was an impressive number of veterans; Modigliani, Signor d'Aragona, who had been the Secretary General of the General Confederation of Labour all through the troubles of 1918–22, Angelica Balabanov, a campaigner of the old internationalist days of 1915 and 1916 at Zimmerwald and Kienthal, and one of Matteotti's sons.

Meanwhile, Signor de Gasperi was in Washington, negotiating a loan. When he came back, he found a string of resignations waiting for him; Signor Nenni, his Foreign Minister, Signor Saragat, the Chairman of the Assembly, and Signor d'Aragona, his Minister of Labour, all wanted to devote themselves to organizing or re-organizing their parties, in other words, to conducting polemics against each other. In three days the daily paper of the new party, *Umanità*, achieved a circulation in Rome alone of 160,000, or twice that of the communist daily, *Unità*. The whole political life of the nation was turned inside out.

On January 20th, Signor de Gasperi resigned. There was for the moment no possibility of forming a less unwieldy coalition, for the Peace Treaty was still to be signed, and to give any party the chance of repudiating it later would have been unthinkable to a statesman of Signor de Gasperi's calibre. The new government, accordingly, was much like the old, with the exclusion of the two protagonists of the socialist brawl. On February 2nd Signor de Gasperi announced the formation of a new three-party coalition of democristians, socialists, and communists, with the inclusion at last of the offending Count Sforza as Foreign Minister. Since it was foreign policy on which not only the Socialist Party but the nation was divided, the peaceable change from a fiery pro-Russian demagogue to the man who has since outrun public opinion, his colleagues, and discretion, in hurrying to meet Marshall Aid and Western Union was a considerable achievement. It was perhaps fortunate that there were rival attractions for public attention at the time: the retrial of the Matteotti murder, twenty-two years after the event, and the mounting tension in Trieste and Pola.

In May came the first national general strike since the great wave of strikes in 1922. It was called in the traditional manner as a protest against some murders in Sicily. The Peace Treaty being by now signed, Signor de Gasperi took the opportunity of resigning and forming a stronger and more coherent government to deal in particular with another urgent difficulty, the still unchecked inflation. He got rid of the socialist and communist ministers, keeping beside the men of his own Party the independent Count Sforza only. As Finance Minister he installed an eminent liberal economist, Professor Luigi Einaudi. It was a peculiarity of the Italian cabinet system to have three ministers concerned with the national finances, the Minister of Finance, the Minister of the Treasury, and the Minister of the Budget. The three posts coexisted simply because no self-respecting party would join a coalition unless it was given some control over financial policy, and the posts had in fact been used as bargaining counters between the parties in all the governments since the end of the war. Professor Einaudi was now put in undivided control of the whole machine by simply throwing the other parties out of the cabinet. He arrived with a short slogan: "All expenditure is bad now, even good expenditure." With a series of deflationary measures that no socialist or communist would ever have dared to carry out or even allow a colleague to carry out without resigning, Professor Einaudi had the lira steady within a few weeks at about 640 to the itself slightly inflating dollar.[1] The further result of Signor de Gasperi's single-party government was to allow the parties to develop a free line of propaganda before the elections, and to clarify the issues on which they differed. There was some need of this opportunity, as there was still no legislative chamber given to regular and unrestricted debate.

Having carried the general story of political changes thus far, we must now leave the parties preparing themselves for the elections to the first free legislative chamber since 1924, and consider the socialists in particular. We have seen what they did in 1943–7; they cleaved fast to the communists, so fast as to provoke a split in their own ranks. What did they want? In three ways

[1] The reader will remember that in 1920 it stood about 18 to the dollar.

the situation was different for them after the war of 1940–5 from what it had been after the war of 1915–18. Abroad, the Russian Revolution was no longer the light of the future, but a rigid totalitarian state. At home, they were no longer the extreme left-wing party; the communists were in all respects more so. In their own consciences were the memory of their part in bringing Mussolini to power and the determination to be warned.

The official socialist attitude to Russia was still the same as in 1917; that is to say, approval and support of whatever was happening there. Phrases like "substantial democracy" (as opposed to the "formal democracy" of the Western Powers), "the vanguard of civilization," "the bulwark of progress," "the friend of oppressed peoples," "the leader of the struggle for freedom," and so on, which had once been the true thoughts of true men, were now used thoughtlessly as slogans for the thoughtless. The honest and intelligent among the socialists and communists now accepted the view made familiar in England by the novels and essays of Arthur Koestler, that it is the duty of thinking men to suffer and submit for the sake of their descendants. This mixture of puritanism and *Weltschmerz* hardly existed in 1917–18. As then, Russia was held up as the model, but if the socialist intellectual of the later time were to describe his idea of Russia to the socialist intellectual of the earlier, the latter would scarcely recognize a follower of the same principles. The outlook of the educated socialist has changed, but that of the uneducated is less sensible to events. The Tuscan peasant votes socialist now, as he did then, because Italy is a poor sort of country and Russia is a fine country, and the socialist politicians want to try to make Italy more like Russia.

As relations between the Russian government and the governments of the Western Powers became worse, so the communists and socialists abandoned their initial position, that "Italy shall be nobody's colony," for one of day-to-day defence of Russian policy and day-to-day attacks on American and to a lesser extent on British policy. We have seen how it was the choice between Russia and the United States that led Signor Saragat to break away from the Socialist Party; his decision was also conditioned by his profound respect for the British Labour Party and its gradualist methods. Now that the British socialist government was in the same camp as the United States, he was able to lay more emphasis on gradual socialism as opposed to demagogic socialism with revolutionary undertones. He and his followers have devoted far more energy to polemics against communism than against capitalism, the traditional enemy of socialism.

In home politics the great issue for the socialists was that of union with the communists. Apart from Signor Saragat and his followers, the Socialist Party was at this time squarely in favour of "unity of action." This was the protection worked out by Signor Nenni against a repetition of the events of 1918–25. There is an interesting passage in one of Signor Nenni's speeches in 1946 in which he points out how a split in the proletarian movement of a country has invariably led to dictatorship.[1] He mentions the divisions between the maximalists and the minimalists in Italy, the spartacists and the reformists in Germany, and the socialists and anarchists in Spain. Another suggests itself at once, that between the Russian bolsheviks and mensheviks. It was almost an obsession with him that all the ills of Italy were due to the incoherence of the socialist movement a quarter of a century before, and that if the socialists and communists were to come to blows again another fascism might be expected. His dominating personality, often compared to that of his old friend Mussolini, held the majority of the Party with him. It was of course this obsession that accounted for his violent reaction against Signor Saragat's breakaway.

The differences between the Communist Party and the Socialist Party were at this time slight, but perceptible. To begin with, the Communist Party had a position in an international organization that the Socialist Party had not, the organization centred in Moscow that was called first the Communist International, then was nameless for some years, then was called the Cominform. The leader of the Italian Communist Party, Signor

[1] Pietro Nenni, *Una battaglia vinta*; p. 109.

Togliatti, had himself held for many years the second post in the Comintern and had broadcast from Moscow to Italy throughout the war until his return to Naples in 1944. He had a hold over his followers that Signor Nenni did not have over his; at least twice he reversed their attitude overnight, once on his first arrival in Italy, about co-operation with Marshal Badoglio, and once when in April 1947 he returned from electioneering in Sicily to call them back to orthodoxy, after they had been preparing to vote into the Constitution a provision that marriage should be indissoluble. The Socialist Party was a democratic party, open to all the vicissitudes of opposition and schism from within; the Communist Party was not. Both parties were united in wishing the installation of a rêgime modelled on that of Russia, but there was a difference which was just perceptible in their approach to the question of how to install it. Signor Nenni, having spent twenty years reflecting on the effects of maximalist propaganda in 1921, was prepared to say that the new rêgime must be installed by democratic methods. In April 1946, he said in a speech:[1] "We have no right to play about with the lives and the future of the workers; as long as there is any possibility of legal action it is our duty to exploit it and so spare the country the great troubles of another civil war." It is noticeable that even here he implies the possibility of a situation in which the socialists would be forced to resort to illegal action. Signor Togliatti, on the other hand, has maintained a deliberately oracular vagueness on the matter of revolution or not. In his speech to the National Congress of the Communist Party of 1948, for instance, he said,[2] "We hear ourselves asked the question whether, in the development of this democratic movement of the masses, we are going to respect the republican constitution, whether we propose to act on legal ground, or to move off it. To this question we have only one answer; up till now, only conservative and reactionary groups, only the privileged castes, only the bourgeois classes,

[1] Nenni, op. cit., p. 93.

[2] Palmiro Togliatti, *Tre minacce alla democrazia italiana*; Rome, 1948; pp. 103–4.

have ever shown themselves disposed to violate the constitution in any way, or even to defend their own interests, hindering the advance of the working class and the restoration of our economic activity. It is you, gentlemen of the bourgeoisie, and your agents, who ought to speak clearly. The question, therefore, does not interest us." His next remark is one that Signor Nenni, with a clearer sense of the consequences of the socialists' errors, would never have made: "It was neither the socialists nor the communists who organized the civil war in 1921 and 1922."

Later in the same speech, he said:[1] "We are following a line of democratic action, but we shall not allow ourselves to be caught unawares by any provocation or by any reactionary plan. We have behind us the experience of the partisan war. Tens of thousands of youths and men who have had this experience have learnt to defend the liberty and independence of the Fatherland by force of arms and, if a situation were to arise, as often happens in the course of democratic revolutions, in which freedom had to be defended or reconquered by force of arms, they would not fail to do their duty once again towards democracy and towards their Fatherland." Time and time again Signor Togliatti has used this mixture of truculent counter-attack and menace. Support of Russian foreign policy was the biggest strain on the socialists' co-operation with the communists, but the old issue of revolution versus reform was another.

This slight difference in the approach of the two parties to the method of installing a socialist régime is not matched by any difference of opinion about the nature of the régime itself, for in that they are both vague. Free use is made of such phrases as "giving the land to the peasants"; Signor Nenni has sometimes mentioned small holdings, and any suggestion of collectivization has been carefully avoided; but there has never been any detailed programme for the structure and administration of agriculture under a socialist state. For industry, on the other

[1] Palmiro Togliatti, *Tre minacce alla democrazia italiana*; Rome, 1948; p. 142.

hand, there is a programme, or at least a panacea for propaganda; it is the famous *Consigli di Gestione*, or Management Councils. These councils already exist in Italy. Standing committees of negotiation between management and labour first appeared, as in other countries, towards the end of the last century. After the war of 1915–18 these committees were strengthened and enlarged, partly after the model of the British Whitley Councils; and we have seen how the Occupation of the Factories in 1920 had as its aim the setting up of mixed committees through which the workers should be allowed some say in the policy of their concerns. One of the last gestures by which Mussolini tried to gain the support of the masses for his republican government at Salò was the institution of such management councils, and at the uprising of April 1945 those which had been formed under this disposition took to themselves a far greater measure of power than had ever been intended. They survived, and exerted a considerable influence over central industrial policy after the war. It was through this influence that decrees were passed forbidding the dismissal of workers in order to make room for the minor fascists when the first waves of those who had been imprisoned were released and returned to their jobs. The result of these decrees was that the returning fascists shared their jobs with those who had supplanted them when they were imprisoned. The huge Fiat works, for instance, was employing 70,000 in 1946, as it had in 1940, and yet its production, owing to war damage and the disruption of imports, stood only at 20 per cent of its 1940 level. The scope and functions of these councils was, however, unco-ordinated. Some of them have at times virtually dictated to the managers; others have been no more than a channel of communication to the workers of the decisions of the managements. A number of bills to co-ordinate them and give them legal protection have been framed by socialist and communist ministers at various times since the war, but the managerial interest in the Democristian Party and the parties which vote with it has always been strong enough to keep them out of the Code. The situation is much like that of the Joint Consultation machinery in England, but more confused and arousing more passions.

The Councils, even in their present form of an incident in a capitalist society, have been hotly opposed by the General Confederation of Industry and it sometimes appears that that body would even prefer that the heavy industries should be nationalized rather than that they should be submitted to the irregular control of the Councils.[1] On the other hand, the Communist and Socialist Parties and the communist-controlled C.G.I.L. have fought for the Councils with every means of propaganda and agitation that they possess. It is much to be doubted whether their chief interest in them is as potential organs for the control of industry under a socialist régime; it is more likely that they foster them as organs to help in the seizure of power by violence in the event of a revolution.

The period between the expulsion of the socialists and the communists from the government in May 1947 and the general elections of April 1948 saw a sharpening of the conflict between East and West in the world, and between their epiphenomena in every country of the West. The outlines of the Marshall Plan appeared, the Cominform was founded, and the Western communist leaders met at Byalystok to decide on their winter campaign. From July 1947 till Christmas of that year, the Italian communists staged a series of disorders of a new type. It was no longer the rough-and-ready method of the loose shouting match or the strike that got out of hand; it was a carefully controlled technique which sought to excite the greatest possible alarm while inflicting the fewest possible casualties and provoking the least possible reprisal. In one town after another a general strike would be called in protest against the troubles in the town before. The communist workers would congregate in the Piazza, sing and shout, and then march to the Prefecture. A Communist Party leader or the leader of a communist-controlled Chamber of

[1] See particularly the memorandum submitted to the government by the *Confindustria* on December 6th, 1946; printed in the pamphlet of the *Confindustria, I Consigli di Gestione*; Rome, 1947; pp. 20 et seq.

Labour would go inside and "negotiate" with the Prefect. After a time he would come out and assure the crowds that everything was all right. That was the minimum; often someone was killed or an enemy paper's offices were burnt out as well. In the words of the *Manchester Guardian*,[1] "With . . . consummate skill the agitation for smashing-up is aroused, fanned, inflamed, and then deliberately put out by 'negotiations' with the local police or with Rome." The two most notable disorders were in November at Milan, where the Prefect was deposed and the offices of the government occupied for a day, and in the south, where the police did not arrive in time to prevent the declaration in one small town of the First Soviet Republic of Apulia.

Two real grievances were exploited, the Italian Social Movement and the de Gasperi Award. The Common Man Party had been losing its following, partly as a result of the personal eccentricity and buffoonery of Signor Giannini,[2] and had been superseded on the extreme right by a new party, built round a nucleus of prisoners of war returned from Russia, the Italian Social Movement, *Movimento Sociale Italiano*. It was an openly fascist party, exploiting the full technique of militaristic pageantry and openly urging patriots to forget all that had happened since 1941. The communists and socialists agitated and demonstrated for its suppression, and they were within their rights, for it is illegal for anyone openly to apologize for Mussolini and the fascist régime. Informations were laid against the weekly paper of the Italian Social Movement, the *Ideal Revolt*, in any number of which could be found such illegal "apologies," but the government did nothing. The other real grievance was local to central Italy. The share-croppers of the central provinces have since the Middle Ages shared profits equally with the landowners.

[1] *Manchester Guardian*; December 12th, 1947.

[2] When, for instance, various elder statesmen were being nominated in the Assembly for the Presidency of the Republic, Giannini put forward the only woman among his followers, an unknown blonde Amazon from Sicily. She received only the sixteen votes of her party, and when the election of de Nicola was announced, Giannini leant across the bench behind him to kiss her hand with a melodramatic flourish.

After the war, Signor de Gasperi, as chairman of a tribunal for the purpose, gave a decision in a general arbitration that the sharing should now be sixty-forty in favour of the peasants. The grievance of the rioters in 1947 was that the award had been only very unevenly brought into effect by the various local governments.

The communist and socialist press drew the lesson from these disorders that Signor de Gasperi could not carry on his government without their co-operation; indeed it may be safely presumed that the disorders had been promoted expressly to give this impression. The influence wielded by communist Ministers of the Interior at elections in Eastern Europe is indication enough of why the communists and their socialist followers sought to be in power in Italy at the first elections to a legislative assembly since 1924. Signor de Gasperi, however, was not to be intimidated. Instead of broadening his government to the left, he broadened it at the centre by taking in the republicans and the Saragat socialists. Within a year of his secession, Signor Saragat found himself a minister, while the orthodox socialists under Signor Nenni were in opposition and, with their allies the communists, had not that opportunity of surveying the elections from inside the government which is so necessary for the success of a modern left-wing party.

At the turn of the year, the election campaign opened and the communists and socialists changed their tactics. They renounced riots and disorders and turned their attention to the gathering of noisy assemblies of representatives from various walks of life who came together without programme or organization and took the title of "Constituent of the Land," "Constituent of the South," "Congress of Democratic Communes," and so forth. The name "*Costituente*" was a throwback to the insurrectionary days of 1918, and it is probable that these bodies, under the full control of the Communist Party, were intended to be the organs through which Italy would be governed in the event of a communist victory at the polls. The communist Garibaldi Brigades of the partisan war reappeared and arms dumps were found.

The government parties made the most of both these developments in their campaign to catch the votes of the law-abiding millions with no political affiliation, and particularly those of the women.

The Nenni socialists, relieved of the cautious councils of Signor Saragat but not without severe internal dissensions, decided to present themselves at the polls in a common list with the communists, in an alliance to be called the Democratic Popular Front. When this decision was taken a further group seceded to join Signor Saragat under the leadership of Ivan Matteo Lombardo, an experienced businessman. With them was the former communist writer, Ignazio Silone. They took the name of "Union of Socialists" and combined with the Italian Workers' Socialist Party led by Saragat to form a common list called "Socialist Unity." The traditional socialist vote had therefore the choice of two lists, the Democratic Popular Front, consisting of the communists and Nenni socialists, who were in opposition and who offered Italy a place behind the Iron Curtain and *Gleichschaltung* to the Russian system, and Socialist Unity Saragat and Lombardo, who were in the government and offered Italy Marshall Aid and the continuation of free democratic methods.

The election campaign was fought almost entirely on foreign policy. With American forces in Greece and North Africa and American coal and *pasta* in their homes, with Signor Togliatti travelling about Europe for consultations with Zhdanov, with the Czech *coup d'état* in February, and with Tito's forces in Trieste, the Italian people felt their decision was crucial both in place and in time. The Pope and the American Ambassador openly exhorted them to vote for Signor de Gasperi, the Russians to vote for Signor Togliatti. It became almost a personal contest between the two men, and Signor de Gasperi, although he continually and heartily repudiated the idea, became a symbol of anti-communism more than of catholic democracy. On April 18th polling took place and the Democristian Party obtained a clear majority in the Chamber of Deputies. To realize the extent of this victory, one must reflect how seldom proportional representation gives an absolute majority to one coherent party, excluding its flanking groups. There were one hundred and five parties registered for the elections, sixteen of which presented "national lists," that is to say, represented more than merely local or sectional interests. The answer of the people to communism was more truly a landslide than we are accustomed to see in a country where a working majority is only obtained by the untidy but very practical expedient of single-member constituencies. Signor de Gasperi continued in office in coalition with the republicans and Saragat socialists, and the deflationist Finance Minister Einaudi was elected first President of the Italian Republic.

After the elections, the Italian socialist movement fell into the last stages of disintegration. In June 1948 the Socialist Party (Nenni) met in extraordinary National Congress at Genoa to pass judgment on yet another movement for breaking clear away from the communists; the movement was headed by Signor Romita, who had been Minister of the Interior at the time of the referendum. No decision was taken. The issue was precipitated when on July 14th a fanatical student shot and gravely wounded Signor Togliatti. The leaders of the Democratic Popular Front seized the occasion for a throwback to the tactics of the autumn of 1947. In the hopes of unseating Signor de Gasperi or at least of forcing their way into coalition with him, they ordered a national general strike through the C.G.I.L. The strike degenerated into disorders with loss of life, and was suppressed by prompt police action. Within a month, the Democratic Popular Front had been broken and succeeded by a loose alliance on the lines of that of 1943–6. In September the C.G.I.L. itself finally fell apart, the catholic workers retreating under their leaders to form an independent organization and leaving the democratic (Saragat) socialists in uneasy collusion with the communists. In September 1948 the extreme left were the communists, united, undismayed, adaptable, and cryptic. To the right of them were the Nenni, or rather ex-Nenni, socialists, for that fiery fusionist had ceased to exercise any official control over the destinies of the Party. They were disorganized, and a prey to the struggles of competing factions. Between the Socialist Party proper and "Socialist Unity" were several individuals and groups who thought that the best way of reuniting the movement was to detach themselves from all the parties and hope that the others would join them. The Lombardo and Saragat groups, as before the elections, had their leaders as ministers in Signor de Gasperi's three-party coalition. Signor Saragat himself was a deputy Prime Minister and Minister of the Merchant Marine, and the chairman of the parliamentary committee for the administration of Marshall funds was a Saragat socialist.

From the confusion of splinter groups and personal rivalries in which the Italian socialist movement lies attenuated, it is not impossible that a leader may appear to build it up again into a sober band of men having at heart the welfare of the Italian people. Nevertheless, in the course of their sixty years of existence the Italian socialists have only once been able to reverse the tendency to disintegration which has stultified the efforts of their best men, and that was when they were persecuted, imprisoned and driven into exile by their enemies.

CHAPTER VI

CONCLUSION

IN seeking a judgment on the Italian socialist movement, one is hampered by the lack of constancy in its ideas. If the movement had had any unity of teaching from time to time and from wing to wing, if it had ever based itself coherently on some recognizable system of ideas, that of Marx, for instance, or that known in England as Fabianism and in Italy as Reformism, it would have been possible to examine the system of ideas, to examine the condition of Italy, and then to examine their interaction, thus arriving at conclusions about their effects on each other and on the worth of the ideas in their setting. But a fundamental unity is just what the history of Italian socialism has not got. This is not peculiar to Italy; the mere fact that the governments of Russia and of England to-day both call themselves socialist is enough indication of the range of systems and attitudes which the word covers. And in Italy in particular the same wide range of ideas has gone under the same name. In 1911 Signor Bonomi and Mussolini were both socialists, in 1919 Turati and Lazzari, in 1946 Signor Saragat and Signor Nenni. Between on the one hand Signor Bonomi, Turati, and Signor Saragat, and on the other Lazzari, Mussolini, and Signor Nenni, there is absolutely nothing in common, except an intermittent wish that this were not so. At no time in the history of Italy has it been possible to say "the socialists want such-and-such."

In default of a real unity, then, one must turn to the formal unity presented to the world under the name of the Italian Socialist Party. Although the ideas have no unity, the institution has. Let us therefore frankly put the question, what good has the Italian Socialist Party done the Italian people? At once we come across the disunity of ideas again, for it was this disunity that gave the Party its most prominent characteristic, the tendency to split. The Party came to birth in 1892 with the main intention of showing its disapproval of anarchism. In 1908 it expelled the syndicalists (Arturo Labriola), in 1912 the reformists (Bissolati and Signor Bonomi), in 1914 the Masons, again in 1914 the interventionists (Mussolini); in 1921 the communists left it (Bombacci and Gramsci) and in 1922 it expelled a second batch of reformists (Turati). In 1930 the peculiar conditions of exile led to the reunion with the reformists, in 1934 to the pact with the communists. Once those peculiar conditions were removed, the process started again; in 1947 the first batch of reformists split away (Signor Saragat), followed by another in 1948 (Signor Lombardo), and by the mitigation of the alliance with the communists in the same year. Two causes have contributed to this tendency to split, one ineradicable and the other a mere political error, the fruit of political inexperience. The first is the over-meticulous clarity of the Latin mind, expressing itself in politics by a passion for detailed and logical analysis of its position and a consequent inability to stay in a party with those who have other views. This national misfortune of temperament is reinforced and allowed to become really dangerous by the system of proportional representation; for when a politician has found that his ideas differ from those of his colleagues, proportional representation makes it possible for him to split away and form his own party and to be sure of at once getting a few seats in parliament. Latin exactitude and proportional representation are for ever reinforcing and aggravating each other in France and Italy, and are likely to go on doing so until it is realized that there is only one way of breaking the vicious circle, that is to abolish proportional representation, since national temperaments cannot be abolished.

The whole-heartedness and abandon with which the Italian Socialist Party has played the game of tendencies, splits, and splinters has not helped it to be useful. A coalition with a socialist minister was always a prospect uninviting to others, for he might at any moment be disowned by his party. But, and this brings us to another leading characteristic, until 1944 the socialists always refused to enter a coalition. Between 1903 and 1912 they held aloof from Giolitti while he passed socialist measures, and in 1919–21 they refused the opportunity given them by the elections of 1919 to govern the country as they wished. In the last resort this is the gravest charge that can be brought against them, for their conduct in both these periods was nothing less than an outright and politically infantile refusal of responsibility. In 1903–12 no harm was done, for Giolitti had his own deplorable methods of getting on without them; but in 1919–21 their position was so strong and their misuse of it so total that in sheer desperation the country turned to Mussolini and fascism. But there was another difference between their two periods of refusing responsibility: in 1903–12 they had refused quietly, in 1919–21 they not only refused but rioted and bred violence as well. Violence was answered with greater violence and irresponsibility with a perverse lust for power. For us, when we seek a more remote historical cause of the downfall of parliamentary rule in 1924 and an explanation of how it came about that fascists and bolsheviks fought over the débris of democracy, there is only one answer; let us put away any national modesty we may have and remember that England is the only country in the world which through two centuries fought for parliamentary rule as a defence against despotism and corruption, and that in all other countries which have parliamentary rule, including Italy, it is only a written copy of the living fabric of English life. The constitution which Mussolini and the socialists tore apart was a scrap of paper written by well-informed Piedmontese professors in the nineteenth century, it was not the life-blood of a people.

In the last two years another scrap of paper has been written in Italy by another generation of professors and politicians, and it lies in the hands of Signor Togliatti and his Russian masters to tear it up, for he disposes of the full forces of both cupidity and bigotry throughout a section of Italian society.

Violence is still in the socialist repertory but the refusal of office is out of it. If any conclusion can be drawn from the short history of free socialism in Italy since the war, it is that both parties, the socialist and the communist, will go to almost any length to get into office. Why? It is impossible to know directly, for there has never been a socialist government in Italy, and in none of the coalitions of 1944–8 have the socialists or communists been strong enough to take any initiative. But an indirect indication of what would happen if the communists were in power may be seen in what has happened when they were in power in the Eastern European republics, for the Italian Communist Party has taken every opportunity of emphasizing its solidarity with those of Eastern Europe. There, what has followed has been a monolithic police-state within the nearly monolithic Russian hegemony. The left-wing socialists, who at present hold *Avanti!* and the title of Italian Socialist Party, cannot be separated from the communists in this, for they have presented themselves in propaganda and at the polls as a mere subsidiary group to the Communist Party. The right-wing socialists, on the other hand, are already in power under the Prime Ministership of the catholic Signor de Gasperi. The longer the coalition lasts, the clearer it becomes that they are merely an appendage of the democristians as the Nenni socialists are of the communists. A particular example will serve; the parliamentary commission for the administration of Marshall funds, under the chairmanship of a Saragat socialist, is being increasingly by-passed in favour of the Ministry of Finance, under a democristian minister. It is not from Signor Saragat and his followers that any positive measures of reform can be expected.

The problem of Italy is the same now as it was in 1900, when the Socialist Party began to have an influence; it is over-population. Italy is a poor country, and parts of it are desperately poor. There were in 1948 two million unemployed and another two million under-employed. In 1861, with a total population of twenty-five million, the average density was 87·2 to the square kilometre; in 1943, with a population of forty-five million, it was

147 to the square kilometre. In France, where the nature of the country is much the same except that France has coal and iron deposits while Italy has not, the density in 1940 was 75·1 to the square kilometre. In 1938, the excess of births over deaths was: in France minus 0·8 per cent, in the United Kingdom 3·7 per cent, and in Italy 9·6 per cent.[1] After the war of 1914–18 the United States were virtually shut to immigration, and after the war of 1939–45 Italy was deprived of her colonies, which provided the hope of emigration to all, even if only small numbers could actually go there. While it lasted, emigration was one means of reducing the pressure of population. But there is another means, contraception, of which no use at all has ever been made in Italy. Italy is the most catholic of all catholic countries, except perhaps Spain, and the attitude of the Vatican to contraception is and always has been stubborn hostility. If an adequate outlet could be found for emigration and if the Vatican would allow its followers to refrain occasionally from creating new souls, so that those which already exist might lead a more tolerable existence, Italy could become a prosperous country within two generations.

Neither of these two matters has received the attention of the socialists. In emigration in general they have always been uninterested, presumably because they thought that a socialist revolution would make possible the exploitation of resources which the capitalists had deliberately ignored out of self-interest, while cloaking their villainy under assertions that there were no such resources. To colonial emigration they have been more or less actively opposed for the same reasons as those for which they have been opposed to colonies in general, that colonies are a manifestation of capitalist imperialism and exploitation of the backward races. They have never given any attention at all to contraception, nor even turned on the Church's attitude to it the irony with which they greeted a campaign for more ample bathing-suits launched by the democristian Minister of the Interior in 1948.

Over-population and its consequent poverty have laid open

[1] Figures from Ivor Thomas, *The Problem of Italy*; Routledge, 1946.

the Italian people to the propaganda of the "proletarian parties." Those parties have not taken practical steps to remedy the poverty which got them their hearing. Early in the century they proposed such steps, and then refused to carry them out. After the war of 1915–18 they held up the Russian Revolution as an example, but they shrank from imitating it when they had the opportunity. As the bolshevik state hardened into an autocracy, they continued to hold it up as an example. For the moment those among them who are faithful to a changing Russia have been squarely beaten at the polls, while those who seek to steer Italy into the ways of democratic socialism have allowed themselves to be outmanœuvred by the catholics. If there is blame, it belongs to the Party leaders, for it is they who have missed the point: that a remedy must be found for over-population.

INDEX

JACKSON LIBRARY - LANDER UNIV.
HX288 .Y6 1975 CIRC
The Italian left : a short history of political socialism in
3 6289 000595048

HX 288 .Y6 1975

Young, Wayland Hilton,

The Italian left : a short history of political

342361

CARD REMOVED

Jackson Library
Lander College
Greenwood, SC 29646